Football, Fascism and Fandom

The UltraS of Italian Football

Alberto Testa and Gary Armstrong

A & C Black • London

Published by A&C Black Publishers Ltd
36 Soho Square, London W1D 3QY
www.acblack.com

ISBN 978 1 4081 2371 3

A CIP catalogue record for this book is available from the British Library.

Note: throughout the book players and officials are referred to as 'he'. This should, of course, be taken to mean 'he or she' where applicable.

Acknowledgements
Cover photograph © Shutterstock
Inside photographs © Getty Images/PA Images/Colorsport
Designed by James Watson
Commissioned by Charlotte Croft
Edited by David Pearson

This book is produced using paper that is made from wood grown in managed, sustainable forests. It is natural, renewable and recyclable. The logging and manufacturing processes conform to the environmental regulations of the country of origin.

Typeset in 10.5 on 14 Sabon by Saxon Graphics Ltd, Derby, UK
Printed and bound by CPI Group (UK) Ltd, Croydon, CR0 4YY

CONTENTS

AT: To my Mum with love.

GA: In memory of Eduardo Archetti whose wisdom, generosity and humanity made him exceptional.

FOREWORD

This is an important book, the merit of which lies in the authors' abilities to present the significance of the trilogy that is Italian football fandom, the prevalence of nostalgia for fascism, and the socio-political history of the Italian capital city of Rome. Unique in its depth of ethnographic detail, the text provides testimonies from some of the main proponents of a particular manifestation of contemporary Italian neo-fascism, a political phenomenon that has attracted much commentary but very little by way of first-hand evidence as to how it is sustained and operates. The authors present to a reader the iconic artefacts produced by two neo-fascist football fan groups, and offer explanations for such groups' persistence and transformation.

The main analysis specifically focuses on the collective sense of identity – and its concomitant moral coda – created and sustained by the supporters of Rome's two largest football clubs, AS Roma and SS Lazio. These groupings remind us of what American political scientist Benedict Anderson termed 'imagined communities'. Such entities – similar to football fans the world over – are characterised by the dynamics of who's in and who isn't. This dichotomy operates primarily at the local level and demarcates those who can and cannot join such gatherings. But a similar notion of distinction has resonance at the national level and affects Italian football loyalties nation-wide. This has produced a labyrinth of football fan alliances and conflicts, which in recent years has taken on a political dimension. As the authors illustrate, the sense of a specifically football-related neo-fascist notion of community draws on sophisticated means of communication via fanzines, websites and radio broadcasts. Central to these processes is both an ideological and iconic resonance that admires and promotes a belief system that locates its origins in Ancient Rome and is synonymous with the First Republic era of Benito Mussolini.

Many 'ordinary' Italians consider the pre-1938 fascist administration as a model of good governance. The same people, however, are quick to deny the racial laws enacted by Mussolini or explain away his alliance with Hitler's Nazi regime. That such opinions can be articulated without embarrassment may reflect the political cleansing that has been conferred on the past by the government of Silvio Berlusconi. The

Premier has relied on other elected members whose politics are of the far-right – none more so than Gianfranco Fini, former President of *Alleanza Nazionale* (AN), a political party that grew out of of the neo-fascist *Movimento Sociale Italiano* (MSI). Fini's AN merged in March 2009 with the *Forza Italia* movement to constitute the centre-right *Partito delle Liberta* (PDL, Party of Freedom) to create a government under the Presidency of Silvio Berlusconi. Fini is now President of the Chamber of Deputies.

With a philosophy embedded in the 2000-year-old ideals of civilisation and democracy, these ideas and the sentiments of the overtly fascist far-right (be they via the formal Party apparatus or via the extra-parliamentary movements) presents the Italian state with a real problem. A rhetoric of hatred underpins much of the neo-fascist proclamations. Opposing such sentiment is not straightforward. Its appeal is not to an identifiable demographic; some sympathisers are 'well-to-do', others exist in run-down neighbourhoods and live cheek-by-jowl with immigrant peoples. The latter populations suffer discrimination and violence, and note the failure of the Italian populace to condemn the neo-fascists in its midst. Over the past decade a sense of hysteria around the 'foreigner' has been built up around the incomers' assumed propensity to drug-dealing, illegal occupation of premises and violence against women. In this ecology of fear, a sense of mission has been articulated by the Italian far-right which has seduced many. The tough talk and public displays of fascist symbolism have become the armour assumed by many who speak of the need for some form of urban resistance and national renewal. Statistically, however, Rome remains one of the safest cities in Europe.

Fascism still fascinates millions of Italians. In 2005, some 50 years after the death of the Italian fascist dictator Benito Mussolini, Italian state television broadcast a documentary titled *Combat Film* which showed footage of Italy taken by Allied forces during the Second World War. Amid these archives was the day following the execution of Mussolini. Viewers saw the body of the man known to his co-patriots as *Il Duce* (the Leader) lying alongside his similarly executed mistress, Claretta Petacci. The broadcast attracted an audience percentage hitherto unprecedented for such a broadcasting genre. This provoked social scientist Robert Ventresca to state: 'In death, as in life, Mussolini's figure exerts an unmistakable influence on the Italian imagination and in politics, galvanizing the public interest as few historical figures can.' After more than five decades Mussolini's ghost is still rattling its chains in 21st century Italy. His legacy remains very evident in one of Italy's most popular cultural practices: *Il Calcio* (football).

The past holds a fascination for both the politically inspired and the devout football follower. This symbiosis has produced a highly politicised fandom in Italy. The soccer *curve* (terraces), including those of Rome, represent in 21st-century Italy the epicentre of a football supporter subculture inspired by fascism. That a place breathtaking in its beauty and referred to by many commentators as The Eternal City is centrally involved in such dynamics should not come as a surprise. As the bureaucratic capital of the Italian state, Rome was re-born during the years of Mussolini's rule and was to provide the most spectacular backdrop to the celebrations of the fascist regime. Celebrations are evident today, albeit on a lesser scale and mainly in the city's Olympic Stadium which hosts both AS Roma and SS Lazio. In the 1990s, as Italy experienced the transition from the First to the Second Republic, neo-fascist sentiments were expressed more frequently in the AS Roma *curve*. Hitherto such words and actions had been the preserve of fans of SS Lazio. For the next decade one could witness these long-standing Roman rivals newly affiliated by a shared neo-fascist ideology: fascist sentiment trumped football loyalty. The two clubs have proud histories and attract large followings. That said Rome had never been the capital of Italian football; the clubs of Milan and Turin have always overshadowed it. This reality has almost metaphorical qualities. The capital is considered by those in the North as parasitic, bureaucratic and prone to Mediterranean vices. By contrast, the northerners consider themselves astute and business-like. The game in Italy thus dramatises the ongoing and ever-incomplete unification of Italy.

Some remember that, unlike the northern cities, Rome did not see the mass mobilisation of its populace resist the fascist regime. Its people, however, were later involved in heroic acts of resistance to the occupying Nazis. Commentators note how Rome and its surrounding regions have long expressed a nostalgia for fascism in a variety of forms and its electorate has voted for fascist candidates far and above national averages. Football has never been inoculated from such sentiment. The first league championship won by AS Roma in 1942 was awarded amid suspicion that Mussolini had obtained favours in high places which benefitted the club. Such details go some way to explaining the synthesis evident in this text between football fandom and the language and values of neo-fascism. The youthful revolutions of 1960s and 70s Italy, with their concomitant radical left idealism, saw their utopian visions opposed in Rome more than anywhere else in the country. The main opponents were neo-fascist sympathisers. Rome might be the epicentre of neo-fascist fandom, but it is not alone. In June 2009 the Italian Supreme Court judged the leader of Verona *UltraS* under the Mancini Laws which punished incitement to racial and ideological violence. The same man had convictions going back 20 years.

Italian sports journalist Corrado Zunino has written of what he termed the 'secret fascination' of Italian football with fascism. The facts speak for themselves. In October 2008, Christian Abbiati, the goalkeeper of AC Milan and the Italian national side, was revealed to be an associate of the Milan-based neo-fascist gathering, Black Heart. When asked to explain his association to the group, he replied: 'I share the fascist ideals of fatherland, the ideals of the Catholic religion and the ability to retain order in society.' The 2006 World Cup winning Italian goalkeeper, Gianluigi Buffon, once appeared in Rome's Olympic Stadium with the number 88 on the back of his jersey. The number is used as a code of identification among neo-Nazis; H is the 8th letter of the alphabet, so 88 is taken to stand for HH which in turn means 'Heil Hitler', the proclamation of the Waffen SS. Ignoring the outrage of Italian Jews, Buffon later wore a T-shirt bearing the phrase *'Boia Chi Molla'* ('To Hell those who give up'). During the 2006 victory parade in Rome the same man posed in front of a statue bearing the Celtic cross (a symbol with neo-fascist resonance) and the words *'Fiero Di Essere Italiano'* ('Proud to be Italian'). The captain of the Italian national team, Fabio Cannavaro, held aloft an Italian flag bearing a fascist symbol while plying his trade in Madrid. In 2007 he lent his name to radio adverts for Eva Perón summer camps run by the Italian radical right. And so it goes on. AS Roma midfielder Daniele de Rossi is public in his support for the neo-fascist Forza Nova party. His former teammate, Alberto Aquilani, now in England with Liverpool FC, has a large collection of busts of Mussolini. Other players are known to have the song *Faccetta Nera* programmed as their mobile ringtone. Players with left-wing sympathies are few or prefer to remain silent.

Such sentiments need an identifiable target – some are easy to hand at football matches. Incidents of racism in Italian football stadia are ever-present. The talented 19-year-old Inter Milan striker Mario Balotelli – born to Ghanaian parents but having adopted Italian citizenship – complained in early 2010 of the racist and fascist insults hurled at him by rival fans, one of whom proclaimed 'There are no black Italians'. Explanations for the proliferation of such attitudes and behaviours have to be found in the socio-cultural history of Italy; a nation that will seek security in its glorious memories yet willingly celebrates foreign models, and is resentful and triumphant in its isolationism. The processes of globalisation have revealed weaknesses in its armour. Over the past 20 years, five million 'new citizens' have entered the Italian peninsula mainly from Africa and Eastern Europe. Among many of the cities, Rome is experiencing the crises and neuroses of modernity but, having avoided the experiences of urban industrialisation, it has some catching up to do. Rome is a bureaucratic city *par excellence* and manifests a demographic that has not changed much in nature in the 50 years since Mussolini took power. The new multi-ethnic presence has provoked in many a nostalgic search which is ethnocentric and exalting of a glorious and romanticised past. The might of history sits alongside – in many senses – the anachronistic cult of tradition. Football fans would recognise this correlate.

While neo-fascists colonise some Italian football stadia they have – as this study illustrates so well – an existence beyond the 90-minute game. In the first decade of the new millennium the historic piazzas of Rome have witnessed fascist-inspired disorder. In early 2000 an American tourist was stabbed by two assailants whose homes revealed to police an arsenal of weaponry and fascist paraphernalia. In the same location in 2006, AS Roma's *Nucleo Eur* gathering established a notoriety that resulted in them being outlawed. Curiously the group also contained fans of SS Lazio. Their collective attempt to occupy a building in the centre of Rome was prevented by the Roman authorities. Days later, graffiti appeared there, celebrating the death of a man murdered by the knife of a fascist. Other areas of socialising have attracted the wrath of neo-fascist fan groups. In July 2009, 24 fans of SS Lazio were arrested for attacking left-wing sympathisers at a rock concert. Italian neo-fascist sympathisers are even prepared to cross borders to proclaim their ideology. In December 2009, a fixture between Austria Vienna and the Basque club Athletic Bilbao was suspended for 20 minutes as neo-fascists lit distress flares whose smoke enveloped the pitch and made visibility impossible. Fans of SS Lazio were involved. Having watched their side play in Salzburg the day before, the Italians joined their neo-fascist Austrian friends in seeking to provoke the visiting Basques who hail from a region with a strong anti-Francoist tradition – a fact which the banner announcing 'Viva Franco' beside the Roman salute reminded them of.

The words and actions of the neo-fascists have unsettled the political status quo of Italy. Football fanatics in Italy have for decades celebrated their position via song and slogan. Many now proclaim their longing for elements of neo-fascism and the pursuit of the eternal yesterday, alongside their football songs. Their stadia cacophonies invoke the might of Roman history and celebrate fascist traditions based in notions of honour and loyalty, parochialism and nationalism. Some among their ranks – as this study illustrates – invoke the tradition of the 'warrior' believing they have a duty today, to rescue a society deemed corrupt, in which elite football clubs and the men who administer the game at the top level epitomise of all that is bad in contemporary Italy. Intolerant of political opponents, the neo-fascist gatherings adopt the pose of libertarians when proclaiming the virtuousness of their cause and the courage of their actions. But many belonging to such groups are quick to claim victimhood when police penalise or oppress their overt displays of neo-fascist sentiment. Such people and their gatherings are discomforting; their neo-fascist logic unsettles the Italian political machine and pollutes the Italian football stadia. This is a story that needs telling.

The authors provide a plethora of detail to explain such processes and account for the reactions neo-fascist fan groupings provoke from both political opponents and state representatives. In such contests people have died and the uniformed agents of the state have been deployed to break the groups. The authors suggest, however, that those celebrating such political sympathies – and their attendant antagonisms – refuse to be cowed and will not fade away. The book is thus essential reading for those interested in both the contemporary attraction of the ideologies of neo-fascism and the unfinished project that is the pursuit of parliamentary democracy and the modern nation state.

Professor Nicola Porro
Faculty of Sport Sciences
University of Cassino, Italy

January 2010

ACKNOWLEDGEMENTS

This project would not have happened without the collaboration of the *Boys Roma* and *Irriducibili* of Lazio. In particular, we thank Gianpaolo, Yuri, Katia, Paolo, Fabrizio T., Fabrizio P. and most importantly Paolo Zappavigna.

A big *Grazie* is due to Dr. Massimo Carboni, editor of *Supertifo* magazine, to Dr. Domenico Mazzilli and Dr. Valeri of the Italian Ministry of the Interior and Italian journalists Franco Arturi, Gabriele Marcotti and Giuseppe Tassi. Gratitude is also due to the webmasters of the ASRomaultras and UltrasLazio.

From the academic world, precious advice came from the direction of Prof. Nicola Porro, Prof. Dick Hobbs, Dr. Malcolm Young and Prof. Richard Giulianotti. The authors are indebted to Professor Emeritus Jennifer Hargreaves for negotiating the bursary for this project. Our thanks are also due to Professor Ian Campbell who, in his capacity as Subject Leader (Sports Sciences) of the School of Sport and Education and as Pro-Vice Chancellor of Brunel University, showed constant trust in both our academic abilities.

Sincere thanks are due to commissioning editor Charlotte Croft and the many pleasant meetings at the appropriate venue of Soho's *Bar Italia*. The editing was conducted with typical efficiency by David Pearson and Kate Wanwimolruk, the marketing was slickly executed by Naomi Webb.

A study of the home of Roman Catholicism would not be complete without our invoking the saints. The prayers dedicated to Padre Pio were answered and the life and works of Don Bosco continue to inspire.

Our thanks are due to our respective wives Helena and Hanafiah for their constant support and love throughout the difficult moments of this venture.

December 2009

INTRODUCTION: THE DARK HEART IN THE ETERNAL CITY

Just like the relationship with an impossibly beautiful but selfish, argumentative and downright mean partner, it is anything but healthy. It fosters pain and suspicion, insecurity and dissatisfaction. You know that – rationally – you should call it quits, but you can't help yourself. You keep going back and, once in a very long while, you glimpse the fleeting beauty and intoxicating warmth that continues to keep you hooked. It's an addiction and an unhealthy one at that. And yet you need your fix and for those who are addicts they know that they sure as hell are not going to get it from a league like the Premiership, where relegated teams are applauded off the pitch, effort is rewarded more than results and Steve McLaren gets contract extension after contract extension. Yes, we're sick. But at least we're real.

Review of 'Calcio: A History of Italian Football'
by Gabriele Marcotti in *When Saturday Comes*

Italy remains utterly unlike any of its European neighbours. The powerful creativity of the Italian soul has always manifest a 'dark heart', evident in a penchant for political turmoil, organised crime and a willingness to embrace political extremism and its concomitant violence. At the same time the Italian nation has fascinated the world with its style, cuisine, sensuality and its obsession with *il calcio* (football). Indeed the great Italian-born polymath (and Professor of Sociology) Umberto Eco opined in exasperation that social revolution was not possible in his native land because the populace put too much of its time, passion and energies into the Sunday afternoon fixtures of the professional football leagues and the accompanying *Totocalcio* state radio football commentary broadcasting.

The hypothesis of Eco informed, to a degree, the years of research for this book which centred on one of the world's most renowned cities – Rome – and its environs known as Lazio. The Lazio region consists of some 5.1 million citizens with Rome, the administrative centre and Italian capital, accounting for some 3.7 million residents. The capital's two biggest club sides are AS Roma and SS Lazio. Their two hardcore fan sub-cultures – *Boys* Roma and the Lazio *Irriducibili* – are referred to colloquially as '*UltraS*', a word too often wrongly presumed to be synonymous with the English term 'hooligan'. Semantics is crucial here; *ultrá* and *UltraS* can be very confusing terms (in English the latter would be considered the plural). They are, however, two ways of conceiving the hardcore, football-supporter faction. For the *ultrá* the football team is the most important thing in their existence; *UltraS* by contrast put the group and its aims before the team so an ideological motif is ever-present. To be an *ultrá* means being anchored to club traditions and not caring about individualistic or sub-group style; their main concerns are football-related passion as reflected in folklore, flags, and any paraphenalia that spectacularise the football *curves*. The *ultrá* use chants from popular songs which represent the city and its football-balling traditions. The *UltraS* (for example the *Irriducibili* and the *Boys*) place great importance on their own personal and group styles reflected *par excellence* in their own merchandising. The *UltraS* favour a football support most visibly and audibly present in the stadium by staccato clapping and chants. The words of their songs are more sophisticated and at times refer to social and political issues. Crucially, the *UltraS* share the same ideals enacted in the football stadium in their everyday life; they follow a code of violence with an ideological imprint. Groups such as the *Boys* and *Irriducibili* denounce the corruption of money in Italian football, but also dislike and manifest a resistance for both Italian and international politics, specifically around issues such as the invasive power of political parties in the Italian society, the housing emergency, illegal and irregular immigration, and the politics of Israel in Palestine. Their appearance was concomitant with the *Tangentopoli* (bribesville) scandal of the mid-1980s and with it a loss of integrity and values across society[1]. Today the word *UltraS* has an

---

[1] *Tangentopoli* describes a political scandal that initially arose around the granting of public works contracts. This then revealed the illicit financing of political parties and the bribery of politicians. In response, a team of magistrates acting under the authority of the '*Mani Pulite*' (Clean Hands) investigation and composed of Antonio Di Pietro, Francesco Saverio Borrelli, Gherardo Colombo and Pier Camillo Davigo, uncovered systematic corruption within the major political parties and illegal payment of monies as normal practice in all public bodies. These revelations caused the estrangement of public opinion from politics, and the eventual destruction, via judicial inquiry, of an entire political class (cf. Barbaceto et al. 2002).

overt and explicit contemporary political element, inextricably linked as it is with late 20th-century Italian political extremism.

Because of their similar, boorish behaviour, it is an obvious assumption to consider both the long-established *ultrá* and the more recent *UltraS* as being synonymous with the hooligans in English football. This is wrong. The word 'hooligan' has its roots in Victorian England and was originally applied to a bellicose extended family of anti-social Irish immigrants living in London. However, the word has since developed a life of its own and has now been applied globally to suspect gatherings of young men whose modes of behaviour are not approved of by the state and its representatives. As a word then, 'hooligan' has no definition in law, but is a label with extraordinary political and symbolic resonance.

In the Italian context, the *UltraS* are perhaps hooligans, but of a very different ilk, because they are now inextricably linked with late 20th-century Italian neo-fascism and a crucial fixture within the new millennium's social milieu. Focusing on the relationship between politics and football in the Italian state, what follows chronicles how various neo-fascist sympathies have been manifest by the Italian electorate since the 1920s, but since the late 1970s support for this political genre has been particularly proclaimed at football stadia throughout Italy. The genre changes shape as new generations appear, but the basic premise remains.

Over the past two decades the link – perceived and actual – between political extremism and football fans has been the subject of academic, political and policing debate throughout Europe. It is not rare to witness manifestations of intolerance and ideological statements referring to regional, national and international issues at football stadia globally. In Italian football stadia, political representation has been evident for decades; politics has been integral to all realms of Italian society and culture since the origin of the nation. As one of the most significant of Italian cultural practices, football has not been an exception. A combination of political theory and the will to action to achieve those goals – or resist the opponent – inspires tens of thousands of young male football supporters. The Italian football stadium might thus be interpreted as a 21st-century social *agorá*, where political opinions otherwise ghettoised in society are freely expressed in pursuit of a wider consensus. The football authorities do not always celebrate this possibility. The

Italian state now does all it can to stifle (and criminalise) such commentary and display.

Employing as its conceptual frameworks the New Consensus Theory on fascism and the ideas of philosophers Julius Evola and Georges Sorel, this analysis hypothesises that the neo-fascist's doctrine manifested by the ideologically-orientated fan groups may be understood as both a consequence of, and a resistance against, the dominant socio-cultural and political values of contemporary Italy and contemporary football. What follows offers a riposte to Eco who failed to consider that social revolution was possible precisely because of the Italian obsession with football, and that the potential for political change might well be facilitated by political advocates at the opposite end of the political spectrum to that which he considered the vanguard.

The final game of the 2003–2004 Italian *Serie A* season – a May Sunday afternoon Roma-Lazio derby – sparked just this kind of debate. Chapter 12 contains a full description of the brutally violent events of that day; suffice to say for now that it placed the true power of the *UltraS* in the international spotlight. One participant in events, Todde, an integral part of the *Boys Roma UltraS* gathering, was arrested for his part in the disorder. He tells his version of events:

> The derby started calmly; there were no violent clashes between *Romanisti* and *Laziali*; the only clashes were against the police. Both us and the Lazio fans were peaceful in the stadium. The problems originated from the *cani sciolti* (groups of teenagers) without tickets who exploited situations in order to enter the stadium free. They started throwing stones and running around provoking a brutal police response. At around 8.30 p.m. when the first half was nearly ended, the rumour that one such youngster was dead was believed by everyone because the conditions for this tragedy to happen were believable. The police had lined up armoured vehicles outside the ground. The most shit in their method were the Guardia di Finanza who are not usually used for this kind of operation, so when they helped the police with their batons they were the most brutal. They used armoured vehicles to

disperse the crowd driving at 50–70 km per hour … under the circumstances the rumour that a youth had been killed by them was plausible. It was possible that a kid stumbled in front of the armoured vehicle. In all this chaos and 'guerrilla climate' the police charged the *curve sud* because many exploited the occasion to enter without paying. The police then opened the gate that joins the Tribuna Tevere and 40 riot police charged and struck indiscriminately those in the piazza. They were unlucky because all the *UltraS* were already in the curve so they answered with violence; the police were cornered, and even the DIGOS with the surveillance cameras were beaten; all the *curve* stood united against 40–50 police who left but upon leaving made threatening gestures meaning 'we will see each other after'. At 9.00 p.m. when the situation calmed and the crowd was watching the match they – 200 police – came back in riot gear and with three jeeps on the pitch perimeter started to launch tear gas in the *curve sud*. These 200 police were out of control but if they get injured they get their days off paid for. This is not the case if we get injured, and believe me you do if they shoot tear gas at you at point blank range. I saw a man receiving 13 stitches in the head because of a tear gas cannister. We cannot go to hospital; if the police find you receiving treatment you get a stadium banning order. Many of us who are injured by the police do not go to hospital; we prefer to take care of the injuries by ourselves. There was no conspiracy that day, just an issue of respect. The *Laziali* believed this boy (a Roma supporter) was dead, killed by the police [It was later discovered that no one had been killed in the skirmish.]. Out of respect they took down their banners and wanted the derby to be abandoned. There is reciprocal respect for death; the *curve sud* do not make banners to ridicule the *Laziali* for the death of Paparelli [a Lazio supporter accidentally killed by pyrotechnics fired by a Roma fan in the late 70s]. I was arrested and evidence presented from photographs that the police took in the square before the match when I was not doing anything illegal. My lawyer told me the police were attempting to prove a link between this image and the incidents in the stadium. In the absence of being charged I faced four days in police custody, 50 days under house arrest, and two months of having to sign daily in the police station at 7.00 a.m., 2.00 p.m. and 9.00 p.m. Currently I sign only when Lazio and Roma play: three times a day for Roma and three times a day for Lazio and this will last until September 2007...

In these skirmishes the forces of law and order have suffered their own casualties. In early February 2007, Inspector Filippo Raciti was killed during an ambush of a police vehicle by 200 youths who were followers of CC Catania before the Catania-Palermo Sicilian derby, in what many observers considered a pre-planned attack by home fans as the visiting fans arrived at the stadium. As the latter were escorted to the stadium, the mob of 200 appeared and attacked them while hundreds more within the stadium ran out of it to join them. In doing so they trapped a police vehicle in the middle; Raciti was in the vehicle. Months previously a police officer was severely beaten on the Catania *curve* by the same fans. The object that struck the deceased was a piece of sink pulled from a wall during the stadium tournament. Other objects thrown at police included rocks, iron bars and fireworks. Raciti's death was attributed to heart failure caused by the impact. The professional football programme was suspended until the next Sunday and his death dominated the news for weeks. Parliament debated the tragedy; the state had to both act and be seen to be acting.

The Laboratory of Bad Ideas?

While football fans rioted and police officers died, the Italian electorate voted and its politicians opined. In April 2007 Romano Prodi's centre-left coalition won the General Election by 25,000 votes, a margin so tight that the defeated President Silvio Berlusconi refused – and to this day still refuses – to concede defeat. In December 2007 Giorgio Bettio, a Northern League town councillor in Treviso, announced in the Council Chambers that should an immigrant commit a crime against an Italian national, 10 immigrants should be punished for the act. Bettio remarked that his rage came about out of a desire to protect his mother, who felt threatened by the presence of immigrants. Prodi's government was brought down in February 2008 when its slender majority was defeated when four senators in the Upper House refused to vote with the government on foreign policy measures. In short, the Union of Christian Democrats would not join a government which included unreformed Communists – Prodi had 27 Communists in his coalition – represented by seven factions. Upon the defeat being announced, the dissenters faced verbal abuse from fellow senators and a bound collection of newspapers was thrown at them from across the Chamber.

The vote centred on a package of foreign policy issues which made the left in the coalition uneasy; it was very similar to what the centre-right had proposed in Berlusconi's government. Three senators for life – one the 87-year-old Giulio Andreotti – and two others voted against the government; another abstained. The foreign affairs issue concerned the deployment of 1200 Italian troops in Afghanistan and the refusal of the Foreign Ministry to bring them home as demanded by the senators (one a pacifist, one a Trotsykite). A further bone of contention was the plan to build a second US military base in Vicenza, which had weeks earlier brought 100,000 Italians onto the streets in protest. The vote was also about the contest between the government and the Catholic Church; the former was seeking to legitimatise civil unions, including those entered into by gay couples. To secure extra support following this defeat, Prodi dumped the civil union legislation. As a consequence co-habiting couples continued to have no rights. Prodi's government was doing well by the standards of Italian politics. His coalition enjoyed a large majority by the *Camera* (Lower House), but a one-seat majority in the Senate. Prodi's government only obtained majority votes by relying on ostensibly neutral senators. Taxes had been raised to recover some of the growing national debt; tax dodgers were being pursued. Restrictive practices so prevalent in the professions were being challenged. But the chaos that is Italian politics won the day. The electoral system that Prodi had won with – and then lost – had been crafted in 2005 by Roberto Calderoli, a well-known exponent of the political party *Lega Nord* (Northern League). The latter described his design as 'a pile of shit'.

Football always offered a distraction from political chaos. However, in recent years football in Italy has been going through a dark phase, more off the pitch than on it. The 2006 World Cup victory of the national team and the 2007 all-Italian Champions League final made up for some lost pride. Talk of a crisis in Italian football is, however, ever-ripe. In recent years, the world of Italian football has been marred by problems such as violence (two *Serie A* matches were abandoned in 2005–6, and in *Serie B* the 2006 season did not even start due to previous serious crowd trouble in which a fan died). Protests and contestations from a variety of professional clubs have arisen in connection with the so-called *'aiuti arbitrali'* championship victories obtained by the help of referees in return for cash or services, the issuing of false passports creating a European ancestry for South American players, the presence of doping – mainly of nandrolone and the apparent approval of its use by the clubs' medical staff – and widespread allegations of match fixing.

The start of the 2006/07 season was delayed because agreement on television rights could not be reached. Over the previous two years television rights amounted to 53.8 per cent of the total income of the top *Serie A* league clubs. The two broadcasting competitors, *Tele+* and *Stream*, started a feud around the distribution of monies which centred on the large discrepancy between the monies received by the big and smaller clubs. Among the former, Juventus, AC Milan and Inter Milan received payments from *Tele+* of E52.3, E48.1 and E48.1 million respectively. Smaller provincial clubs like Verona, Perugia and Piacenza received less than E10.1 million each. The difference for the clubs contracted to *Stream* was less notable but still discriminatory. The amount paid by the rights-holder for the Juventus-Perugia fixture was five times the amount paid by the same rights-holder for Perugia-Juventus. In this way the financial gulf between the clubs inevitably increased. The aforementioned top sides also had political power that the others did not. This brought huge resentment and accusations of corruption at the top level of the game. In Italian football money talked and everyone connected to the game believed that success could be bought.

A month before the 2006 World Cup Final, hosted by Germany, Italian football was embroiled in an enormous scandal. Phone taps, authorised in 2004 and focussing on key footballing personnel in Turin and Naples, revealed a world of bribery and match-fixing involving a gang of six men. These included Luciano Moggi, the General Manager of Juventus; Antonio Giraudo, the Chief Executive of Juventus; and Innocenzo Mazzini, a Deputy President of the FIGC (Italian Football

Association); a referee also implicated was shortly to represent Italy at the World Cup. The six had between them manipulated the outcome of the entire *Serie A* season and championship. Four of the *Serie A*'s most famous clubs – Juventus, AC Milan, Lazio and Fiorentina – were implicated in the match-fixing. In a showcase trial at the Olympic Stadium in Rome, Juventus, Lazio and Fiorentina were relegated to *Serie B*. Juventus were also stripped of their 2004–5 *scudetto* (championship). Their 2005–6 *scudetto* was awarded to Inter Milan. AC Milan remained in *Serie A*, but with a 15 point reduction to start the season. All six men subject to the inquiry were banned from any involvement with football for between five years and 30 months.

Some five months later after a series of appeals and arbitration hearings, Lazio and Fiorentina were re-instated in *Serie A*, with penalties of three and 15 points respectively. AC Milan also started the season in *Serie A* with a reduced eight-point reduction and retained their place in the Champions League. Juventus failed in their attempts to get their punishment lifted, but their season in *Serie B* saw their point deduction reduced to minus nine. Juventus did not take their punishment lightly. Having exhausted the sporting appeals process, they sought justice in the civil courts to overturn the sentence and receive damages of £88m which, if awarded, would bankrupt the Italian FA. Their appeal argued that they did not attempt to influence referees. While there was no disputing the evidence that Luciano Moggi, in his capacity as Juventus General Manager, had made hundreds of calls to FA officials seeking specific referees for his club's matches, the issue was more about ethics than law. He had, they argued, acted against the principle of the sport, but had done nothing wrong in the eyes of the law. Consequently, they argued the punishment served out to Juve was wrong. No evidence existed to show that anyone acted on Moggi's request. In his defence Moggi explained his actions as 'lobbying' – an integral feature of democracy. As General Manager of a corporate entity with a Stock Exchange listing, he was, he argued, doing business as it should be done. By contrast, the world's footballing governing body FIFA was implementing a morality to serve entities that existed for recreational sports purposes. Such regulations and those who upheld them were at odds with what football clubs had evolved into. Meanwhile the Italian national team won the World Cup.

Over the past 25 years, Italy has won one World Cup and its clubs have seven Champions League titles. This is a remarkable feat if one considers that the 1963 Inter Milan victory in the European Cup was the first significant Italian victory since the national team won the 1938 World Cup. Between 1963 and 1970 Inter and AC Milan won four European Cups and one Winners Cup. The national team won the 1968 European Championship and came runners-up in the 1970 World Cup Final. Italian football was globally loved, and at times was both sublime and enchanting. The game manifested the best and worst of the Italian soul. That said, the world of *il bel calcio* (the beautiful game) was ever ugly. As far back as 1927 Torino were stripped of their title following revelations of bribery. In the late 1970s Milan and Lazio were relegated for their part in match-fixing. Some 20 years later the Juventus club doctor was found guilty of doping his players throughout the 1990s. His 22-month suspended prison sentence was overturned on appeal.

The Republic of Football
Football in Italy determines the circulation of about 80 per cent of the total monies spent on sports. Over the past few seasons Italians have spent hundred of millions of Euros on admission tickets for football matches and football magazines and on the football betting game called *Totalcalcio*. If we compare that amount of money with some of the nation's biggest industries, football finds itself almost at the top. His Holiness Pope Jean-Paul II in his Sunday '*Angelus*' spoke many times about the powerful effect that football exerted on any Italian province and Italian social life generally. The common saying that 'football is the foundation of the state' exceeds the meaning in Italy. Nowadays such a relationship is felt more than ever. During the *Campionato* (*Serie A* Championship) there is a typical Sunday scenario for all Italians. Following lunch, families and friends gather in football clubs or bars with pre-paid TV channels, or at home to follow the TV or radio stations. Everywhere you can hear the commentator's voices, particularly via the radio programme *Calcio Minuto Per Minuto*. Following the match, there is the unmissable TV broadcast of *90th Minuto* with the first interviews with coaches and players, accompanied by the '*Schedina*' whose holders hope for a points accumulation numbering 13

in the *Totocalcio* lottery, and therefore a fortune in winnings. *Totocalcio* is an Italy-wide phenomenon – one might say 'I did 13' to explain unexpected good luck. A victory in important matches sees hundreds of fans in cars, on scooters, bicycles or other vehicles created specially for the occasion roam the respective city's streets blaring their horns in celebration. The same kind of behaviour, with obviously some differences, reminds the older people of what happened 60 years previously in the Italian piazzas where loudspeakers blared with the voice of Mussolini as he attempted to excite his people about the imminent war.

Il calcio support in its various manifestations involves participants taking upon themselves various roles and identities alongside the like-minded. These impermanent structures are at times very pragmatic. Many football rivalries are embodied in decades-old parochial, urban and regional chauvinisms which, at times, offer possibilities for verbal and occasionally physical violence. At times hostilities transcend the parochial and present political beliefs in opposition to the state, and involve attacks on the state's uniformed representatives. Such collective action is dependent on agreement as to what is symbolically and culturally relevant to the participants. This, in turn, is responsive to the wider national, and occasionally global, political milieu.

01

CHAINS OF MEANING

In October 2008, world champions Italy played a 2010 World Cup qualifier against Bulgaria in Sofia. Notable among the Italians in the crowd was a group of about 150 supporters who, sporting Celtic crosses on their chests, enacted the Roman salute during the pre-match playing of the Italian national anthem, and chanted *'Duce, Duce'* throughout the match in honour of the long dead Italian fascist leader Benito Mussolini. This activity outraged the Italian media, who reported the incidents and thus made the newly formed *UltraS Italia* instantly notorious. However, when interviewed by the Italian newspaper *La Repubblica*, the President of the *Osservatorio Nazionale sulle Manifestazioni Sportive* (the National Observatory on Sport Events of the Ministry of the Interior), Dr Domenico Mazzilli, set out to play down the events in Sofia, arguing, 'The chants '*Duce, Duce*' and the Roman salute during the national anthem are not a crime in Bulgaria … I am not a sociologist but crimes are specific to the country in which they occur. Until now this group has been calm, now let's see what really happened and we will act in the future. But what of the Bulgarians who showed disrespect to our national anthem with whistles? Even if this is not a crime surely it is a rude behaviour.'

This episode illustrated to Italy and to the world what seemed to be yet another manifestation of Italian-induced, football-related intemperance normally blamed on the *ultrá* (hardcore supporters). However, to more interested parties it also confirmed not just the existence but the increasing strength of the *UltraS Italia* – a set of supporters who are keen to publicly express their ideological influences.

To begin an investigation into the behaviour of notorious Italian football supporters, it is essential to examine the setting for most of their activities – the football stadium. Each week a football stadium becomes the venue for a broad range of collective behaviour as well as providing a wide variety of associations for supporters. For more than 40 years now, since the 1960s, the activities of the *ultrá* in the *curve* (the place in the stadium where the home team's hardcore supporters are located, so-named because of the curve of the stadium) have become renowned for their visual and oral choreographies. Whether it's the singing, the songs, the gestures or the sometimes violent behaviour of the supporters that gather there each week, the stadium plays host to a ritual event that differs from club to club and stadium to stadium. These activities are carried out each week in front of an audience of other supporters (*tifosi*) who have usually seen it before, expect it and sometimes even admire it. It is as though the collective experience of the crowd permits this kind of behaviour in the confines of the stadium, in which a kind of micro-system is created for the duration of the match.

Identifying who these supporters are has been an area of interest for many years. But, of course, the reality is that they are, usually, just ordinary young men who for the most part live their lives like others but whose behaviour changes when they go to the football. The correlation of the word *tifo* (football fan) with 'fanaticism' is thought to derive from the medical pathology of typhus, an illness classic symptoms of which alternate phases of illness and well-being. A football fan in Italy is thus characterised in the public eye as being influenced by phases of 'normal' behaviour, which are set alongside temporary periods of (football-related) abnormality. For example, active *tifo*, *ultrás* and *UltraS* do not always see the entire match as they busy themselves in a variety of tasks on matchday (a paradox and an absurdity in the eyes of 'ordinary' fans who pay their admission to watch the football). Those leading the chants will usually turn their backs to the pitch to face fellow supporters as they urge them on to voice their encouragement of the team and to create a spectacle. Some will dedicate great amounts of time outside the stadium prior to the match in co-ordinating group operations, such as fighting with rival fans, and initiate or at least maintain the social order of this micro-system.

The significance of the *UltraS* groupings, therefore, has been crying out for an inquiry, even though any proposed investigation was going to be notoriously difficult. These groups do not readily welcome the non-partisan; nor do they easily tolerate the intellectually curious. Enter *Football, Fascism and Fandom*, the first study of the *UltraS* from the privileged view of 'in the field'.

The research for this book is focused on two *UltraS* groups. The first is the *Boys*, followers of AS Roma, who have been notoriously neofascist in character since 1972, and who are the oldest *UltraS* group in Italy. The second is the *Irriducibili*, who follow SS Lazio, and who, since 1987, have attained a notoriety based on toughness and violence both inside and outside the Italian borders. The *Irriducibili* display and maintain a strong oppositional attitude towards the Italian state for, as Giovanni (age 40), one of their leaders, explained, 'I do not want to be too judgmental or maybe just judge the politicians, but there is a certain culture prevalent in Italy that favours chaos and moral degradation. We elect the wrong people and we have a wrong attitude towards the *res publica* (public interest).'

The *Boys* Roma

02
THE SET-UP

While the subject of this book is clearly a study of one aspect of the city of Rome and the region of Lazio that surrounds it, what follows would not have been possible without the input of the English city of Sheffield. For it was there that the Old Harrovian schoolmasters of Sheffield College taught their pupils – the sons of the Victorian middle class – the principles of an invasive new game played with a ball. Ideally the game was to be played with the ethics of 'fair play' and 'sportsmanship' that were central to the genre of the middle class gentleman-amateur. The boys were so enamoured by what they were taught that some of them went on to found what was the world's first football club – Sheffield FC – in 1857.

Within no time at all, however, these pioneers discovered that the Corinthian ideals of playing the game were easily and constantly subverted by the need to win. Those attracted to this new game, with its basic rules, often brought their own version of how it should be played. So, from its very beginnings, the game of 'Association Football' witnessed the urge for victory and the desire to achieve this by conflict and intimidation, running alongside the pursuit of victory that utilised tactical manoeuvre and superior athleticism. Football was never just about the playing the game; it was also about victory and performance. Soon it needed an audience because spectators enhanced a performance, and footballers were soon to learn, in the same way as thespians in the theatre, that the responses of the audience were instructive as to how well they – the footballing actors – were performing.

For 100 years this was enough. But by the middle of the 20th century, in the mid-1960s, audiences in and around English football began to make their own contribution to the weekly social drama. The terraces at Sheffield's two professional football clubs, Sheffield United and Sheffield Wednesday, witnessed early manifestations of what was to become a national and then an international disorderly spectacle; quickly branded as 'football hooliganism'. A plethora of responses from politicians, police sources, press and media spokesmen poured forth. Academic commentary followed, most notably from Sheffield-born criminologist Ian Taylor, who put forward the explanation that the hooligans were working class youths rebelling against the 'modernisation' of the game that had started in the 1950s. But these insights were strictly based in the academic domain; few members of the academia would seek to venture out into the terraces to see what was really happening and seek a greater truth.

As hooliganism got worse and began to affect more people all around the country, this lack of scientific investigation was eventually addressed, firstly by sociological debate and then much later in a plethora of biographies penned by the hooligan participants themselves. These varied accounts made it apparent that the game itself and its fans were bound together in a (footballing) world that was essentially based in conflict and passion.[1] Of course, in a city like Sheffield such passion and conflict was not just confined to football. The place had a centuries-old reputation for political radicalism and indeed in the 1980s was the self-declared core of the 'People's Republic of South Yorkshire' with its oft-proclaimed antagonism to the principles of the government of Margaret Thatcher. Since that time the conflict and passion that the game of football carries all over England has been infected by a new set of socio-economic demands such as the break-up of the traditional idea of 'society', the need to belong, the celebration of success at all costs and a political system (even under a Labour administration) that sees (and in many instances ignores) the ever-wider disparities between the economically privileged and those at the bottom of the heap.

Today, it seems, the concept of 'sportsmanship' in the game has all but vanished at the elite level. Players dive to deceive and deliberately handle the ball to win games. Matches are fixed and referees are regularly abused by fans, players and managers. Retributive tackles are executed months after the original sleight. And the now all-seated English spectator continues to applaud success no matter how it is achieved. Amid them are sections of men who for 40 years have been willing to fight those who might deny them their sometimes violent part in these occasions. Throughout all this, however, the English terraces have remained largely free of political activity. There was a degree of activism in and around football in the late 1970s and early 1980s by the

---

[1] The world of the Sheffield football hooligan was examined by Gary Armstrong over the decade 1986–96. This prolonged ethnographic inquiry produced *Football Hooligans: Knowing the Score* (Berg, Oxford). Published in 1999 and now in its third reprint, this text was the first to utilise a methodology renown to Social Anthropology, and the world of those considered 'hooligans' was represented like never before. The individual hooligan behaviour was contextualised as the significance of the local culture was presented. The research provoked many to ask if what was applicable to Sheffield (and indeed the UK) was replicated elsewhere. An appetite to address that question informed this book and the years of research to write it. The choice of Italy was a consequence of visiting the country at the time of the 1980 European Nations Championship and a fascination with the Italianate politics of Malta which lies 60 km off the southern tip of Sicily and produced the 2008 text, co-authored with Jon Mitchell, *Local and Global Football* (Routledge). Football and politics were ever intertwined.

far-right National Front (NF) and its later associates such as Combat 18. This was contested in leaflet campaigns and music festivals by the left-leaning Anti-Nazi League and the solid-left Socialist Workers Party. Despite the presence of far-right sympathists at a number of grounds around the country on matchday, often selling copies of the NF magazine *Bulldog*, none of this came to any large-scale fruition compared to what seemed to have been occurring elsewhere in parts of Western Europe; or what was to occur in parts of Eastern Europe after 1989 and the demise of the Soviet bloc. As these differences developed, however, one issue did still link the various genres of 'hooliganism', and that was a willingness to resist the impositions of the powerful.

The purpose of this book is to look beyond the work of the English academics and consider those situations where a political dogma or vision had an influence on events in the football world. The focus for the research was to be on venues where fascism and the far-right perspectives had occurred and been influential. This inevitably led to the volatile Italian situation, the country where fascism had its origins and dogma laid down; and where a far-right vision of reality still seemed to be pervasive and closely tied to some factions of football support and behaviour. Traditional right-wing tendencies have had a resurgence in Italy in recent years and there has been a dramatic increase in members of neo-fascist youth groups. Some eight years ago, a mere 20 out of 400 high school students (aged 15 to 17) elected in the *Consulta Provinciale Studentesca* (District Students' Youth Council) represented the far right. By 2007, neo-fascist representatives were in the majority and managed an annual budget of E80,000 provided by the national government. Data from 2009 records that there are now at least 50,000 neo-fascists in Rome.

Rome was chosen as a suitable centre of study for other reasons too. Firstly, the Lazio region and its major city have a strong political tradition. Secondly, the city's football enthusiasm is dominated by two main teams, both of which have banks of clearly visible right-wing supporters on the *curve*; and thirdly because these supporters have a history of disorderly conduct that has often carried noticeable political baggage. One aim was to come to an understanding of the influences on, and the actions of, the far-right supporters of AS Roma and SS Lazio and to see how they operated and were sustained.

There were many other questions to be answered: was their existence to be best explained by a need to satisfy a 'macho' need for conflict? Was it simply xenophobia? Was it the case that the game provided an image and metaphor of the Imperial Roman ethos which, it seemed, these groups still favoured? Was it, perhaps, a remnant hangover of a desire for control and state power that the Italian fascist Benito Mussolini had once embodied? To answer these questions, and to seek out further details on how the *Boys* and the *Irriducibili* functioned and operated, some scientific fieldwork was essential. To do this, and to achieve any true understanding of this 'political hooliganism', required a route-map into the research process and an Italian (in fact, Roman) native. The crucial figure is Alberto Testa (referred to henceforth as AT) who originally began this research as a student at Brunel University and who was given the task of accessing the semi-closed world of the *UltraS*. He explains how this access was negotiated later in this chapter.

At stadia across Italy *curve* embrace a political ideology, be it *rossa* (red, communism) or *nera* (black, neo-fascism), in part because of the social and political history of the area in which the football club and stadium exist. The result of this is that, generally, a *rossa* city, such as Livorno, will mainly attract left and extreme left fans, while a city that is traditionally *nera*, such as Rome, will have *curve* that are predominantly formed by centre-right and extreme right supporters. Unlike the stadia of England, then, the *curva* is not only important as a sector of the stadium where people can discharge a collective passion for their favourite football team, but it is also important as a location in which the 'rebels' of the city can find space to voice their political beliefs and often their opposition to the current state of affairs of Italian society.

Rome's main football stadium, the Stadio Olimpico, where both Roma and Lazio play, is one of the most important venues for the gathering of the city's youth. It has two 'symbolic' territories: the *curva sud* for the *Boys* and the *curva nord* for the *Irriducibili*. Cesare of the *Irriducibili* (aged in his late twenties) noted that the *curva* allowed fans, 'to express our ideas to public opinion and show that we are not only *UltraS* or, like the media affirms, "thugs" but people with a brain, able to think and unwilling to be ghettoised or unheard.' The *UltraS* see the *curva* as their 'territory', as a home to be guarded and, if necessary, defended from outsiders. According to Antonio, a 19-year-old member of the *Boys*, the *curva* is a venue into which you can welcome friends or 'whoever wants to know our world free of preconceived ideas'.

The choice of the *Boys* and the *Irriducibili* as the central focus of this book was made for a number of reasons. The 'groups' are respected among similar *UltraS* groups for the extremism of their ideology. Many Italian *UltraS* regard them as the example to follow. This dynamic of emulation, together with the nature of Italian fascism – which in its modern form tends to encourage uniformity of individuals via shared values, myths and beliefs – suggests a certain degree of transferability of the findings to other similar Italian groups. The logic of the *Irriducibili* is similar to the *Boys* regardless of the teams that they support, so the logic of those studied might be similar to other neo-fascists, such as the *Boys San* of Inter or the *Settembre Bianconero* of Ascoli. Based on such possible transferability, this micro-scale study has macro-scale implications in terms of a better understanding of the whole Italian *UltraS* phenomenon.

The main difficulty in gaining access to these groups is their intense dislike of any media attention as they have always deemed that it represents them 'unfairly'. In addition, there is a 'paranoia' concerning the constant police surveillance and intelligence gathering to which they have been subjected in the past. Suspicion towards 'outsiders' is strong; a trait shared by any radical right group due to their perception of persecution by the state.

Ethnographers seeking to study extreme political groups face another difficulty. Ideally they need to balance ethical convictions – which could lead them to expose and hinder the very groups they are studying – with impartiality. This can be problematic because the *Boys* and the *Irriducibili* both espouse an ideology with which few sociologists empathise. For instance, it is difficult to accept their discourse on 'race' or their viewpoint on the use of violence. For Todde (a 28-year-old law student at the University of Rome and a member of the *Boys*) violence was normally only kicks and punches; however, in a confrontation before a European fixture a Man Utd fan threw a bottle of beer in his face and attempted to 'glass' him. Still livid in his recollection, Todde admitted he knocked out his opponent and, as his head lay on the concrete steps, he attempted to jump on him. This is not acceptable behaviour in today's society. However, luckily for everyone involved, Todde was prevented from taking his revenge by colleagues aware that his brutal reaction could easily have resulted in the death of the opponent.

At this point it is important to state the reasons for our research into these groups who, as we have already seen, often indulge in morally indefensible behaviour. Investigating their activities, and those of similar groups such as the National Front (NF) in England in the 1980s, can lead to accusations of giving them the 'oxygen of publicity', but understanding them can bring solutions to the problems they create. English sociologist Nigel Fielding defended his research into NF activities in 1981 saying, 'My reply is that while my instinct was to reject these beliefs as forcefully as they were expressed, to have done that would have prevented me from building up a picture of the beliefs and their significance for members. It seems necessary to me that we appreciate how deeply felt these beliefs are, for we must tackle them realistically and in recognition of the fact that their advocates are as human as ourselves.'

We faced a stark choice when deciding how to gain access to the two *UltraS* groups. We were reluctant to attempt to infiltrate them for a number of reasons: it would have been ethically unfair because it involved deception; it would not have allowed for formal interviews; and open discussions would have been hard to come by. So we decided that AT would approach the groups openly, declaring his interests and his role as a researcher on a book. It is appropriate here for AT to describe how research access was negotiated in his own words:

For the purpose of gaining entry into the social word of the *Boys* and the *Irriducibili*, a minimum of knowledge about the *curva* way of life and values was needed. In this, I had an advantage over my academic colleagues given that I had a childhood passion for football combined with a similar passion for martial arts. In the early 1970s, my family moved from the north of Italy to Rome, a move that resulted in me watching an SS Lazio side win its first ever *scudetto* (championship) as a five-year-old. The Lazio and *Azzurri* (the nickname of the national team) striker, Giorgio Chinaglia, became a personal hero of mine. My choice of club, while inspired by our relocation, was also influenced by sartorial issues. The sky blue and white colours of the Lazio team shirt and the eagle insignia of the club appealed to a child unaware of the significance of aesthetics and emblems. Suffering many times for the incompetence of the team, I have remained faithful to the *biancocelesti* (white and light blues).

An education during the 1980s at a Catholic high school of repute in the city saw my passage from a simple *tifoso* to something more. I started playing football at a high level with the *Eur-Olympia* club, which is connected with AS Roma, while training in karate and judo. I found it hard to juggle the various demands on my time and, after a successful trial with a feeder club of SS Lazio, I was forced to make a tough decision – football or study? The familial commitment to big fees for an education without a commitment from their son saw a parting of the ways. Leaving active football, I dedicated my life to my studies, practising martial arts and sometimes going to watch Lazio from the perspective of the *curva nord*. My football watching activities came to a stop in 1989 as they were replaced by my study of law at the University of Naples. My martial arts training continued during university. In 1998, as I left Italy for what was presumed to be a short language study experience in the UK, my Lazio scarf and flag were packed in my luggage.

While on my 'London adventure' I maintained my Sunday matchday character as a fringe Lazio hardcore supporter from a distance. While waiting on tables and serving at Carluccio's deli near Oxford Street, I decided to put my knowledge of the *curva nord* to use, studying not only languages but also social sciences and, in particular, the behaviour of Italian football fans. As part of my research I began to return to Rome and revisit my former colleagues on the *curva*. I found people willing to talk to me. The *Boys* and *Irriducibili* knew me as a son of the Eternal City. They knew where my family lived; if I was not one of them, I was not too distant either. The years that I had lived in London provided me with a distance from my Roman past that was helpful for this project. I had gained new perspectives that helped me to under-stand my past more clearly upon my return. My perceptions were more astute as I had learned new ways of thinking. I was similar to those whom I sought to study, but I was also different. The *UltraS* I spoke to were aware of this distinction.

I knew that my first requirement was to find 'gatekeepers' to facilitate ongoing access to groups of interest; negotiation for such entry was necessary. I used my knowledge of the characters on the *curve* to select two such gatekeepers likely to be the most knowledgeable. Following this rationale I chose a man called Todde among members of the *Boys* as he was part of the *direttivo* (the equivalent of a 'members committee') and was knowledgeable about the Roman and national neo-fascist world. Among the *Irriducibile*, I selected a character called the Boxer, who, at 40 years of age, was one of the historical leaders of the group.

Gaining access to the *Boys* proved not to be problematic. However, the *Irriducibili*'s nationwide notoriety had produced constant negative exposure in the Italian media and ongoing scrutiny by the police, which made any approach to its leaders difficult; an outsider needed to pass through a series of 'filters' in order even to speak to someone.

I contacted the *Boys*, – a small group who number 200 and are just one group among others who meet in the *curva sud* – via mobile phone (a number was advertised on their website), which resulted in an appointment with one of their senior members in the *sede* (head office) in San Lorenzo, one of Rome's oldest districts in the centre of the city. Once in the *sede*, I underwent an examination of sorts, which, to my astonishment, was conducted by a woman, Francesca. I found her to be an important member of the *Boys direttivo*. She had earned a high level of respect in the otherwise exclusively male group. Francesca was an attractive woman in her 30s. She was not only working at the head office, but was also a keen sportswoman who had trained in the Korean martial art of tae kwon do. She fired several testing questions at me; she recollected a recent deceit by a person who had introduced himself to the *Boys* as a researcher, but who was actually a journalist intending to write an exposé on the group. The journalist later published what she considered lies about them. Despite this, she eventually agreed to my somewhat vague request to be allowed to 'hang out' with the group. Confirming my anxieties, Francesca warned me to be careful because if any member of the group mistook me for an undercover police officer then I might be physically assaulted. For this reason she said that Antonio – who at 19 years of age was one of the youngest in the group but also very trustworthy – would keep an eye on me.

I had already met Antonio a few times in the company of Todde. At the time Todde was working in the *Boys'* head office but was not able to go the matches as he was a *diffidato* (banned from the stadium). So Antonio accepted the role as my 'minder'. He was curious about my presence and my living in London, a city that he considered admirably 'cool'. Despite the 'cool effect' I brought with me, Francesca's warning became a reality. I was invited by the group to watch the Roma-Lazio fixture of 2005 from their position in the *curva sud* and, while using a tape recorder to record notes and chants, I was approached by one individual who asked me in a threatening way if I was a *guardia* (police officer). Antonio immediately came over to speak with me to show that I was accepted and hence staved off possible violence. After a few more meetings at the head office and the emergence of mutual empathy inspired by my previous university background in law, Todde became my gatekeeper. I was in.

Gaining admission to the *Irriducibili*'s world was more complicated. The group is far bigger in membership – some 6–7,000 people gather each week in the *curva nord*. I began by trying to contact the Boxer, a man who had a Rome-wide reputation. One matchday, I asked the men selling *Irriducibili* merchandise at the stadium for his whereabouts. They became increasingly agitated and hostile as I questioned them. I decided not to persist with this line of inquiry. Overhearing my request, another supporter explained that the Boxer was a person with strong personality is known by every Lazio footballer, the club management and all regional sports journalists. But he could not give me much other information. Having failed to meet the group at the stadium, I pursued them to their head office near the Roman working class district of Ostiense, where they held meetings and prepared banners and choreographies for the matches. The owner of an adjacent shop told me that the office was rarely open because of a supposed constant surveillance by the DIGOS, an elite anti-terrorist police unit that operates in every Italian province and is accountable to the State's anti-Terrorist police.[2] Because of these fears, the *Irriducibili* meetings were discreet with no routine programming

---

[2] The *Divisione per le Investigazioni Generali e le Operazioni Speciali* (DIGOS) reports directly to the *Direzione Centrale della Polizia di Prevenzione* (Central Directorate for Anti-Terrorism Police). It was established in 1978 via decree of the

or timetable. I moved on then to the *Irriducibili*'s merchandising warehouse, where they produced dedicated designer label hats, jackets, shirts, scarves and stickers, as well as other merchandise. Endless security 'screenings' from the workers in the warehouse followed in order to be permitted to speak to anyone even close to one of the four leaders.

Having taken phone numbers with a promise to call back, the wait for a response from a representative of the *Irriducibili* became longer and longer. Knowing the importance of the *Irriducibili* to the proposed research, I decided to play my trump card – I got my mother to call the warehouse. Sounds funny, but in Italy *La Mamma* is the fulcrum of the family and of society and revered by all, even in these circumstances. She explained to her interlocutors that I would fail to receive my PhD if I was unable to speak with the Boxer. This highly emotive and symbolic avenue of pursuit got me what I wanted; the Boxer agreed to meet. The meeting was during a Lazio-Inter match in 2005, where, as usual, he was very busy with preparations for the *curva* choreographies and chants. At the same time he was the only leader who was not banned from the stadium, and thus had the responsibility to lead his 'warriors'. After asking about the research, he agreed to be the gatekeeper. He had

---

Minister of the Interior in the context of the reform of the Italian Secret Services. The aim of the unit is to investigate and repress:

- national and international terrorist organisations
- subversive associations that promote social divisions inciting violence for racial, ethnic, or religious motives
- associations that pursue the destruction of the independence and unity of the Italian State or the change of the constitutional order by illegal means
- military or paramilitary associations
- links among national and international terrorist organisations with the flows of clandestine immigration and international weapons traffic
- secret and sectarian associations
- informatics terrorism
- phenomena of group violence promoted by ideologies
- episodes of violence at sports events accomplished by organised factions.

The increased occurrence since the 1990s of episodes of racism and violence linked to extreme political ideologies at football events has become more and more the focus of DIGOS investigations. The DIGOS operate a special 'Supporters Teams' unit, which is in contact with the official representatives of the football fans clubs existing in every Italian province. The aim is to gain intelligence on the activities of hardcore *UltraS* factions and monitor them in order to prevent them creating disorder at and around the football stadia of Italy.

relatives in London and he liked the city but, most of all, he was impressed that I was working abroad as an academic. We agreed that no information about the *Irriducibili* would be discussed with the *Boys*, and vice versa, and from that moment access to the *Irriducibili*'s social world became a reality. After further negotiation I was also permitted to meet three other *Irriducibili* leaders – Giorgio, Giovanni and Federico.

I stayed in regular contact with the Boxer until he was arrested in 2006 with the other three *Irriducibili* leaders for what became known as the 'Lotito Affair'. In 2005, the *Irriducibili* accused the Lazio president Claudio Lotito of financial speculation – at the expense of the team – in his effort to build a new stadium for the club. The dispute soon spiralled with numerous threats made against the president. The *Irriducibili* declared their support for former player Giorgio Chinaglia, who was trying to take advantage of the dispute and facilitate the purchase of the club by an elusive Hungarian-based business group. Chinaglia himself was subsequently arrested and found guilty of financial manipulation. The leaders of the *Irriducibili*, while declaring that they were unaware of any details of Chinaglia's investment group, were also arrested on similar charges (*see* chapter 13). At the time I was unable to go to Rome and speak directly with the Boxer about the matter because he was under house arrest. One of my friends went to the *Irriducibili*'s warehouse to collect a scarf for me and find out what she could. She called to tell me that the warehouse had been raided by the police the previous day. She was told to go to a shop in the centre of Rome to collect the scarf. In doing so, she found the owner of the shop to be nervous and reluctant to show her any product that bore ideological symbols; however, upon mentioning the Boxer by name, he revealed a hidden scarf. Following these events, via different sources – including Todde – I was to learn details of a long-term police operation targeting the Roma-based *UltraS*.

What follows in the subsequent pages of this book is the result of research into two 'unloved' groups of Italian football supporters. The investigations afford the groups a sense of indulgence not usually permitted by their critics. What they also present is an evaluation of the groups' shared social world in a process both ongoing and unfinished.

The *Stadio Olimpico*, home ground of both AS Roma and SS Lazio

03

THE STADIO OLIMPICO
AND ITS HEROES

Rome's two teams, SS Lazio and AS Roma, both play at the *Stadio Olimpico*, the city's main sports stadium. It was originally built as part of a sports complex – the *Foro Mussolini* – commissioned by *Il Duce* himself and designed by Enrico Del Debbio to give the Italian capital a 'sports city' ethos, symbolising the prominence that the Italian leader gave to sport in his pursuit of a fascist-led national identity. Construction of the stadium began in 1928 under the direction of the architect Luigi Walter Moretti. It was named the *Stadio dei Cipressi* (Cypress Tree Stadium) and opened in 1937. During the fascist period (1922–43), the stadium hosted sports events, parades and rallies, and in May 1938 was the site of celebration for the visit of Adolf Hitler. After Mussolini's death in 1945 the complex was renamed the *Foro Italico*, the name it retains today. In December 1950 the architects Carlo Roccatelli and Annibale Vitellozzi began work on enlarging the stadium, by then known as the *Stadio dei Centomila* (Stadium of the One Hundred Thousand – because of its increased capacity). Ultimately it was renamed the *Stadio Olimpico* in honour of the XVII Olympic Games that took place in the city in 1960. The stadium hosted both the opening and closing ceremonies and the athletics competition. Since then it has been used to stage many of the Italian national team's matches as well as other major international sports events.[1] But the stadium is also important in reflecting social demarcations in the city because it hosts the fixtures of both the teams supported by the *UltraS* in this study.

At the beginning of the 20th century, football in Rome was in a rather chaotic state. Five professional clubs existed within its boundaries: Football Club Roma (f. 1901), Roman (f. 1903), Alba (f. 1907), Fortitudo (f. 1908) and AS Lazio. The latter, founded in 1900 as a sports association, established a football section 10 years later. Matters became more complicated in 1922, by which time no fewer than eight teams represented the capital: Lazio, Roman, Juventus, Fortitudo, Alba, Audace, Pro-Roma and US Romana. Some of these long forgotten teams were quite successful, particularly during the amateur era before 1930. In 1922 Fortitudo were runners-up in one of the two national league cham-

---

[1] The stadium was restructured for the 1990 World Cup hosted by Italy. The *curve* were brought nearer the pitch by nine metres; more seats were covered; plastic seats and two large TV screens were installed for broadcasting. The capacity of the stadium was reduced to 82,000 (all seater) making it 14th in the list of the world's largest football stadiums and second position in Italy after the *Meazza Stadium* in Milan. The stadium hosted several *Italia '90* World Cup matches including the final between Germany and Argentina (http://puntosport.net/gli-speciali-di-puntosport/i-templi-del-calcio/11782/stadio-olimpico-roma.php).

pionships. In 1925 and 1926, Alba also finished second in the same competition, beaten by Bologna and Juventus respectively. However, this proliferation of clubs so diluted the city's football talent that to improve its status, Italo Foschi, an important Roman representative of the political party *Partito Nazionale Fascista* (PNF), reached an agreement with the management of Alba, Fortitudo and Roman to develop a new club that would embrace all three of them and that would promote football, cycling and athletics. The new club's constitution was signed on 22 July 1927 and Italo Foschi, Secretary of the Roman Fascist Federation, became the first president of the newly merged AS Roma club.

Foschi's first aim was to gather together Roman sportsmen for what he intended to be a great club that could compete with the dominant teams of northern Italy. The club adopted the colours of the city (yellow and red) and its She-Wolf emblem.[2] The new management eventually selected the players they wanted to keep from the three clubs that they had enveloped; a task that took several days. The role of coach was given to an Englishman, William Garbutt, who had previously led CFC Genoa to the *scudetto* (championship) in the 1923–24 season.[3]

During the 1920s Rome boasted four sports stadia. The *Stadio Nazionale*, capable of holding some 30,000 spectators, was used mainly for athletics. In 1927 it was turned into the *Stadio PNF* by Mussolini, but renamed again after the war as the *Stadio Flaminio*. SS Lazio played at the *Rondinella*, while the *Madonna del Riposo* stadium hosted Fortitudo, Pro-Roma and Audace. For AS Roma, Italo Faschi chose the all-wooden *Motovelodromo Appio* because it was big enough to hold the supporters of the three member clubs of his newly formed association. It was here that AS Roma played its first match in July 1927 – a friendly game against the Hungarian side Ujpest, a match that AS Roma won 2-1. The club finished the 1927–28 season, its first in the national championship,

---

[2] According to legend the She-Wolf took care of the twins Romulus and Remus – future founders of Rome – after their grandfather Numitore was driven out from the Alba Longa kingdom by his brother Amulio. The latter wanted to throw the twins into the Tiber in order to avoid their claim to the kingdom.

[3] William Garbutt coached Roma between 1927 and 1930. He was one of the first professional coaches in Italian football. Originally from Stockport, south of Manchester, Garbutt had at one time played professional football in England with Blackburn Rovers.

in eighth place. In March 1928 Renato Sacerdoti[4] took over as club president and immediately began to build a new team, buying Fulvio Bernardini from Inter and Eusebio and Rudolph Volk from Fiumana. The 1928–29 championship saw 32 teams competing, with AS Roma finishing third behind Torino and Milan. In March 1929, AS Roma played its first official game in a foreign country, a friendly in Paris against Club Français; the visitors won 5-0. In November that year the AS Roma team played its first official match at *Campo Testaccio*, a new stadium built to hold 20,000 supporters, beating Brescia 2-1. In the first season at their new ground – the first since the establishment of a national professional league – AS Roma suffered just one home defeat and finished sixth in the table.

But the parochial nature of Italian football was soon challenged by the Roman club's importation of high-calibre players from South America. The summer of 1933 saw the arrival of three Argentinean championship winners (all of Italian origin): Enrique Lucas Gonzales Guaita, Alejandro Casanova Scopelli and Andrés Stagnaro. During the 1933–34 season, the most loved player was Guaita, known as the *Corsaro nero* (black pirate), a nickname derived from his characteristically shrewd and opportunistic *gol di rapina* (stolen goals). He established an all-time goalscoring record during an Italian championship that season, scoring 28 goals in 29 matches. In the summer 1935, on the eve of the war with Ethiopia, the three Argentinians left Italy fearing they would be conscripted into the Italian army. After a decade of good results, AS Roma eventually won its first *scudetto* in 1942, the first time a team from the centre-south of the peninsula had won the national title. The victorious team was by this time managed by an Austrian, Alfred Schaffer, who built a formidable side with a reliable defence led by the outstanding goalkeeper Guido Masetti. The *scudetto* victory was due largely to centre-forward Amadeo Amadei who was ever present during the 30 league games, scoring 18 times. Roma finished three points clear of runners-up Torino. World War Two interrupted the team's progress and the league was suspended in 1944, but resumed

---

[4] Renato Sacerdoti was a wealthy Jewish banker. Perhaps because of his ethno-religious background he is one of the least remembered yet one of the most capable presidents of AS Roma.

two years later. The post-war period was a difficult one for the club; they suffered relegation to *Serie B* in 1950–51, blaming their demise on lack of money, but were promoted again the following year.

In the early 1950s enthusiastic supporters created *L'Associazione dei tifosi romanisti* (the Association of Roma Fans) in an attempt to demonstrate to the rest of Italian football their togetherness and passion. By the end of 1952 at least 80 supporters' clubs had joined the association, giving it a membership of around 24,000. At the same time, a fan magazine *Il Giallorosso* (The Yellow-Red) was founded by Angelo Meschini and Memmo Montanari, the historical leaders of the AS Roma supporters, assisted by the brothers Mario and Peppino Catena with the collaboration of lawyer Alberto Sacca. The club's status rose further at the start of the 1953–54 season with the signing of Alcide Ghiggia. A World Cup-winning right-winger from Uruguay, he not only played in the 1950 World Cup Final against Brazil but also scored the winning goal in the 2-1 victory. In the 1956–57 season, Roma's president, Renato Sacerdoti, keen to secure international recognition for the club, organised a tour in Venezuela where the team played tournament games against Real Madrid of Spain, Porto of Portugal and Vasco da Gama of Brazil.

In 1961, AS Roma won their first European trophy, beating Birmingham City in the final of the Inter-Cities Fairs Cup, a tournament for clubs representing cities that had hosted an international trade fair. They won the Italian Cup in 1964 and again in 1969 but were unable to secure the big prizes at home or in Europe. However, Roma did feature in one particular game that changed the nature of knockout football forever. They were drawn to play Polish side Gornik Zabre in the semi-finals of the 1969–70 European Cup-Winners' Cup. The first match, in Rome, finished 1-1; the second leg ended 2-2. A play-off (in Strasbourg) produced another 1-1 draw and the match was decided on the toss of a coin. There was outrage across the football world at this method of deciding who went through to a major European final. As a result, tossing a coin to decide the result of a drawn tie was abandoned and a system of penalty shoot-outs was introduced.

There was little else for Roma fans to shout about, apart from financial difficulties, until the 1979 appointment as club president of Dino Viola, a senator for the Christian Democrats (and a close friend of

Giulio Andreotti, one of Italy's most prominent statesmen). Viola brought two essential qualities to the club: the passion of the true supporter and involvement in global finance. His wish was for the city to have a team that could compete with the rich northern teams, most notably Juventus. His wishes came true straightaway with back-to-back Italian Cup victories in 1980 and 1981. Then, in 1982–83 the club won its second *scudetto* with a team coached by the Swede Nils Liedholm and led on to the pitch by their Italian captain, Agostino Di Bartolomei.[5] The team also featured Brazilian midfielder Paulo Roberto Falcao and Italian midfielder Bruno Conti, who had won a World Cup with the *Azzurri* in Spain in 1982. That same season striker Roberto Pruzzo became the club's second highest ever goalscorer with 106 goals, an achievement bettered only in 2004 by Francesco Totti. The following season, 1983–84, saw them win the Italian Cup again and reach the final of the European Cup, facing Liverpool at the *Stadio Olimpico*, their home ground since 1953. Ironically, they lost the match on penalties after a 1-1 draw.

Viola's presidency ended when he died in 1991. He had been at the helm during what had been a golden era for the club, albeit tainted by allegations of political favouritism, and he proved a hard act to follow. He was succeeded by Giuseppe Ciarrapico, a Roman publishing tycoon, who brought a different political affiliation to the post. Ciarrapico's neo-fascist inclination is perhaps best reflected in the composition of the financial group of which he was a part. The CEO of this organisation was the neo-fascist Giulio Caradonna, an MSI (*Movimento Sociale Italiano*) MP from 1958 to 1994, who remains close to the neo-fascist Forza Nuova party. Ciarrapico's poor management and judicial problems arising from alleged fraudulent bankruptcy saw him replaced in 1993 by the business tycoon, Franco Sensi, who died in 2008. Under Sensi the club stabilised and results improved. Roma won a third *scudetto* in 2000–01 and finished as runners-up the following year under the management of Fabio Capello, who left the club in 2004.

Since then there have been a bewildering number of coaches including Cesare Prandelli, former player Rudi Völler, Luigi Del Neri, Luciano

---

[5] Di Bartolomei committed suicide in 1994 after a long period of depression.

Spalletti and Claudio Ranieri. For the team, the search for football talent became ever more global. The club signed the Ghanaian Samuel Kuffour, the Brazilian Rodrigo Ferrante Taddei and the Congolese Shabani Nonda from Bayern Munich, Siena and Monaco respectively. Having won the Roman derby 2-0 in January 2006, Spalletti established a record of 11 consecutive victories in *Serie A*, but could not secure the much-coveted *scudetto*. Yet the crowds still flocked to the matches, with an average of 40,000 *Romanisti* at each home game in the 2007–08 season, a campaign which Roma finished in second place behind Inter.

In the history of AS Roma, relations with its close 'neighbours' have always been the source of football antagonism. The first Roman derby of the Italian championship was played at Lazio's *Stadio della Rondinella* on 8 December 1929, when AS Roma won 1-0. Worried about the possibility of pre-match tensions between rival supporters, the local authorities implemented strict safety measures, with hundreds of police officers, *carabinieri* (military police) and soldiers of the fascist party militia mobilised to control potential disorder. The return leg was played at Testaccio in May 1930. Again the *giallorossi* (Roma) won, this time 3-1. Almost inevitably, the proximity of two clubs' supporters meant they simply could not enjoy a cordial relationship, and they began fighting. Little did they know or care that they were starting a tradition.

Then, as now, there were more Roma than Lazio fans. Supporters of AS Roma consider their club the 'people's club'. Some say that enmities between the two sets of supporters has its roots in the fact that Lazio rejected the city's colours back in 1900, a decision incomprehensible to locals and something that drove the working class inner city dwellers into the arms of AS Roma. They remain somewhat disparaging towards the *Laziali*, who are traditionally drawn from the middle-class districts of the capital and regions outside of the city boundaries. The AS Roma fans are clearly happy to denigrate the virtues of the *Laziali* motherhood, as this chant in the Roman dialect illustrates:

La mamma del Laziale
je piace er sesso orale,
e se je metti 'n dito raja come un mulo,
je piace pijallo ar culo.

The Lazio fan's mom
likes oral sex,
and if you put a finger in she brays like a mule,
she likes to take it in the ass.
(Boys Roma chant: Roma–Lazio Derby, May 2005*)*

In addition, they invariably refer to their SS Lazio fan rivals by using the derisory term *burini*, a term that suggests they are uncouth country dwellers.

It is interesting to note that historically the two sets of supporters also had political differences. AS Roma's hardcore supporters leaned to the political left even as they co-existed with small extreme right groups, while Lazio fans have always been neo-fascist. However, today the majority of the two sets of fans share a similar political ideology as this statement made by a prominent member of the *Boys* demonstrates, 'We have respect for the *Irriducibili* and I guess the respect is mutual for us and Paolo [Paolo Zappavigna – the former leader of the *Boys*]'. The power of neo-fascist ideology, thus, goes beyond and supersedes any Roman football rivalries.

The roots of Societá Sportiva Lazio football club can be traced to the late 19th century and are linked to Italian colonial adventures in Africa, specifically the Eritrean campaign. On 1 March 1896, 16,000 Italian soldiers attacked the 70,000 strong army of King Menelik II in Adwa in East Africa. The Italian soldiers fought to the end, but were defeated, with approximately 7000 casualties. The defeat ended the Italian-Abyssinian war and was one of the few successes of African military resistance against European colonialism. This defeat dealt a mortal blow to Prime Minister Francesco Crispi's government, which collapsed two weeks after the battle and was brought down by a people fed up with the national colonial exploits.

Back at home people looked for other things to fill their time and, among a number of proposed new ideological ventures on offer, sport was given a higher status and was soon to play an important role in shaping the future of Italy and its national consciousness. A number of exclusive sporting clubs opened for business on the banks of Rome's

River Tiber, and were intended to occupy the leisure time of Roman nobility and intellectuals with sports such as swimming, boating and cycling. Naturally, these clubs – the *Canottieri Remo, Canottieri Aniene, Rari Nantes Roma, Canottieri Tevere* and *La Romana* – soon became social arenas too. Unfortunately, for those Italian youths not born into the upper echelons or in possession of an elite educational background, the possibilities for practising sports were scarce. Of the few options for the less well off were the Talacchi brothers' *Capannone* (Big Shed) and the *Pippa Nera* building, both sites of intense and passionate sporting competition, but mostly disorganised. One frequenter of the latter locale was Luigi Bigiarelli, a Roman-born officer of the elite *Bersaglieri* corps and survivor of the battle of Adwa. In January 1900, keen to pursue sport, something that he saw as an antidote to the horrors of war, and fed up with the disorganisation of the existing facilities, Bigia-relli and his brother Giacomo founded the *Societá Podistica Lazio* (Lazio Running Club). Their normal route was along the *lungotevere* in front of the *Piazza Della Libertà*.

The name did not include the name of their city, as others had already claimed that title, instead they opted for a name that encompassed the city and beyond. Choosing Lazio, the Italian region within which Rome is the biggest city, they adopted the white and blue colours of the Greek national flag in honour of the nation that founded the Olympic Games. Both in its origins then and its position today, Lazio exists as more than a football club, offering 35 sporting activities and counting among its supporters some of Mussolini's descendants and survivors of the Italian royal family, such as the descendants of the Princess Mafalda of Savoia, who died in 1944 in the Nazi concentration camp at Buchenwald.

The first two years of the club's existence were busy, with its members participating in regional running competitions. In 1902 the SS Lazio club members came into contact with football when the game was introduced to the city by Bruto Seghettini, a member of the Racing Club de Paris. The new sport immediately took hold among the youth of the club and, as the game began to diffuse throughout Rome, the SS Lazio football team became unbeatable. As a result of their performances, the team was invited to play in the first central-south football championship held at Pisa in June 1907, where they competed against Pisa, Livorno and Lucca. The newly nicknamed *biancocelesti* (the white-light blues-in honour of their team's strip) played three matches in one day, winning them all. In the years before the First World War, SS Lazio was at the pinnacle of Italy's centre-south football community, although the team had no opportunity to demonstrate its skills against representatives of the northern championship. However, soon after Italian football had got back on its feet following the conflict, SS Lazio won the southern championship in the 1922–23 season under the talented leadership of Fulvio Bernardini, one of the best players of his era; they only lost out to Genoa in the national championship play-off.

Italian history contains several examples of a symbiotic relationship between football and political intrigue, and during the time of the fascist regime SS Lazio became embroiled in this duality. The link between fascism and the Lazio team is most obviously personified by Giovanni Marinelli, Administrative Secretary of the *Partito Nazionale Fascista* (PNF) until 1943. An accountant by profession, Marinelli proved efficient in organising the newborn PNF's economic resources. But he was also a man of action who was involved in several violent attacks carried out by the Blackshirts within the PNF[6]. In 1924 he was implicated in the murder of the socialist leader Giacomo Matteotti and, partly because of the disgust of the Italian public regarding the case, he was relieved of his post and arrested. But by 1926, Marinelli had regained the prestige and status he had temporarily lost, and was re-appointed to his old position with the PNF. In 1935 he reached the top of the fascist establishment when he was elected as a member of the Grand Council of Fascism. A devoted football fan, Marinelli was a supporter of SS Lazio, an association which is not surprising given that Mussolini's family members were also fans of a club whose core support was drawn from the rich Roman districts in the north of the capital, where sympathy for fascism was strong. Such a socio-demographic association remains in place today, in districts such as Aurelio, Salario, Vescovio and Trieste, and also in Eur, where the presence of neo-fascist parties such as *Forza Nuova* and *Movimento Sociale Fiamma Tricolore* is very strong.

---

[6] wearing a uniform of black the Blackshirts (Camicienera) were the paramilitary henchmen of Mussolini's political movement. They were officially titled the National Security Volunteer Militia.

But Marinelli's connections with the club developed further. Towards the end of the 1920s it became clear that the Rondinella stadium needed refurbishment. With a new stadium, commissioned and built by the PNF, due to open soon, Lazio wrote to the fascist authorities requesting permission to use it as their home ground for the 1927–28 season. Their request was denied and Marinelli did not intervene on their side as he wished to avoid accusations of favouritism. But in 1931 a contract signed between the fascist authorities and the Italian Olympic Committee (CONI) handed management of the stadium to CONI while the PNF retained some control over the venue for its political purposes. Within weeks Marinelli had used his indirect influence and the club was granted use of the stadium for 42 months at a paltry rent of 60,000 lire per year. This arrangement, which ended in 1935, was a great honour for SS Lazio, because the luxurious new stadium was a symbol of the new Italy of Mussolini and signified the importance that fascist ideology gave to sport as a means to build a new physically and mentally strong generation. The arrangement was that the athletic facilities remained under the control of CONI while, in exchange, SS Lazio invested money in the facility, paying for the construction of the cycling track and issuing contracts for the ground staff.

Marinelli's ongoing support for the club was crucial. In 1938 he was presented with a report revealing mismanagement of the stadium by SS Lazio officials. According to the document, the club paid a very low rent yet collected monies by charging individuals and federations to use the stadium, even though it was ostensibly open to all sports federations free of charge. Although Marinelli was angry, he spoke privately to the SS Lazio president, Eugenio Gualdi, at the same time complaining about the deplorable state of the dressing rooms and toilets. The problems were promptly addressed and the club spent 250,000 lire improving the facilities. In 1939, when the stadium was becoming an economic burden for the club, the SS Lazio management wrote to Marinelli asking him to consider their predicament. He replied immediately informing them that their annual rent had been halved. Marinelli's help was evident on the pitch too. In 1939 he assisted in the purchase of the left-footed forward Gino Colaussi from Triestina, a member of the Italian national World Cup-winning team in 1938. The northern club was naturally unwilling to let their player go. However, Marinelli used his influence and spoke directly to a local official of the city of Trieste and the player's transfer was announced shortly afterwards.

Although still in a position of political power, Marinelli ceased to help SS Lazio any further from 1940 by which time Italy was at war. Despite these indirect favours, prestige and good commercial conditions provided by the fascist regime, the club had not been able to collect any major trophies on the field. However, they remained at the top of the Italian football tree and the team featured such players as striker Silvio Piola who still holds the *Serie A* goalscoring record with 274 goals. But it was not until 1958 that coach and former player Fulvio Bernardini and team captain Roberto Lovati led SS Lazio to their first trophy, beating Fiorentina in the Italian Cup final. The club's first *scudetto* arrived in 1974 thanks in large part to the goals of striker Giorgio Chinaglia and the management skills of Tommaso Maestrelli.

But the club had peaked and some bad years followed. A number of players began to leave SS Lazio, including Chinaglia who made the move to the USA to join the newly formed NASL. This league attracted many of his contemporaries who were nearing the end of their careers and who saw the potential of earning comparatively huge wages. Chinaglia was a success in the USA and made both his home and fortune there; others were not so lucky. For instance, Luciano ReCecconi, an important member of Maestrelli's *scudetto*-winning team: in 1977, he and three friends went into a local jewellery shop owned by Bruno Tabocchini who had recently been the victim of two armed robberies. Knowing of Tabocchini's misfortune, Re Cecconi decided to play a joke on him saying, 'everyone stop, this is a robbery'. The shocked shopkeeper did not recognise the player or spot the ironic nature of his statement and reacted by shooting him in the chest. Re Cecconi died instantly.

Things got much worse in 1980 when SS Lazio was caught up in a match-fixing scandal involving the management and players of AC Milan, Avellino, Bologna, Palermo and Taranto, in which the outcome of matches was decided in advance to favour betting syndicates. Lazio was found guilty and the club paid for its involvement by demotion to *Serie B*. Although not an isolated incident in Italian football, the scandal was widely viewed by the club's supporters as seriously tarnishing what they considered to be the highly-regarded, patrician name of the club, with the ultimate football disgrace being a subsequent (but eventually successful) battle to avoid relegation to *Serie C*.

It was not until 1992 and the arrival of food tycoon Sergio Cragnotti that the club eventually regained some pride. A lifelong and passionate supporter, Cragnotti changed the fate of the club by investing a considerable amount of money to buy new first team players and, at the same time, restructuring the youth team. During the Cragnotti era, SS Lazio qualified for five UEFA Cup competitions, and finished second or third in *Serie A* in consecutive seasons in the mid-1990s thanks mainly to the goals of skipper Beppe Signori. In 1997, Sven-Göran Eriksson took over as manager and attracted skilled players such as Roberto Mancini, Christian Vieri and Chilean striker Marcelo Salas to the club. With the help of such stars SS Lazio won seven cup competitions in three years. This growing success was crowned in 2000, the year of the club's centenary, when they won their second *scudetto*. This success resulted in Eriksson leaving in 2001 to manage the English national team.

The years since then have not been successful on or off the field. An economic crisis that engulfed the Cirio food company (the club's biggest shareholder and owned by the Cragnotti family) was not helped by under-performing players who were receiving high wages. Neither Dino Zoff nor Roberto Mancini were able to do anything about it and eventually the Cragnotti family sold its stake in the club. On the edge of bankruptcy, SS Lazio was then bought by the property developer and cleaning tycoon, Claudio Lotito, who brought local hero (and former player) Paolo Di Canio back from his highly controversial sojourn in England. Loved by all of the *curva nord* – and not only for his football skills – Di Canio was considered a real *Laziale*, an *UltraS*, and most importantly an *Irriducibile* (*see* chapter 9).

Being an *UltraS* means believing in a philosophy of life in which you must – ideally – be prepared to agitate, articulate and ultimately assault in pursuit of a variety of aims. While there are similarities between the *UltraS* of Roma and Lazio, the two groups differ in a number of particularly important areas.

A flag of the *Boys* Roma, with the image of a double-headed axe

04

ROME AND GLORY

The evolution of Roma's *ultrá* can be traced back to the late 1960s when groups of young fans – the majority aged around 16 years – began to gather in numbers on the *curve* of the Stadio Olimpico. These were the first organised, hardcore AS Roma fans. As was then fashionable, the names of the various groups were borrowed either from military heroism such as *Arditi* (elite storm troopers from the First World War) and *Eterna Legione* (the infantry of the Ancient Romans), or from predatory animals like *Lupi* (Wolves) and *Pantere* (Panthers). A few years later, at the beginning of the 1970s, the *Boys Roma* were formed and, right from the start, they displayed a neo-fascist ideology in the language, actions and methods of support for their team.

In 1977, the *Fedayn, Pantere* and *Fossa dei Leoni* gatherings were collectively known as the *Commando UltraS Curva Sud* (CUCS). This fusion was considered necessary to strengthen the sense of unity among AS Roma supporters. The CUCS first appeared at a Roma-Sampdoria fixture, advertising its existence with the longest banner (42 metres) ever seen in an Italian *curva* at the time. All the other AS Roma groups spontaneously gathered under this banner. Over the next few years, the CUCS came to national prominence, respected by similar groups because of its organisational capability and its ability and willingness to fight. From the end of the 1970s until 1987, the CUCS took its place as one of the most important Italian supporter groups, manifesting all the important characteristics of Italian hardcore football fans: consistency in numbers and cohesiveness in choreography and 'spirit', which was considered an illustration of loyalty; loudness in chants; and a willingness to trespass into 'territories' belonging to rival fans at both home and away games.

But this shared enthusiasm for bad behaviour, which brought the CUCS together in the first place, was also the reason for its demise. In 1987, there were disagreements among the various factions as a result of a decision made by the club. Under instruction from president Dino Viola, AS Roma sold team captain Carlo Ancelotti to AC Milan and replaced him with Lionello Manfredonia, a former SS Lazio player hated by Roma supporters as the personification of their closest rivals. He had, unforgivably, once made insulting gestures to the *Romanisti* during a derby game. Manfredonia's arrival split the CUCS into two – the old CUCS who were prepared to forget the insult, and the CUCS-GAM (Group Against Manfredonia) who were not. The radical and tougher elements of the new group then shifted the *curve* ideology to one that supported both the football club and the City of Rome. Adopting the slogan *Roma e Gloria* (Rome and Glory), underlined not only the pursuit of football glory but, just as importantly, the glory of the capital city, the one-time centre of power of the Roman Empire. Around the time of the split, a third group of supporters also emerged and took their place in the *curva sud* – the *Opposta Fazione* (Opposite Faction). This group, proud of its neo-fascist ideology, was notably 'hard' in fights and offered no compromise in its opposition to the football establishment.

From the late 1980s and inspired by *Opposta Fazione*, political ideology became more evident among the hardcore AS Roma supporters, an important step in the emergence of the first true *UltraS*. The days of the CUCS were numbered. Changes in the *curva sud* were unstoppable, many of the *vecchi* (older leaders), disappointed at how their world was changing, decided to retire and the group began to lose its ascendancy. Other groups such as the *Boys* began to take over. An account of this transition exists in a self-penned document obtained from a member of the *Boys* in 2005: 'The *Boys* brought a massive contribution to the CUCS acting with a behavioural logic that was tough and intransigent... [But] many misunderstandings and a thousand differences [one was the political ideology promoted by the new groups] provoked them to leave the CUCS and exist autonomously. The *Boys* wanted to be an "action group" capable both of facing the "enemy" immediately and commanding fear... During that period, the *Boys* were always the first to look for a battle (against rival fans) and never found anyone capable of making them retreat. In spite of the many difficulties – warnings from the authorities, repression from the police – we were always at our place to defend the city and the shirt. It has not been easy, but today we are proud to be still admired and feared. We have never hidden and never will.'

Such a statement underpins the pride that the members of the *Boys* have for both their history and their beliefs. Since their formation in 1972, as the above document explains, the *Boys* have sought to be an elitist group. Despite the 35 years between their inception and the research conducted for this book, the beginnings of the *Boys* are still considered a road map by some contemporary aficionados. A perfect representative of this group is Todde, the man who became the contact with the *Boys*. He originates from a middle-class family, lives in an affluent district of Rome, studied law at university and has a passion for history, especially that of the Roman Empire. He is a man clearly able to articulate his opinions and beliefs despite the potential risks of being considered a 'hooligan thug'. His justification for the formation of the *Boys* is informed: 'In 1972, a neo-fascist called Antonio Bongi took the first steps in the evolution from the *Furie Giallorossa* (Yellow-red Furies) to the *Boys*. The political sympathies of the *Furie Giallorossa*, their rivalries with other groups and their anti-system oppositional style were displayed long before the *UltraS* movement had taken its first steps in Italy. The *Boys San* (Inter) (1969) and the *Boys Roma* (1972) were the pioneers of the *UltraS* thinking; of a behavioural style to be adopted seven days a week not only inside the stadium and not only during a meaningless football match that lasts only 90 minutes ... '

The above passage demonstrates not only the sophistication of the *UltraS* arguments used to cite historical and political events when describing the evolution of the groups, but can also be considered a 'world-view' or at least the foundation of a distinctive cultural trait that makes a fundamental claim on the identity of group members.

Looking at the first known photograph of the group, which was then in the *curva nord*, Todde said:

> They are all kids, you can see it from the faces. They gathered in the *curva nord*, which was – and still is – occupied alternate weeks by Lazio fans or by other teams' supporters. There was no place for them in the *curva sud*, because they were the antithesis of the typical *curva sud* Roma fans who were mainly communist in sympathy back then. Their motto was: *Odiati e Fieri! Boys Roma oltre la morte!* [Hated and Proud! Boys Roma beyond death].

While talking, Todde produced a sheet of paper containing words written by Antonio Bongi, which recalls the origins of the Roma *UltraS*,

> 'We were in the *curva nord* and we had the right [negotiated with the club officials] to have our own banner and four free tickets to every match. We arrived at the stadium when the gates opened because we needed to position ourselves. I remember being impressed by the Torino *UltraS* who already had 50 banners in their end when we got there; I tried to emulate them to save our voices. We started our chants when the referee whistled for the beginning of the match. We had 200 drums, megaphones, even electric trumpets connected to car batteries that made an infernal

noise. We organised the buses to go to away matches and every now and then even the mothers of some of the members joined us! I remember yellow-red trains [the same colours as the Roma team kit] with carriages packed full of Roma supporters.

I then had my first experience with violence. The first fight astonished me. It was at Torino in 1973. The *UltraS* of Torino – notorious left-wing sympathisers – came to our end with sticks and wearing motorbike helmets. They stole our banner and attacked us. They tore and burnt the banner of the RC Giuliano Taccola [a Roma *Ultras* group] in the Maratona end; perhaps the most beautiful banner of the *Giallorosse* ... There were political divisions evident even in the stadiums. In the *curva sud* groups such as ours appeared. A banner appeared on the *muretto* (the small wall – a part of the Stadio Olimpico) proclaiming *Guerriglieri della Sud* (Warriors of the South) with their extreme right-wing ideology. On the opposite side there was the *Fedayn* from Quadraro-Cinecitta[1]. They were communists; their leader Roberto Rulli was a well-known militant and idealist. The *Fossa dei Lupi* (the Wolves Den), led by Stefano Scarciofolo and Vittorio Trenta, were from Monte Cervialto. The *Brigate Giallorosse* came from Torrespaccata. The *Commandos Lupi* was organised by guys from Monteverde. Then there were the *Pantere Giallorosse* (the Panthers) and other minor groups...

Although the history of the group is important for understanding its cultural roots, an interview with Marco, a 20-year-old current member of the *Boys*, provides a snapshot of the group in the 21st century:

Q: How does a Roma supporter become a member of the *Boys*?

M: It is a pretty close group... it occurs mainly through friendship. We are a group with a strict organisation. We have a strong nucleus

---

[1] The Quadraro district is home to a considerable number of both Roma *Fedayn* (the oldest of Roma's supporter groups) and Lazio *Irriducibili*. It is a populous working-class district of Rome that traditionally supported the politics of the Italian Communist Party (PCI).

at Pomezia (a small township outside Rome), another nucleus at Cerveteri (another Roman township) and another in Rome. We have some problems meeting mostly because of the distances involved but hold evening meetings over a pizza or beer. We meet weekly. If Roma play in the afternoon, we meet at 11 in the morning at our head-quarters; if Roma plays at 8.30 in the evening, we meet at 6.30.

Q: How many members are active in the group?

M: Thirty; then we have people who pay for membership but as I see it only do so for fashion, being one of the *Boys* is pretty cool. They want 'to be' but not to 'belong' and they do little for the common good of the group. 'Active' means coming to the stadium regularly, helping with banners and so on … we are a 30-strong elite, the others within the group number around 200.

Q: I hear the *Boys* have some selection criteria to avoid the *cani sciolti* [a slang phrase that refers to youths who cannot be relied on]. Can you explain how selection is made?

M: The group grows via contacts; for instance I belong to the *Boys* and I can introduce a friend. Members of the group then see if they like him or not and eventually he becomes part of the group or he is rejected. In this way there is an informal selection and we have time to impart the ideals and values that he should possess in belonging. Our group is based on friendship and most of all trust… you must understand that in extreme situations in the street, it helps knowing your mates will help you. You also see how a guy performs in the street. If you are afraid in the street, you are afraid in the stadium. We have a special sign for members of our elite group, the insignia of the rising sun [symbolising the re-birth of fascism – *see* chapter 10], which is worn on our hats.

The sense of togetherness is important to the members of the *Boys*. The *UltraS* fight 'their' battles in what they perceive as unfriendly locations, in Italian society – where their ideology places them as 'strangers' – and within the football stadium where their very existence is challenged by the Italian authorities, the football institutions, *UltraS* of other teams and the police. For this reason, the *curve* and their *sedi* (seats) are considered places of refuge where they can share their feelings with their peers, or in neo-fascist terms, with their *camerati* (comrades).[2]

Q: So, basically, you have a group within the group?

M: Yes, you can get our membership card and come with us to the stadium but only 'the elite' are the vanguard of the *Boys*. You understand who is part of the elite because when we are about to start action the people displaying the rising sun are at the front. We have a defining chant repeated three times when we begin confrontations with our opponents [be they police or rival *UltraS*]. A leader shouts, *Chi siamo noi?* [Who are we?], which is repeated three times. The collective answer in rhyme is *Contro il sistema la gioventu si scaglia, boia chi molla e' il grido di battaglia* [Against the system the youth fight, damned are those who give up the battle chant]. There is a strong structure and sense of order. This can only be understood by taking into consideration that ours is a way of life that exists beyond the stadium. We have our own language and dress code. We call each other 'comrade' and also give the Roman salute. Members often have a Celtic cross tattoo or pendant. We are, you might say, a subculture within both the stadium and society.

Q: How is the group structured?

M: We have a charismatic leader – the 'big boss' Paolo Zappavigna [known as Zapata] – and we have the *nuova guardia* (or *direttivo*) consisting of five guys. Then come the 'ordinary' guys.

The *Boys* leadership has changed several times since the group was

---

[2] This term derives from the word *camera* (room) and evokes feelings of privacy and intimacy and a common safe location (Dechezelles, S (2008). The Cultural Basis of Youth Involvement in Italian Extreme Right-wing Organisations. *Journal of Contemporary European Studies*, 16 (3), 363–375.).

formed, normally through violence. As with many male groupings, new individuals appear and challenge the existing leaders with shows of strength and threats followed by actual violence. The most recent change in leadership was brought about in 2001 by two cousins, Paolo Zappavigna and his cousin Guido, one a 'warrior' the other a politician. Paolo was the toughest and was in control of the group until his death in 2005 in a motorbike crash. In 2001, they found the *Boys* in a poor state; there were members of the group that were considered out of control, disrespectful to the hierarchy and quickly prone to violence for its own sake in and around the stadia. For the cousins this was not the *UltraS* code. Such reprehensible behaviour had to be stopped – consequently the cousins, together with other members of the *direttivo,* re-established order. Crucially, because the group was only one among half a dozen in the *curva sud*, they were left alone to sort things out for themselves.

Q: Marco, how do you become a member of the *Boys' direttivo?*

M: Seniority in years as well as charisma – in the *direttivo* there are people aged 25–30.

Q: So why are you in the *direttivo?*

M: Because I am charismatic! [laughs]…

The concept of 'charisma' emerged constantly during several interviews as an attribute admired and desired among members of both the *Boys Roma* and *Irriducibili.* This is something that the *UltraS* have in common with other extremist gatherings, both political and religious, and seems to be their way of making sense of group dynamics. It was evident that both *UltraS* groups had at their apex a charismatic leadership – Paolo Zappavigna for the *Boys* and Giorgio, Federico, Giovanni and the Boxer for the *Irriducibili* (*see* chapters 5 and 8). A charismatic leader, not elected or officially appointed in any way, 'is obeyed not by virtue of a custom or a law, but by virtue of the faith he inspires'. They are considered to be the leaders because of their exceptional personal merits. For members of the *UltraS* such men are not only respected by their ability to fight but also for the strong convictions they hold on how they lead their lives.

Q: How do you agree on the messages displayed on your banners?

M: Some 80 per cent of the ideas start from the 'big boss'; if the youngsters want to propose an idea this is taken into consideration democratically by the *direttivo* who analyse it and give their evaluation. The idea is studied and revised until Thursday, then on Friday and Saturday three or four *Boys* prepare the banner in two or three different places. For derby games, the preparation is longer with more people working on them because the banners are sometimes very large.

Q: How does the group find money for its activities?

M: From selling stuff [hats, scarves, stickers, shirts, sweatshirts, flags and so on] – 10 per cent of income goes to the *Boys* as a group and 90 per cent goes to the shop owner. Then we have a membership fee and other monies come from collections at the stadium. There's a box where other supporters, if willing, can leave donations.

Q: Which *gemellaggi* [group twinnings] do you have?

M: Our *gemellaggi* are political; the only real friendships in Italy are with Taranto at home and abroad with the *ultrá Sur* of Real Madrid. The *ultrá Sur* often come to Italy and are also allied with the *Irriducibili*. Our 'big boss' introduced them to the boss of the *Irriducibili*. We also have political *gemellaggi* with Benfica of Lisbon and Panathinaikos of Athens who share our ideology.

We have problems, however, because not all our *direttivo* can travel abroad due to restriction orders on their movement [*see* chapter 13 for details on legislation aimed at neo-fascist membership]. You have to consider that we [Roma neo-fascist *UltraS*] have a specific hate for the English based on our ideology; we are not like the *Irriducibili* who have some sympathies for them because they share the same style. We are first Romans then *UltraS* – our style of supporting is Italian not British! The English are a shit race by nature, they are arrogant. There is an old saying, *dio stramaledica gli inglesi*[3] [God curse the English!]. We support the Irish Republican cause.

Q: Are there any other team's fans that you particularly dislike?

M: The fights with other groups arise mostly out of tradition; an exception is Siena. This is a hate born in our generation and our people that will continue in 10 years' time and longer [Siena fans are renowned 'communists', which elicits particular hostility from the *Boys*].

Marco mentions an important element here, one that differentiates the *UltraS* behaviour from other, more traditional hardcore supporters (*ultrá*) and that is that political ideology not only strongly characterises the *UltraS* actions as football supporters, but also directs their lives outside the stadium. The very fact that AS Roma *UltraS* have forged *gemellaggi* is a political act based on ideology. Such twinnings are generally based on the value of *rispetto* (respect), which means that only other groups sharing a similar outlook or 'logic' can achieve this status. The *UltraS* only respect *camerati,* and will do so regardless of nationality. The Roma *UltraS* collectively have twinnings with comrades from Benfica (Portugal), Hammarby (Sweden) and Real Madrid (Spain), while the *Irriducibili* has twinnings with Espanyol, Real Madrid, Werder Bremen and Lokomotive Leipzig (Germany), Panathinaikos (Greece) and Paris St Germain (France).

Also important is the Roma *UltraS* reluctance to make twinnings with English supporters. The *Boys* are more vehemently opposed to the English than the *Irriducibili*, who have in the past established a twinning with a few Chelsea fans. The *Boys* articulate aggression, as Marco demonstrated in the previous statement, towards anything from the UK, though this sentiment is not without contradictions, considering

---

[3] A slogan created for the first time by Italian journalist and fascist Mario Appelius during the Second World War.

that quite a few members see London as a 'cool' city. But it is an ideological hatred, most likely a part of their Italian neo-fascist make-up. Anti-English sentiments are traceable to the Second World War and arise from the role that the UK played in the defeat of Italian fascism. However, Marco's hostility towards the English is not shared by everyone in the neo-fascist world and is certainly not reciprocated by extreme right groups in the UK. The neo-fascist *Forza Nuova*, for example, chaired by the Italian-born Roberto Fiore and quite popular among the *Irriducibili*, has close links with the British National Front and the UK Third Position. The UK Third Positionist magazine *Political Soldier* has a web store titled 'Final Conflict' that sells merchandise of national and international neo-fascist groups and the *Irriducibili* and its paraphernalia are quite trendy items within this world.

A tattoo belonging to a member of the *Irriducibili*

05

'DARE, BELIEVE, BE RECKLESS'

Although Lazio supporters have always had strong links to the neo-fascist youth movement, the first modern *curva nord UltraS* group – the *Commandos Monteverde Lazio* – appeared among their ranks in 1971. They sought a public profile by holding up an impressive 22 metre banner. The SS Lazio team's success in winning the 1973–74 *scudetto* attracted new recruits from the swelling *curve*. Distinct groups began to become visible: the *Folgore* (named after an elite parachute regiment of the Italian Army that is much admired by neo-fascist youths) emerged, followed by the *Boys* and the *Marines*. Some of the latter groups combined to constitute the *Eagles Supporters* in 1976. The *Eagles Supporters* put on spectacular matchday displays, accompanied by drums, smoke bombs, confetti and thrown rolls of toilet paper. Their gatherings averaged 2,000 members per game, which increased to 5,000–6,000 for important matches, particularly against Juventus and Roma.

A few years later, in 1978, the overtly neo-fascist *Vikings* appeared in the *curva sud* and displayed on their banners the Viking *drakkar* (a type of ship) and the sun (*see* chapter 8 for an explanation of neo-fascist symbolism). The ideological imprint of this group did not impress everyone on the *curva nord* and in the late 1970s fights often broke out between supporters of the extreme right (including the *Vikings*) and the more moderate *Eagles Supporters*. The 1980s saw a significant increase in the notoriety of the SS Lazio *UltraS* throughout Italy. They became respected and feared by many other Italian hardcore supporters for both their passion and the originality shown in their choreographies and chants. Such admiration brought alliances with similar groups from Bari, Torino and Trieste. Again, success bred success, this time off the field, with the appearance of *Gruppo Sconvolti*, *UltraS 74* and *Gruppo Rock*. In 1987 there was a sea change; this was the first season in which the central wall of the *curva nord* did not display the Vikings' banner, in its place was the banner of the *Irriducibli* – a group that has since developed into the main force of the Lazio *curva*.

The 1989–90 season was significant for the *UltraS* as both Roman teams played home games at the Flaminio stadium while their own Olimpico was being refitted for the 1990 World Cup. Though the Flaminio was a smaller ground, the atmosphere at matches was better as the seats and the supporters were nearer to the pitch and the players. It was the perfect place for confrontation. It was no coincidence that the same season was characterised by strong repression of the *UltraS* by the authorities, who were keen to avoid hooligan-related publicity prior to the World Cup[1].

---

[1] From htp://news.lazio.net/2004/03/22/ultras-uniti-nella-guerrigli-ansa/ and http://ultraslazio.it

During one conversation with the SS Lazio gatekeeper, the Boxer, he produced a document written by the *direttivo* of the *Irriducibili*, which outlines the group's view of its origins and evolution:

Our story started in the 1980s when the Italian *UltraS* movement was passing through a period of renewal. Many small factions were appearing at the various ends [of the Olimpico] aiming to present a strong *mentalita* (attitude), uncompromising in its philosophy against the system [as represented by the Italian authorities and the Italian football establishment] and which was no longer evident in the existing groups, who we believed had lost their initial vitality. Every Lazio home match was organised meticulously; our new group met in a *bisca* (amusement arcade) in the Monteverde district and came up with the idea of wearing football scarves coupled with sewn-on football patches in the British style. In the meantime, co-existence with the *Eagles* became tenser. Quarrels began over the different ways of supporting the team (but most importantly) because the fact was that many were leaving the *Eagles* to join our group. A Lazio-Barletta game saw the first scuffles between the two factions that needed police intervention.

The *Irriducibili* appeared on the national stage for the first time in mid-October 1987 during a Lazio-Padova *Serie B* match. We invited everyone committed to Lazio to meet at the *muretto* (a small wall in *curva nord*) and dislodge the *Vikings* who always gathered there. The name *Irriducibili* [literally the 'immovables'] was original and suggested we would not compromise with the club or the media as many other fan groups had done. We wanted to support our team without *moralismi* (being judgemental) and criticising the previous behaviour of the *UltraS*, which had created tension among the Lazio support. We wanted to assert our independence, to disassociate ourselves from the past and from the other supporters and even the club. So, for example, we arranged our own transportation for away matches. Instead of taking the bus provided by the supporters club we chose the train, which gave us independence from scheduled travel. This proved popular and large numbers of fans began to travel with us. We adopted as our mascot a character called Mr Enrich, a little man who kicks furiously – the kick signifies rebellion against the political and football system.

Although not officially confirmed by the *Irriducibili*, the figure of Mr Enrich may well have been derived from Andy Capp, a British newspaper cartoon character created by Reginald Smythe in the mid-1950s. Andy Capp was a politically incorrect and aggressive caricature of the English Northern working class man. The *Irriducibili* caricature is younger than Capp and wears different clothing – buttoned down sleeveless 'polo' shirts and a 'pork pie' hat popular in the British Skinhead subculture of the late 1960s.

Since the late 1980s, the *Irriducibili* have controlled that part of the *curva nord* closest to the pitch. To enter, one must be known or invited, and must pass the gatekeepers – members chosen variously by virtue of their fighting ability and their willingness to challenge 'outsiders'. The *Irriducibili* make it their business to know everything that occurs on the *curva*. On entering this area, one can clearly see men collecting money to fund the social campaigns (*see* chapter 6), as well as the materials used to make the banners and the pyrotechnics crucial to the matchday spectacle. No extortion is practised and no unofficial 'tax' is levied on those who enter; all contributions are voluntary.

In this space, the *Irriducibili* began to control the content of the banners and the nature of the chants. From here, the matchday organisation was co-ordinated, with fans watching the match, discussing the game and providing a wide variety of commentary, be it insulting, encouraging, political or simply anti-establishment. The self-appointed leaders, armed with tannoys, would urge the rest of the crowd to join them. At times, the *Irriducibili* would single out people who were not singing and insult them. The ordinary (i.e. non-*Irriducibili* and non-*UltraS*) fans in the immediate vicinity who were not participating would face criticism from the protagonists, and be encouraged to be more participatory with comments along the lines of: 'Come on boys, let's sing all together for our team; why do you fucking come to the stadium if you don't support your team?' On occasions, the group leaders would send a few of the *Irriducibili* to speak to the non-participants, to encourage them in the virtues of vocal support.

The Boxer's document elaborates further on the origins of the *Irriducibili*:

The *Irriducibili*'s beginnings were difficult. We had some flags bearing our name but we were different from the 'ordinary' *UltraS* because we were more unpredictable. 'Being original' was our motto and every time the more ordinary fans looked at us, they wondered what we would have organised. At a Lazio-Verona fixture, drums were first used for supporting the team. Before a Lazio-Ascoli fixture we published for the first time the *Mr Enrich* fanzine, which became very popular on the *curva nord*. In December 1987 at a game in Genoa, nearly all the Lazio supporters travelled by bus – but we used the train. We all met up at the railway station and led a parade of Lazio fans all the way to Genoa's Marassi stadium. This became the new way to 'introduce' ourselves to rival supporters. From that day all Lazio fans knew that for every away match there was an unofficial *biancoceleste* (white and blue) train with us on it, all wearing the *Mr Enrich* insignia. We became the self-appointed vanguard of Lazio.

The 1989–90 season was the one that Lazio played in the Flaminio stadium. We were against the refurbishment of the Olimpico, considering it a waste of public money and voiced this opinion in chants at the stadium. This was also the year of serious, constant and heavy police repression. The first *diffide* (stadium banning orders) were issued against us, limiting our personal liberty and giving police the power to ban those whom they considered 'dangerous' from the stadium. The first serious battle between the *Irriducibili* and the riot police occurred during the Lazio-Atalanta fixture; a similar battle occurred at the Roma-Lazio game when we voiced our condemnation of the *diffide* with a famous banner that stated *Dio salvi gli UltraS* (God help the *UltraS*).

The 1990–91 season saw a return to the now totally changed Olimpico. We did not like it and immediately produced a banner that read, '*Dodici in campo? Solo quando lo vogliamo noi!*' (Twelve on the pitch? Only when we want it).[2] We decided to strike, refusing to bring banners or chant for the first half of each match; no other *UltraS* did this. We also put on choreographies for the derby, exploring and demonstrating our feelings on a banner that read, '*Lo spettacolo colora la curva, la solidarieta la rende grande*' (The show makes the *curva* alive, but solidarity makes it great!). We were accused in the media of not caring for our team. On the contrary, the *Irriducibili* wanted to show that support was not compulsory and that other values also counted, most of all friendship – especially with the guys that were banned.

The 1990s were also the years when the Union Flag emblem of Britain was adopted, as the global flow of players provoked and generated a new set of symbols at Lazio matches. In 1992, SS Lazio signed the English international, Paul Gascoigne. In response, the *Irriducibili* made a banner that depicted a pint of English beer over the message 'it's ready for you', in honour of his somewhat notorious alcohol consumption. During the 1992–93 season, the food tycoon Sergio Cragnotti became president of the club and brought new hope to the supporters and the team. The same year saw the dissolution of the *Eagles Supporters*, as the *Irriducibili* became the new leaders of the *curva nord*. The group's power and influence spread and included dealings with the new president, something also mentioned in a document in the Boxer's collection:

In the 1995–96 season, after we stopped Cragnotti selling Beppe Signori, we became the most creative *curva* in Italy. In 1996 the coach Zdenek Zeman was sacked and Dino Zoff replaced him; the Roma derby saw the players received in the *curva nord* by a massive Mr Enrich that covered the *curva* and a giant 'Lazio' made up of blue balloons. In the 1997–98 season we produced four great choreographies: a giant imperial eagle with our motto *Osare,*

---

[2] The slogan stressed the importance of the *tifosi* as the twelfth player as they encouraged the team never to give up. Many Italian sports journalists have acknowledged the importance of the *tifosi* when commenting on the performance of Italian teams.

Creder, Spavaldi di Essere [Dare, Believe, Be Reckless]; the symbol of SS Lazio with the writing *Nobilta' UltraS: da Sempre* [Noble UltraS: Forever] and the banner *Noi Piu' Forti dell Indifferenza* [We are Stronger than the Indifference] as a way of protesting against police repression. In January 2000, to celebrate the club's centenary we created a museum at the Olimpico containing effigies of the club's renowned historical figures ranging from founder Luigi Bigiarelli to Beppe Signori.

The 1995–96 season was indeed important for the *Irriducibili*, perhaps marking the start of a period in which the group's influence was at its best. Their new fanzine *La Voce Della Nord* (The Voice of the North) was published for the first time, soon becoming the magazine of choice for the whole *curva nord*. Taking advantage of Cragnotti's arrival, they quickly made it clear that they were the voice of the club's supporters. There is no doubt that the demonstration they organised outside the club's headquarters in June 1995, following an announcement of the intended sale of top scorer Beppe Signori to Parma, did force the club to change its mind. In 1999–2000, as the club celebrated its centenary, the fans did likewise. Before the Lazio-Bologna fixture in January 2000, the *curva nord*'s celebrations began at 10 a.m. at the *Piazza della Libertá*, where Luigi Bigiarelli and his friends began their morning runs back in 1900. Over 25,000 supporters paraded from the piazza to the stadium where the *curva nord*, and in particular the *Irriducibili's* choreographies, provided the real entertainment of this day, based on a photo-mural of the great people in SS Lazio's history. In the tradition of the world's greatest football clubs, and with an eye to history, SS Lazio won its second *scudetto* in that same season.

The *Irriducibili* control the *curva nord* through a mixture of the charisma they project and the fear they exude. Those who poke their noses into *Irriducibili* business or those who are seen as a threat to the group are dealt with summarily, either there and then on the *curva*, or later on outside the stadium. But they are careful in their use of threats and physical assaults. Violence is only used when necessary. The hegemony of the group and their leaders among the *curva nord* youth is palpable. The young *tifosi* think that being an *Irriducibile* is 'cool' and enjoy wearing their hats, sweatshirts, T-shirts and other merchandise. In turn the youngsters' peripheral status on the *curva* has served them well. They can recount in school on Monday their brush with the powerful *Irriducibili*. Their daring is rewarded by the possibility of being considered 'hard' by association.

To bring matters concerning the group up to date, one of the *Irriducibili*'s leaders, Giorgio, was interviewed. Aged somewhere in his 40s, Giorgio is not only one of the historical leaders of the group, but has also been linked in several Italian media reports to the neo-fascist political group *Forza Nuova* (*see* chapter 6). Inevitably, a link was drawn between the party and the *Irriducibili*. However, this assumption was found to be incorrect. Giorgio is a very confident individual, eloquent and passionate in his convictions, as was demonstrated by what is known in Roman circles as the *due pizze in faccia* (two pizzas in the face – a derivative of Roman slang meaning literally 'two slaps in the face') episode. The incident occurred in August 1999, when the president Cragnotti announced that supporters would have to pay an entrance fee to watch the squad train at Formello (the club's official training ground to the north of the city). Furthermore, he said, if supporters wanted to follow SS Lazio to away matches, they could do so only by using Francorosso tours[3] – a company that offered tickets and travel at a higher price than the *Irriducibili*. The latter started a campaign of protest at the stadium through banners and chants. In response, the SS Lazio management appointed as mediator Guido Paglia, the communications director of the Cirio food company, one of Cragnotti's businesses. During negotiations Paglia promised to try to rectify the problem. However, this promise was not honoured, thus infuriating the *Irriducibili*. The battle lines were drawn. In October, the SS Lazio management banned the *UltraS* from the training ground. In response, the supporters met for a fan summit at a Rome hotel organised by the *Irriducibili*'s *direttivo*. At the meeting, Paglia accused the *Irriducibili* of being the main cause of the dispute. In response, Giorgio gave Paglia two slaps in the face and a kick in the buttocks. Despite this, negotiations continued, with the club eventually agreeing to abolish the entry fee to Formello and to allow the

---

[3] A large Italian travel/holiday company owned by Alpitour.

Irriducibili to continue selling away game packages. It was a victory that showed how much influence the *Irriducibili* had at the time.

A formal interview was arranged with Giorgio while he was working at the group's merchandising warehouse. He first talked about his upbringing:

> I was living in a district of Rome in the 1970s called Quadraro, a place where exponents of *Autonomia Operaia* [a left-wing, extra parliamentary political movement] lived. You cannot understand what it meant for a kid like me aged 14 to have ideology. In that period, being a Roma fan meant being communist and being a Lazio fan a fascist, so at times I had lots of fights and took beatings from these people [communists]. The satisfaction was when I grew up and became *figlio di mignotta* [literally 'son of a bitch', but actually meaning smart in fighting, respected and feared]. I was not a kid any more – from that time those who opposed me had to be careful.

A more formal Q&A followed:

Q: When did you first become a member of the *Irriducibili*?

G: The *Irriducibili* were begun in 1987 but we all have a past in other Lazio groups; we [the leaders] have roughly 25 years of militancy in the *curva*. They originally called us the *cani sciolti* (meaning bad boys) and then in 1987 we created this group.

Q: Why did you choose the name *Irriducibili*?

G: It's taken from an old choreography we produced. The name also reflects the nature of the group and many members identify themselves in the word.

Q: Who chooses such words and symbols?

G: Sometimes we [the *direttivo*] choose them; otherwise the young propose them to us. We have an office for group activity, a sort of 'ideas factory', where we meet and exchange proposals. The same procedure is adopted not only for the choreographies but also for banners on topics that do not have anything to do with football. The group is very attached to the symbol of the imperial eagle and the motto that truly represents us is under the eagle and reads, *Osare, Credere, Spavaldi di Essere* [Dare, Believe, Be Reckless].

Q: What is your employment status?

G: My job now is pursuing the commercial possibilities of the *Irriducibili* [merchandising, distributions of the products etc]. There is a commercial part of the *Irriducibili* that goes under the 'Original Fans' brand. We supply our products to shops in franchising agreements throughout the Lazio region and abroad. The label is represented by an old English cartoon character of the 1970s called Mr Enrich – a non-conformist rebel; he is as we are – against the 'system'.

One interesting feature of Giorgio's statements is that although he comes from a working class background, similar to his colleague the Boxer, as one of the leaders of the *Irriducibili*, he is in charge of a group with many members from middle class backgrounds. This social dynamic is also present in the *Boys*. This cross-class element has been characteristic of Italian hardcore *tifosi* since they first existed.

It illustrates the point that among the *UltraS* the ideological glue of fascism is stronger than that of class-consciousness. The *Boys*, for example, can count well-educated individuals among those in their group leadership. The *Irriducibili* and the *Boys* include individuals studying at university (often reading law); others are successful shop owners or running small businesses, some have solid working class origins and others come from the poor Roman districts. The *UltraS* are not gathering by virtue of socio-economic determinism; they bond because of their shared enthusiasm for both the football clubs and Mussolini's ideas.

One element that both the Boxer and Giorgio omitted from the group history was the challenge that the *Irriducibili* experienced to their *curva nord* hegemony. After all, it is human nature that whenever there is power there is resistance. The *Irriducibili* were forever claiming both football and ideological purity. Despite this claim, they were to face accusations of compromise due to their merchandising business. In 2006, the *Irriducibili* suffered a schism that resulted in the creation of a group called the *Banda Noantri* (Our Gang).[4]

To understand the *Irriducibili-Banda Noantri* relations, one might compare the situation to that of the old *mafia*, not because this analysis agrees with such a correlation – so often used by the Italian media to make sense of the *UltraS*[5] – but because of the similarity in how new leadership of such groups emerge. Every *UltraS* group was founded by overthrowing the established entity. This overthrow was usually accompanied by accusations that its predecessor had grown fat and lazy or drunk on the power and complacent with regard to the group's reputation. The one who takes power will inevitably face a similar threat to its hegemony at some point. The *Irriducibili* were no different. In 2006, they faced accusations that they had lost their willingness for confrontation. The *Irriducibili*'s merchandising operations led to allegations of being more concerned with appearances than action and fighting. They were challenged with the insult of *embourgoisement*; that they had compromised and were now money-driven and pursuing a form of branded notoriety. Years before, in overthrowing the *Eagles*, the *Irriducibili* had stated their dislike for any kind of market in the *curva*, even using the mantra: *No al Mercato in Curva Nord* (No to the market in *curva nord*). In the eyes of their emergent critics, the *Irriducibili* had betrayed one of their founding principles.

The *Banda Noantri* sought to re-establish in the *curva*, in their own words, 'A model of pure *UltraS*'. They were similarly neo-fascists, but did not display their banners, in order to avoid police attention. The group was originally composed of some 40 men aged between 18 and 28 who identified themselves as 'pure and tough', always ready to fight – as the *Irriducibili* had previously espoused. Uncompromising and

---

[4] This group evolved later into the *In Basso a Destra* (Low on the Right), which is still present on the *curva nord*. The name indicates both the location in the *curva* where the group is located and their political orientation.

[5] *See* chapter 12 for an evaluation of the relationship between the Italian media and *UltraS*.

feared, this group was considered by the *Irriducibili* as akin to the Casuals – a collection of football hooligan groups present in Britain in the 1980s. They were an extreme version of the *Irriducibili*.

But the apparent schism was more ideological than actual. Codes, norms and respect were extended among the comrades, especially when they shared space in the stadium. The *Irriducibili* and the *Banda Noantri* remained comrades; their ideology maintained a climate of coexistence, even if it was disturbed by occasional disagreement. The story of Gabriele Sandri throws light on these dynamics. Sandri was a Lazio supporter and was known to the SS Lazio *UltraS*. In 2007, he was shot and killed by a police officer who was intervening to stop a fight between Juventus and Lazio fans at a petrol station along the Arezzo motorway, approximately 120 miles from Rome. Sandri worked as a disc jockey in exclusive Rome nightclubs and was a proactive campaigner against drug use in such establishments. Originating from an upper middle class background (his family owns a clothes shop in the affluent Balduina district), Sandri was also a comrade who was regularly among the SS Lazio *UltraS* gatherings at *Piazza Vescovio* in the Trieste district, part of what is known as Rome's *Zona Nera* (Black Zone) because of its populace's sympathies for the Far Right.[6] Significant figures of both the *Banda Noantri* and the *Irriducibili* were in the car in which Gabriele Sandri was travelling before he was shot. They travelled as friends and stood together as they buried their mutual friend.

The traditional hostility between the two opposing terraces of the *Stadio Olimpico* is important in that it can be used to gauge the power of an ideology. Historically, the two groups were divided for a whole range of

---

[6] From the 1970s, this location witnessed the emergence of neo-fascist groups and gatherings of youths sympathetic to such ideologies. The district is also remembered for the death of Francesco Cecchin, a young member of the neo-fascist *Movimento Sociale Italiano* who died in 1979 having fallen from a wall in Via Montebuono while running away from a gang of radical left-wing militants. In the eyes of the latter, Cecchin was guilty of posting far right electoral posters and needed to be taught a lesson. The local branch of the far right *Forza Nuova* party annually commemorates the death of Cecchin in nearby Via Benaco, where the local branch of *Azione Giovani* (Youth Action, the youth movement of *Alleanza Nazionale*) is also found. In the nearby Piazza Vescovio stands a 'Scottish' pub called *Excalibur*, which is very popular among the Lazio *UltraS* (II Messagero 29/06/07).

reasons, based on the love for a different team. In recent years, however, and defying any historical enmities, a shared neo-fascist ideology has made the two *curve* of the capital city less hostile towards each other. Indeed, the two groups have turned their antagonism against the State and the Italian police. This coming together has brought into focus a number of startling similarities, in particular the highly structured nature of both gatherings, clearly illustrated by two interconnected ideological traits, namely a strong group unity and elitism. The groups each manifest an internal cohesion fostered by ideology and culture, which provides the base of the intensity of the relationship between the groups' members and the construction of 'other' supporters. The *UltraS* are also elitist. Elitism is a deeply ingrained trait of the Italian neo-fascist youth movement and is represented here in the way that members of the *Boys* and the *Irriducibili* portray themselves as 'super-hardcore supporters', always against any compromise with the hyper-commer-cialisation of modern football and ever-ready to 'act' both socially and physically to promulgate their general ethos and specific style of supporting. In these groups today, the concept of being 'true' or 'more true' is one of the most important ideas that emerge from this study. An understanding of the subject is needed to help grasp the logic of the modern *UltraS*.

The funeral of Gabriele Sandri, a Lazio fan shot dead by police in 2007

06

AN EMERGING SOCIAL MOVEMENT?

Since the beginning of our constitution, we have had clear ideas about politics in the stadium. We believe it cannot be avoided, because every man, hence, every UltraS has his own ideals and beliefs, and it seems right that, especially in this place of aggregation, he can display them.

Juventude Crociata – Padova FC *UltraS* group

This statement is a good example of the strong sense of ideology that exists among Italian *UltraS*. If you add this to the behavioural and cultural elements of these groups it becomes clear that Italian *UltraS* activities are manifestations of an emerging social movement. Social movements do not originate from a vacuum; they arise from experiences of the individual members. These groups constitute at least in part a particular response by one section of Italian youth towards the social, cultural and political restrictions that they encounter within the broader social system. The *UltraS* are a good example of this process; they find their roots in both the Italian youth neo-fascist and hardcore football supporters' movements. A social movement is defined here as a 'collectivity acting with some degree of organisation and continuity outside institutional channels for promoting or resisting change in the group, society, or world order of which it is a part.'[1] Before developing the idea that the *UltraS* represent a social movement, it is helpful to examine the origins of the *UltraS* and how they have developed from the wider Italian hardcore supporters – the *ultrá*.

The *UltraS* grew out of *ultrá* gatherings. Until the mid-1990s the term *ultrá* was used to describe all hardcore Italian football fans, regardless of their politics. *Ultrás* were invariably males between the ages of 16 and 40, who indulged in various forms of anti-social behaviour, and in particular violence. The word *ultrá* comes from French political discourse. During the Restoration period (1815–1830), the word *ultrá-royaliste* described partisans loyal to the Absolute Monarchy. The *ultrá-royaliste* championed the interests of property owners, the nobility and the clergy. They were the supporters of authority and royal tradition in opposition to the philosophies of human rights and individual freedoms favoured by followers of the Enlightenment.

During the 1950s, Italian football was characterised by a generally relaxed and informal fan culture. Fan club offices were places to buy match tickets and gather with the like-minded to listen to the State radio commentary when the team played outside of town. A football match was a parochial event and a social gathering, and while episodes of violence did occur, they rarely got out of hand. There were, on

---

[1] This definition is taken from Simi et al. 2004

occasion, scuffles between opposing fans, usually based on long-standing district and regional rivalries, and fights sometimes occurred among groups that supported the same team over on-the-pitch incidents.

Some say that the *ultrá* first appeared in 1959 during a match between Napoli and Bologna, when 65 people were injured following a pitch invasion. Others claim that the first real violent clashes between fans occurred during the 1970s. But it was in the late 1960s that Italian youth first began to show signs of restlessness. This often took the form of social insubordination and sometimes hostility towards authority. The appeal of this kind of behaviour developed further over the next few years until it seemed that Italian politics (and trade unions) had lost the hold they had on both youthful and general public opinion. It was in this environment that the *ultrá* first appeared.

At first it seemed as though the younger generation had simply turned its back on politics and were looking instead to the sports arenas for excitement and conflict. Fans on Italy's *curve* began to identify themselves by sporting team colours, adopting symbols and marking out their territories. But even at this time ideological divisions in Italian society, reflected in cities and regions, were usually mirrored by the political sympathies witnessed at the local football stadiums. This era saw the formation of left-wing hardcore football fan groups, including the AC Milan *Brigate Rossonere*, and the *Brigate Gialloblue* of Modena. On the opposite side were Verona's *Brigate Gialloblú*, and the *Boys San* of Inter-Milan (formed by members of the *Fronte della Gioventú* – the youth movement of the Italian neo-fascist party MSI).

These groups, together with the *Boys*, can be considered the first manifestation of the *UltraS*. However, when they first formed they were not really political. The era between 1968 and 1977, when the whole of Europe was in political uproar, was the turning point. Disillusionment at the failure of the protest movement brought about a hardening of political opinion.

The changing fan culture and its associated anti-social behaviour came to a head in October 1979 when a SS Lazio fan, Vincenzo Paparelli was killed by an incendiary fired from the *curva sud*. The same day, football-related violence occurred in the cities of Ascoli, Milan and Brescia, causing many injuries and widespread criminal damage. There was uproar in the press. Public opinion forced politicians to act. There were calls from the State to eradicate the *teppisti* (thugs). The police subsequently began targeting the most notorious individuals and carried out house searches of those they suspected. They raided the headquarters of fan groups, seizing banners, drums and other paraphernalia.

The escalation of the hardcore football fans' violence between the 1970s and early 1980s indicates the transformation of the phenomenon. It was in the 1980s that the Italian hardcore football fan movement reached its apex in terms of the number of participants and episodes of violence. The development of a complex of friendships and rivalries was regulated at first glance by the logic of the 'Bedouin Syndrome' by which a friend of an ally is a friend, and the enemy of an ally is an enemy, though new rivalries developed quickly for a variety of reasons.

The State's response was an increase in security measures, most notably the installation of CCTV cameras and the use of hand-held metal detectors at stadium entrances. Football stadia took on the appearance of fortresses with riot police surrounding the vicinities and parading in large numbers clad in riot gear. While the new policing techniques reduced episodes of violence inside the stadium, a 'dislocation effect' resulted in an equivalent rise in violence outside the stadium, in town centres, railway and subway stations. Added to this, a developing Italian political crisis provoked contempt for traditional forms of political aggregation. The increasing alienation of youth from mainstream politics saw many of them turn to football. Individual and collective political hopes, joys and frustrations surfaced like never before in the stadium.

By the mid-1980s, new gatherings had joined the *curve*. Among the traditional factions, younger formations had appeared who celebrated their ability to break boundaries. These were the *cani sciolti* (mavericks) – a term first coined by the organised *ultrá* groups to describe youths who were difficult to control. These youngsters did not recognise themselves as part of a pre-existing fan group – nor did they seek such an association. They did not originate out of schisms within the established groups; they were autonomous from all pre-existing fan constitutions. The majority of this new demographic, invariably aged between 14 and 16, were lacking in political consciousness and had little historical knowledge of the *ultrá* movement.

The new *curve* formations represented an Italian society that, during the 1980s, celebrated individualism, self-indulgence and ostentation. As a consequence, the era saw a refusal among much of its young generation to participate in matters that were political or required a sense of dedication. The names of the *curva* groups reflected this ethos; names with political connotations were substituted by those linked to psychological conditions and drug and alcohol consumption. Examples of these gatherings were the *Sconvolti* (Deranged), *Kolletivo Alcoolico* (Alcoholic Group), *Wild Kaos* and *Arancia Meccanica* (Clockwork Orange – from the controversial 1971 Stanley Kubrick film that presented a futuristic vision of violent nihilism). The 1980s ended with serious incidents of fan violence. In 1988, during an Ascoli-Inter Milan match, Nazareno Filippini was killed after being repeatedly punched and kicked by a group of hardcore Inter fans. On 4 June 1989, during a Milan-Roma game, a Roma supporter, Antonio De Falchi, died of a heart attack following an assault carried out by rival supporters. Dislike of and opposition to these new groups was evident in the more notorious *curve*, such as Roma, Milan, Bergamo, Naples and Genova, who took on the title *Vecchia Guardia* (Old Guard). Such gatherings emphasised the principles of collective unity and group collaboration that had first inspired the origins of the hardcore football supporters' movement. It is, perhaps, in this period that the ideology of the Old Guard hardcore football fans became more political.

From the early 1990s onwards, the notion of ideology grew on the Italian *curve*. Hardcore supporters groups throughout Italy more frequently displayed common emblems or mottos related to neo-fascism on their banners. The stadium became a setting in which it was permissible to express both concepts of selfhood and collective political will. It is no surprise, therefore, that the 1990s was a decade of profound political and economic crisis for Italy. An entire political system was falling apart under the acts of *Tangentopoli* (*see* chapter 1); public opinion was tiring of corrupt politicians. The electorate punished the distrusted political parties, which were decimated in the corruption inquiries of the Italian magistrates. Sentiments of political renewal were represented by extreme parties, such as the MSI (which subsequently became *Alleanza Nazionale*), or by new political parties such as Silvio

Berlusconi's *Forza Italia*, founded in 1994, and Umberto Bossi's *Lega Nord*, founded in 1996. The era also saw increased popularity of national revolutionary movements on the extreme right, such as *Forza Nuova, Movimento Sociale Fiamma Tricolore, Fronte Nazionale* and the reaffirmation of extreme left ideological parties, such as *Rifondazione Communista* (the new Communist Party).

In 2009, Dr Domenico Mazzilli, a high-ranking officer of the Italian police and later President of the National Observatory on Sport Events of the Italian Ministry published a report confirming the existence of 58 *UltraS* groups with more than 15,000 members throughout Italy. The *UltraS* are, thus, a relatively large nationwide grouping that interacts across regions. While they are not an imminent threat to parliamentary democracy, their very existence is a stain on the Italian body politic. The political concern that they carry with them is two-fold; they are prepared for violence and they are unpredictable with unknown potential.

Although originally set up in opposition to each other, each group supporting its own team, the rise of ideology and a parallel development of political awareness during the last twenty years have given the various *UltraS* something in common. For the *UltraS*, shared causes are their very survival; they have common opponents (the police, media and football institutions); they use similar tactics, such as supporters' strikes, in which they refuse to support their team to draw attention to a particular matter. Further shared elements are a willingness to engage in violence, public protest campaigns and maintaining a recognisable organisation, which, in the last two years, has seen the emergency of the newly founded *UltraS Italia* (*see* page 160). Collective identity is a sense of 'we' based on cohesion and solidarity around which individuals act. As we have seen, traditional rivalries can be put aside to oppose perceived persecution by the State against their common way of life. The city of Roma has witnessed the capability of the *UltraS* in their struggle against the Italian State. In the last few years the *UltraS* of AS Roma and SS Lazio have gradually united in their resistance against the State, its repressive laws and the police, often in preference to clashes against rival fans. While aware of differences, Marco (of the *Boys*) underlines the comradeship between the two groups:

The leader of our group had a personal friendship, based also on the same ideological outlook on life, with one of the leaders of the *Irriducibili*. When he died in 2005 all the *direttivo* of the *Irriducibili* attended his funeral and raised their hands doing the Roman salute in sign of respect. We are more explicit and openly political than the *Irriducibili*. We produced a banner stating 'No American peace on my land!' We are anti-NATO [they do not want American military bases in Italy]. We are against Italian soldiers in Iraq; we do not want to waste Italian blood for an American war.

In 2007, the death of the Lazio *UltraS* Gabriele Sandri (*see* chapter 8) provoked an unprecedented violent reaction from *UltraS* groups throughout Italy. Groups from Taranto, Milan, Rome, Parma and Torino challenged the police in protest against the killing, but also in rage against the repression of the football stadia and the cumulative measures that the Italian state had undertaken against them. A common theme of the chants was '*Polizia – Assassini*' (Police – Murderers); anti-police graffiti appeared on the walls of cities such as Milan, Rome and Padova. In Rome, the reaction of the Roma and Lazio *UltraS* in the streets – further aggravated by the decision of the authorities to cancel the AS Roma-Cagliari match a few hours before kick-off – was extremely violent. Some 20 police officers were injured in the disturbances. As a result, a number of *UltraS* were arrested and charged with offences pertaining to terrorism.

Sandri's funeral in November that year attracted more than 5,000 mourners. Banners displayed at the ceremony demanded justice for his death and condemned what they perceived as the 'crazy' repression by the State. The disorder that followed Sandri's death was, in the words of the Italian Minister of Interior, Giuliano Amato, a manifestation of 'a blind rage, led by madly criminal minds subversive against the police, its vehicles and its symbols.' Without revealing his sources Amato also informed parliament of planned disorder, subversive articulations and diversionary tactics employed by those seeking 'to attract the police and *carabinieri* around CONI (the Italian Olympic Committee building), to leave the police barracks unattended with the intention of making their attack easier.' In this case, the behaviour of the Italian police force was exemplary. In one instance, the *UltraS* did attack the police barracks, which were full of weapons, ammunition and vehicles. The law allowed the police in such circumstances to shoot to protect the public; skill and professionalism saw the police hold back and avoid a possible tragedy. However, images of the riots, which were broadcasted globally, were not good for Italy's reputation abroad.

Similar dynamics are emerging among other *UltraS* groups throughout Italy. Few in Italy would ever imagine the possibility of hardcore *tifosi* of Juventus and Roma sitting together in the stadium and watching a football match. Nevertheless, this is precisely what is happening with the *UltraS Italia,* who gather to watch and support the national team as a symbol of the concept of *Patria* (native land).

In 2009, Todde, who had recently become involved with the *UltraS Italia,* explained this new group. According to him, their membership numbered approximately 600 and the *camerati* of Lazio, Roma and Inter had recently joined the 'project'. Other members were drawn from Juventus, Ascoli, Verona, Udine, Trieste, Napoli, Genova and elsewhere. Todde gave his explanation for its formation: 'Although there was an attempt to organise ourselves at the national level before Sandri's death [referring to the first emergence of a national group called the *Vikings Italia*], after Sandri's death and the injustice carried out against one of us, there were more interactions among all of the groups and one of the results was the *UltraS Italia.*'

On the occasion of Sandri's death, for the first time, many *UltraS* throughout Italy displayed banners in their stadium and wrote about the death on their websites in honour of Sandri and in solidarity with the *UltraS* of SS Lazio. They were also supported by the punk group ZetaZeroAlfa, who still display on their website a picture of Sandri, demanding 'Justice for Gabriele'.

In Todde's analysis, the same logic that allied members of the *Irriducibili* and the *Boys* applied to the *UltraS Italia*. Even if many of the members are neo-fascist sympathisers, they consider themselves autonomous from any political party. The national mobilisation of the *UltraS,* which is pertinent to their being considered a social movement, is expressed by their direct actions. The *UltraS*' direct action takes several forms. At its most primitive, it is exhibited by the presentation of common banners containing messages of accusation and defiance. At a higher level, as shown previously, it is evidenced by social campaigns that they perceive as 'just'. Direct action is also demonstrated at an organisational level via their (pirate) radio programmes, which they use to explain and spread their ideas. While many of these messages have become little more than a constant background noise, when an issue of real importance arises, the *UltraS* can mobilise and confront the State. Although it seems unlikely that the *UltraS* will emerge as a formal, organised organisation, the sense of an emerging movement is present, based on a common foe and a common strategy of opposition.

As the *UltraS* groups have developed they have gone through similar events, have achieved certain success, been subjected to similar pressures and prejudice and have, naturally, evolved a certain similarity of thought. Their successes have seen them develop legitimate expectations and, as these rise, so does a conviction that these expectations will never be satisfied. In such power-orientated groups as the *UltraS*, the psychological strain of this 'deprivation' is diluted by a belief in a structural solution (in their case comprised of campaigning and lobbying of the Italian parliament and in acts of violence if necessary), conceived against the larger social structure outside the group. It is this same discontent that leads the *UltraS* groups into action.

Armed with righteousness and the *curve* from which to explain their causes, the *UltraS* are a potentially powerful interest group. The recent and sudden escalation of tougher laws and state repression have promoted a perception among them of blocked expectation and an accompanying sense of outrage at the injustice and inequity of the situation. Such a sense of grievance increasingly leads the *UltraS* to see themselves as outcasts and in conflict with the state and the media. The latter, of course, have sided with the state. Consequently, the group's rhetoric of discrimination has increased. However, the groups have developed a number of ways of dealing with this discrimination. Among the most relevant is 'social creativity', whereby the groups respond to discrimination by defining themselves as superior to others. They think of themselves as 'pure', not polluted like the 'others' by the commercialised logic of modern *calcio*, in which mercenaries (the players) are idolised. The

UltraS feel that their ethical stance justifies their violence and way of life and makes bearable the perceived social stigma. They believe that it is 'morally' worth it. Another key strategy for coping with discrimination lies in social support and a sense of bonding. The ideological and cultural traits that make the *UltraS* feel strong are also those that create a feeling of belonging and strength throughout the movement.

There may, however, be another facet of the *UltraS* grievance that merits evaluation; this relates to their nature as an 'extreme' youth movement. The pervasive sense of dissatisfaction by the Italian youth is mostly related to their expectations of an efficient political class that works in their interest. Traditionally, Italian politics has been unsympathetic and blind to youth. The *UltraS* do not trust Italian politics. Such anti-political discourses are a common theme among Italian youths and these feelings are widely present throughout the whole *UltraS* movement. The *UltraS* do not miss any chance to declare their dislike for Italian politics and their incompetent youth policies; Marco (of the *Boys*) explains:

> I do not like politics and do not follow it! I am an extra-parliamentary; I follow the Third Position – the 'revolutionary' position. The Italian system is putrid; if the tree is sick to the root, it cannot give good fruits. The problems are not the fruits that need to be changed, but the tree that needs to be eradicated or at least cured. Sometimes I agree with Bertinotti [the leader of *Rifondazione Communista*,[2] and former president of the Chamber of Deputies]. The extreme left and right converge on some issues …

The term 'putrid' used by Marco can be considered a fair representation of the mood of the youth of the *curve*. In 2009, the international organisation *Transparency International* polled Italians to determine what they believed to be the most corrupt organisation in the country. Astonishingly, 44 per cent of the participants pointed their fingers at the Italian political parties. One influential journalist posed the question, 'Why is the political power in the hands of the old?' He identified the

---

[2] A recently formed Italian far left political party (founded in 1991)

advanced age of the politicians as one of the main causes of the malfunction of the Italian political system; young politicians are under-represented and not in key positions to exercise power. His article concluded that Italy is far from achieving the requisite of a just society – namely having a system based on meritocracy. In Italy, a career, especially in the state-controlled domains, is accomplished only by personal recommendations and a seniority that greatly demotivates its youth.

A recent study of the Italian political class suggests that, in the Italian parliament, individuals of poor political skills, but loyal to the party, function merely to reinforce the leadership that has chosen them. Too many MPs are elderly professional politicians. The study concluded that Italy is a country that exists on political immobility, in a society that is fragmented and lacking a strong political and institutional framework. It is a country that has a significant public debt and that, instead of introducing much needed reforms related to education, health and justice – to name but a few – is instead blocked by litigious local and national leaders who promote a system based on political parties and not on people. Furthermore, Italy is a nation wherein governments, regardless of political line, are unable to erase organised crime in the regions of the south; not by chance these regions experience higher youth unemployment rates – often more than 30 per cent.

Many commentators agree that Italian politicians have traditionally employed a systematic way of doing politics, where concessions and favouritism are institutionalised and where conceding favours to obtain votes has developed into a consistent and non-written rule. The majority of Italian politicians have never been employed outside the political arena. Politics is their only means of revenue, which makes them inclined to adhere to a systematic and methodological administration of power to survive and obtain an income. This situation creates conflict, protest and resistance, especially among the youth, who are the most penalised.

The perceived inefficiency of Italian politics, political parties and protagonists has provoked opposition among the whole electorate. The well-known Italian journalist Eugenio Scalfari published an article in *La Repubblica* in 2007, which crystallised *UltraS* attitudes, '… Growing is the number of Italian citizens who totally refuse this political class …

There is a growing refusal of 'these' political parties, of 'these' politicians ... It is a total refusal on all levels: taxes, public order, legality, inequalities, freedom. Thumbs down on everything. They [the political class] need to go.'

This attitude is reinforced by the recent emergence of a popular movement organised by the renowned Genovese comedian Beppe Grillo who, during his stage and broadcasting career, was a vociferous critic against the malpractice of Italian politics and its politicians. He said:

We are against right and left; we do not have hope anymore... this should have been the government who would have changed everything. We need young people and new ideas, not policies originating from 'pensioners' of 70 years old! The aim [of this manifestation and movement] is to 'kick them out from the palace' and most of all to express our dislike and weariness of a political system which is more and more millions of miles away from the citizens and their needs.

The protest gradually took shape via the comedian's internet blog and, during a tour of Italy, found its first public manifestation with a protest meeting held in Bologna's Piazza Maggiore in September 2007. The main objective of the movement was to 'clean' Italian politics of its so-called rationalisation, wipe out its professionalisation and expose its lack of ideals. The Bologna meeting, called 'V-Day' (Vaffanculo Day, or Fuck off Day), aimed to collect signatures for a petition urging the creation of a new law to make politicians with criminal records ineligible for parliament (25 MPs in Parliament in 2007 held such a status). The movement also sought to disallow Italian citizens from being elected as MPs if they were in the legal system awaiting a verdict. Another aim was to get rid of the 'professional politician'. To this end, the protesters proposed that no Italian citizens could be elected as an MP more than twice and that anyone elected had to come from a grassroots selection procedure, and not be parachuted in by a party system. Some 50,000 signatures were collected.

The inability of the Italian state to respond to the concrete needs of people, especially its youth, who see their existence as increasingly uncertain in this political framework, can be said to have contributed to the creation of an ideological vacuum. Within this vacuum the search for security and certainty has promoted a number of extreme ideologies founded on 'action', among them the neo-fascism of the *UltraS*. Italian novelist (and sociologist) Umberto Eco has termed this 'Ur Fascism' in which action is taken for the sake of action and whose proponents would argue that there is no struggle for life, but rather a 'fight for life'. According to this, pacifism is collusion with the enemy; action is good in and of itself, and must be implemented without reflection. As Giorgio reflects, 'I am waiting for that day when I will be in a piazza in Roma to "take" Rome with the others. I could be 50 years old or older – it does not matter – but the rage that we have with this political system is huge. This society – and I refer to modern society, not only Italy – creates privileges; many people have jobs so low paid that they cannot afford to marry or have children – they can therefore be tempted to "deviate".'

Giorgio expressed once again the populist nature of the *Irriducibili*, a feeling shared by the *Boys* that has spread throughout the Italian *curve*. The *UltraS* do not believe in the Italian State and, while supporting their teams, they use the stadium for their own pronouncements. Such a statement implies an apocalyptic vision of Italian society; they suggest that Italians must be awoken in order to eliminate the inefficient politicians. This discourse is clearly subversive in nature.

The *UltraS* movement stands against the immobility that is dominant in Italian society. The groups will fight for their ideas no matter what the outcome is and no matter the medium used. As Eco recognised in his reflection on fascism, in any mythology, the hero is an exceptional being who regards death as the ultimate reward for an heroic existence. As Antonio (of the *Boys*) argues, 'Who dies or is a victim of this state in our groups is not forgotten and will be always remembered.' The heroes celebrated by Italian *UltraS* are people who fight for their ideals. Their heroes are the deceased – the 'fallen', like Paolo di Nella, who was killed in Rome in 1993 while putting up posters for the MSI, attacked and hit on the head by a gang of left-wing activists. As Eco notes, for those devoid of alternative social identities, 'Ur-Fascism', makes a privilege of being born with a sense of nation going back to the Roman

Empire, of being Italian, the inheritor of these ancient and venerable values, cults and histories. Significantly, the *Boys* and *Irriducibili* sport the colours of the Italian flag in their merchandise.

Of course, the feelings ascribed to the *UltraS* are not reserved for them. For many, modern society lacks meaningful relationships, beliefs, strong values and a sense of place. In modern cities, there is an absence of strong points of reference. As the *UltraS* have a soapbox from which to speak, they speak for many. The Boxer recognises this fact. He describes his reason for the response that it provokes, 'When we speak about issues such as the Palestine *Intifada* and Saddam Hussein's Iraq they do not like it; they do not like political topics at the stadium because they could create a consensus; this scares politicians who cannot control votes. This is the reason for the strong police repression...'

The *UltraS* are careful in their selection of causes outside the Italian context. Their sympathy for the Irish Republic cause arises out of their seeing Ireland as a nation that forever resists an imposed discourse via myth, legend and song – and ultimately violence. The Irish nationalist population celebrates the warrior; the nationalist murals are admired, stressing, as they do, a sense of identity through symbols, non-conformist heroes, and nationalist sentiment. The Palestinian cause offers the same appeal. Such support is not required, it is what such people symbolise that matters. Giovanni was at pains to explain the wishes of the *UltraS* to be heard and counted:

For a while, a well-known and popular extreme left-wing newspaper [*Il Manifesto*] wrote dedicated articles about us and praised us for our social battles against drugs and paedophilia; ironically they said we were fascist because we did not know how to be communist. How ignorant! Many do not know that the social doctrine of fascism has many things in common with the revolutionary left. Unfortunately, in Italy, fascism has been always depicted as reactionary while from the beginning it was nothing like that; but these things are taught in the history books that our children study, where many things simply follow dominant ideology... for us, communism has been reactionary while real fascism was revolutionary.

The ideology of the Italian neo-fascists, as expressed by the *UltraS*, has revolutionary power, and has found an outlet in the Roman (and in the Italian) *curve*. Giovanni elaborates:

> Until the emergence of our group, everyone thought that the typical *UltraS* was an imbecile who went to the stadium to watch the match, perhaps drunk and seeking violence. We want to send a message to the public; the *Irriducibili* showed the public that *UltraS* can think beyond football. We did this firstly with our fanzine and then with our radio programme. Via these tools, we could express our opinions and defend ourselves from media attacks; this was the main reason why we started radio programmes. The fanzine promoted the *Irriducibili* during the games; our radio show keeps it alive all week. We wanted to underline that the *Irriducibili* are Lazio *UltraS* but they are also citizens wishing to have their opinions heard. We have been pioneers; we try to make other *UltraS* realise that we are a potent lobby and we can make a difference at the elections.

Giovanni's statement stresses the status of the *agorà* of the Olimpico. *Agorà* is an ancient Greek term meaning 'public meeting place'. In Ancient Greece it was a place intended primarily for public assembly. Only later was it also used as a marketplace. *Agorà* is the location where the *oikos* (private dimension) and *ecclesia* (public dimension) meet. It is the location where private problems are dealt with in a meaningful way. This locale is used to articulate, not just to draw narcissistic pleasures or to search for some relief through public display, but to collectively seek the tools that are powerful enough to lift individuals from their privately suffered misery. It is the space where ideas may be born, take shape and be considered for the 'public good'. It pursues the 'just society' or at least provides comfort in a sense of 'shared values'. The Italian football stadium is one of the few remaining Italian modern social *agorà*. It is a site where not only football, but also ideological opinions – often the antithesis of notions of political correctness – and direct actions are freely expressed in the pursuit of a wider consensus and resistance. Todde confirms this opinion:

> The football stadium allows us to bring our battles – via the media – to 40 million Italians. Before, in the stadium you would rarely find socio-political issues raised by *UltraS*. It is the only place that we can speak freely about our ideas without being charged with subversive association. In other places, we would be repressed. We are people who do not want to be made stupid by consumerist repression; we want to discuss and to confront. The stadium 'ends' belong to us and here we can express who we are and impose our rules. We go to the stadium and articulate our ideas because the state does not allow the individual to speak freely because of rampant political correctness. We fight this lack of freedom mainly with negative campaigns, but when the state allows us to express our values, we also send constructive and positive messages.

The stadium provides a liminal arena – outside of normal society – for the public performance of behaviour not normally acceptable to that society. Once there, the *UltraS* use words and symbols to debate, similar in a way to organised religion where the believer gives substance to the symbol, as the symbol gives the believer form. The stadium – or *agorà* – becomes another means of identification for the *UltraS*; at the same time a place for the socially excluded and a locale where the *UltraS* can resist repression.

The roots of the political ideology which inspires the *UltraS* lifeworld is oppositional, as it is in all Italian neo-fascist youth groups. The main patterns of *UltraS* reasoning: the *non omologazione* (non-conformity), authenticity, tradition, adversity to modernity and the 'warrior spirit' – together with the *UltraS* way of conceiving issues related to national identity and race – unveil the ideological and also cultural traits of the *UltraS communitas*. These have spread to all corners of the country and are now united by their common strategy of opposition to the police and the State.

Like all social movements the *UltraS* indulge in 'framing'. The *UltraS* are constantly 'framing' their messages. 'Framing' and ideology are two sides of the same coin, and helpful in interpreting the *UltraS* way of life.

They are different but connected. While ideology – supported by culture – represents stability and provides certainty and values to social groups, 'framing' is flexible, unpredictable and is responsible for the construction of their meanings. When opposing the 'others' or fighting their battles, the *UltraS* make choices and erase some information. Put simply, the *UltraS* package the reality, leaving out what does not fit and keep that which can create a consensus. 'Framing' is the key, for example, to understanding the *UltraS* recruitment dynamics among the *curve*. The framing of social stigma and the sense of persecution create a consensus in the group and serves to proselytise their cause to the Italian neo-fascist world. Todde explained that many youth with neo-fascist ideological sympathies approach groups such as the *Boys*, identifying with their plight, enraged by what they perceive as a police persecution against fascists.

'Framing' processes have implications not only at micro but also at macro level. In the current Italian social and political context, the *curva* and, more generally, the football stadium, re-affirms its social status and function as an *agorà*, a site of communication, one of the few surviving places in which a group may jointly express sentiments of rebellion and collective identity. The *UltraS* ideology is meaningful; they are organised and interact both locally and nationally, they are present throughout the country and are able to mobilise themselves to fight common 'enemies'. A climate of hate and vendetta ensues, diffusing progressively among the Italian *curves* led by the *UltraS*, which has repercussions for the Italian public order.

But some messages are unclear. One particular example is their attitude to race. This is a complex issue. The two groups are particularly offended by accusations that their attitude to race resembles that of the Nazis. Federico (of the *Irriducibili*) provided the following story in response to such accusations:

> I am against anyone who calls me a Nazi! What I do not like are people who come to my country and commit crimes; Albanians and Romanians are destroying Rome with their camps. But I am not racist. One day, I was waiting in my car at the traffic lights and, as usual, there was a young female gypsy who was trying to

clean the car windscreen and was asking for money. Suddenly, a municipal police officer [traffic police hired by the Mayor with less power than ordinary police and who are usually not armed] started to mistreat the girl. I jumped out of my car and almost kicked his arse. I hate injustice!

In this account, the anti-system stance of the *UltraS* was stressed over and above racial prejudice. Such an account shows the complexity of the racist dimension. Racism exists within the *UltraS* movement; it is expressed in the stadium and it has different dimensions. It is ritualised; it is ideological (specifically prejudiced towards Jews, who are always identified as 'Zionists') and reflects the broader worries of many Roman-Italian citizens regarding what some see as the State's mismanagement of illegal immigration (especially from Eastern Europe), which is widely perceived as a threat to the security of the city. However, the root of their racism is 'oppositional'. The *Boys* and the *Irriducibili* are hostile to anyone outside of their world, regardless of race and credo and this is one of the most important traits they have in common with other Italian *UltraS*. As they are popular in the *curve* and connected nationally we can, therefore, see in them the emergence of both a social movement and a common oppositional strategy against the media and the police.

UltraS put on a spectacular demonstration of their passion, which covers politics as well as football

07

POLITICAL IDEOLOGY AND THE *UltraS*

Nessuna resa nessun lamento; linea di condotta … combattimento!
(No surrender, no complaint; how do we behave … we fight!)

The chant of the curva nord

When Federico (aged 40, and co-leader of the *Irriducibili*) was interviewed for this book, he vehemently stressed that it would be irrational for any individual to try to join the *Irriducibili* without possessing neo-fascist sympathies. It is through fascist ideology, he elaborated, that the *Irriducibili* define themselves. When asked what role he thought political ideology played in the *curva*, Antonio, a member of the *Boys* answered, 'We are openly fascists and we think that everyone can see this in the *curva*... symbols, banners, chants express clearly what we think. Politics is present in everyone's life so why be surprised that it is also present in the stadium? You cannot imagine the pleasure we have in burning pictures of Che Guevara at the stadium! Even when we fight, politics play an increasingly important part...'

Consequently, all who claim membership of the *Boys* or the *Irriducibili* must be prepared publicly to proclaim their adherence to the main tenets of fascism. Ideology gives meaning and justification to the *UltraS* actions and reinforces the cohesion of the groups and their individual identities. An evaluation of the *UltraS* would not be complete without an elaboration of the roots of their ideological credo.

The impulse for political action among fascists and their heirs through the 20th and 21st centuries is promoted by the perception of both crises and decadence in the political, social and economic domains of Italy. Italian fascism in its original form – before the movement became a party and took power in the 1920s – functioned as an evolutionary dogma, agitating for radical changes in the social, political and economic realms of the nation. Fascism played this role because of its radical socialist roots. But what defines Italian fascism? There are various theories but they all seem to agree that at its heart it is a need to right the wrongs of those in power, by revolution if necessary. It is populist because, even if an elite class rules the state, the legitimacy of political power is conferred by the people. But it is not simply a counter-revolution, it is 'a rival revolution: a rival of the communist one that claimed to be the only one entitled to the label.'[1]

The fascist response to communism seeks a 'phoenix-like' renewal in a revolutionary political and cultural order, embracing all 'true' members (believers) of the national community. In defining what it means to him to be a fascist, Giovanni (another of the co-leaders of the *Irriducibili*), stresses the revolutionary element of this ideology, 'For me, a fascist is

---

[1] Quoted from American academic Eugene Weber (1974).

not on the right of the political spectrum; the right is the party of the industry and the rich. Defining yourself as 'right' means not being 'fascist' but being something else. Mussolini was socialist and fascism has social roots. Fascism was never pro-capitalism and anti-communism; it was revolutionary, a Third Way.'

Fascism was born in Italy after the First World War, animated by a strong socialist and radical component supported by the Revolutionary Syndicalists (RS). Revolutionary Syndicalism originated out of the extreme left faction within the Italian Socialist Party. The RS claimed that, in an economically underdeveloped Italy, socialists had to appeal to national sentiment to win over the masses and dramatically improve industrial production. In such an underdeveloped economy, only the nation could pursue the necessary economic progress. This political vision is identified as National Socialism. Two factions co-existed within the movement – the pro-bourgeoisie (conservative) and the revolutionaries (or Socialist-Movimentists). It is the latter faction that has had most influence on modern Italian neo-fascist youth groups like the *UltraS*.

The message of the Movimentist fascists was simple and social in nature: they wanted *socializzazione* to transform the economy into one in which the means of production of industry and services would pass from private to public hands. A new system, called Corporatism[2], would overcome class struggle; workers and employers would be united in corporations that were controlled by the government. The instigator of this political strategy was Nicola Bombacci, a friend of Mussolini and a former communist, who became *Il Duce*'s political advisor during the period of the Italian Social Republic in 1943.

After the Second World War, the fascist elements in the *Movimento Sociale Italiano* (MSI)[3] had within its structure the same division between moderate conservatism and revolutionary Movimentism. The

[2] Corporatism was intended as a 'Third Way' between capitalism and communism based on the principle of class harmony over class conflict. It is a political system in which legislative power is exercised by the *corporazioni* that represent the nation's economic, industrial and professional groups.
[3] Constituted in 1946, the *Movimento Sociale Italiano* (MSI) continued the legacy of fascism after Italy became a constitutional republic. It maintained 10 principles, including Italian territorial unity, the independence of the nation and, contrary to some suppositions, the promotion of a European Union based on equality and justice.

party's youth, regardless of their class, were naturally drawn to the latter. Revolutionary doctrines appeal to the young, the unemployed and the underclasses – those who benefit least from established society. The fascist Movimentists wanted to harness and aggregate their anti-system protest and use it to radically change the State system. They organised *Campi Hobbit* (so-called in honour of the main characters in the mythological world of J.R.R. Tolkien), which articulated neo-fascist sentiment against modernity. The camps were social events where people met to play music and debate about issues such as the media, unemployment, the condition of women and ecological problems.

During the late 1970s and early 1980s, the movement centred around Pino Rauti. As a leader of the group *Ordine Nuovo*, Rauti spoke out on issues including anti-capitalism and Third Worldism, which argued that the underdevelopment of the Third World is a consequence of Western colonialism. Rauti strenuously opposed the more moderate, conservative faction within the MSI, which was inclined to align itself with the ruling Christian Democrats. Today Rauti's ideological inheritance is evident in the policies of Mayor of Rome, Gianni Alemanno, who was the youth leader of MSI's *Fronte della Gioventú* from 1988 to 1991. Alemanno promoted the ideological agenda of the Movimentist wing of the MSI. However, during the 1995 MSI Congress, held under the leadership of Gianfranco Fini[4] in the city of Fiuggi, the party shifted its position on the political landscape, adopting a classical conservative perspective and in so doing rejected its fascist legacy. This decision, while important from a democratic point of view, created a huge controversy within the neo-fascist world, as Giovanni clearly articulated:

Q: Who do you think are the worst enemies and conversely the best friends of the Italian radical right?

G: That is very easy to answer. The worst enemies are people from our background and tradition who became 'moderate' for greed or power – people such as Gianfranco Fini and all his friends in *Alleanza*

---

[4] Gianfranco Fini, President of the Chamber of Deputies and former president of *Alleanza Nazionale*, is one of the leaders of the newly formed *Popolo della Libertà* (PdL) and is a popular Italian political leader.

Nazionale. The worst thing for us is to cease the battle against this system in Italy; we value anyone fighting the system, even if they have different ideology from us. For instance, we did a banner praising Carlo Giuliani who was killed by the police during the Genoa G8 protest because we value warriors even if their politics differ from ours [*see* chapter 13]. People who fight for their ideals often pay a high price.

During the 1995 congress, the MSI's change of political direction saw the party change its name to the *Alleanza Nazionale* (AN). The congress is now known as 'the schism of Fiuggi' since a faction of the MSI did not join AN, but remained faithful to the post-fascist ideology of the old party, forming a new one called *Movimento Sociale Fiamma Tricolore* (MSFT) led by Pino Rauti. Alemanno remained in AN promoting the ideas of the Movimentists albeit in a somewhat more moderate fashion. Alemanno later became the leader of the AN faction *Destra Sociale.*[5] He was perceived by the *Irriducibili* and the *Boys* as the only respectable politician in the party because, unlike Fini, he did not reject his political roots. During the 2006 Rome Mayoral electoral campaign, the *Irriducibili* supported Alemanno and occasionally displayed banners in the Olimpico urging others to vote for him.

The Movimentist brand of fascism is present today in the majority of the Italian neo-fascist youth groups and is certainly recognisable amid the *UltraS*. There are at least three neo-fascist groups that ideologically influence the *UltraS*: *Ordine Nuovo*; *Terza Posizione* (whose legacy is present today in *Forza Nuova)* and *Casa Pound Italia*. These groups all claim, in one way or another, to be followers of the philosopher Julius Evola and the previously mentioned 'socialist' ideas of Nicola Bombacci.

Ordine Nuovo (ON) was one of the major Italian post-war, neo-fascist youth groups. Its roots can be traced back to the magazine *Imperium*. This publication, which began in the late 1940s, aimed to

---

[5] The *Destra Sociale* promotes a social economy providing a range of services to citizens including the most disadvantaged groups. It promotes a strong defence of traditional values and national identity; among its political priorities are found demands for efficient regulation of immigration, the protection of environmental heritage, the promotion of Italian history, art, architecture and food. The *Destra Sociale* is an important political component of the newly formed PdL.

organise former neo-fascist youth. However, *Imperium* published only four editions before being shut down by the Italian government in 1950, charged with endeavouring to reconstitute the Fascist Party, which became a crime under Prime Minister Mario Scelba's law passed in June 1952.[6] Among the members of the *Imperium* editorial board were Pino Rauti; Giano Accame, a journalist and former member of Mussolini's Social Republic who died in 2009; and philosopher Julius Evola (1898-1974). The magazine's editorial line consisted of an idealistic, ethical and ideological intransigence, which made the magazine required reading among the Italian neo-fascist youths.

Between the 1940s and early 1950s, the ideas evident in *Imperium* spread among the younger members of the MSI, who took a revolutionary stance against the perceived decadence and corruption of the Italian political system. They saw traditional fascism as a method of leading the battle to regenerate Italy. The MSI leadership did not appreciate these ideas. They had accepted democratic methods as a means of obtaining power and were seeking to develop a reliable, moderate European, conservative-right political party image. Younger members of the party formed the ON in protest at the collaboration of the more senior members of the party. The ON was against collaboration – even strategic collaborations with democratic political forces. ON youths were considered the 'tough and pure' of the Italian neo-fascist world. ON believed that the MSI leaders had betrayed the original aim of its foundation, namely 'the continuity' with social and political battles fought under the experience of Mussolini's Social Republic. The ON detached itself from the MSI in 1956 at the party's fifth national congress in Milan. According to the ON's doctrine, the two most important values of the neo-fascist militant were 'order' and belief in a spiritual elite. Adherents considered themselves akin to heroes fighting to defend traditional values.

Stated simply, Evola's philosophy condemns modernity and democracy and promotes elements of totalitarianism and racism. Against notions of

[6] Mario Scelba was the Italian Prime Minister from 1954 to 1955; he is remembered in posterity for the promulgation of Law No. 645 which forbade the exaltation and defence of the fascist regime and the Fascist National Party. See http://associazionedic-costituzionalisti.it/materiali/atti_normativi/XIII/pdf/I1952_00645.pdf.

egalitarianism and fiercely anti-communist, Evola sowed the seed of what became known as the Third Position. In doing so, he promoted values that were opposed to those presented by the Italian bourgeoisie, as he sought a revolution to produce a 'traditional society' that, while based on the concept of the state, was radically different to Italian society. Tradition was central to Evola's doctrine (as it is to the *UltraS*). The society promoted by Evola was anti-democratic and based on superiority of birth. He suggested that only individuals born to the higher caste were capable of reaching the most elevated levels of spirituality and therefore power. He indicated that society should be built on the values of ancient civilisations, the population divided hierarchically according to natural qualities evident in the individual. Such differentiation was inherited and not based on economic or material criteria; the noble caste, however, were at the top of the hierarchy. The warrior caste in any society, Evola argued, should also be located at top of the social hierarchy – above even the priest caste. Evola's 'warriors' manifested important traditional virtues: obedience to authority, love of discipline and order, a willingness to sacrifice (both others and self), a capacity for great courage and a sense of honour. The ethos and spirit of the warrior is evident in many *UltraS* statements. Giovanni articulates this idea as follows: 'We will always fight for socially important topics, especially if "some" want to discourage us. We are not doctors, lawyers or sociologists; our destiny is to fight both the football "system" within the Lazio management and fight Italian society for our ideology.'

For neo-fascist warriors, such as Giovanni, the first battle was against oneself; the warrior forever fought his weaknesses. According to Evola, modern man has less capacity than the warrior has to win over his negative ego and could be easily charmed by temptations that pervert the spirit. In the ideology of ON – and generally in all Italian neo-fascist youth groups – there is a constant negative reference to modernity, which, as shown later, is also expressed by the *UltraS*. This expression manifests itself in a criticism of a society in which materialistic values are believed to have dominated spiritual ones – the small trader over the hero.

ON ideology rejected modern institutions as well as both Marxism and capitalism because they were systems based on the triumph of materialism and economics rather than politics and spiritualism. At the same time, ON ideology rejected elements of group identity and concrete political and social ideas, focusing instead on the broader abstract notions of nation and people. ON promoted a heroic, elitist and warrior vision of life based on anti-egalitarianism, anti-democracy and anti-communism. Their target was to recover 'traditional values', such as honour, hierarchy and loyalty; firstly from within the individual and then, once internalised, to be preached using exemplary behaviours defined against the ever-increasing societal moral degeneration. For ON, the master race was the Aryan people, who were represented *par excellence* by soldiers, military heroes and warriors, and exemplified by the Nazi regime's SS and the Japanese Samurai and fighting orders.

Terza Posizione (TP) was founded in 1978 and is widely acknowledged as the natural evolution of a youth group called *Lotta studentesca*.[7] It was intended to destabilise the current constitutional framework of Italy and to seize power by creating a state that rejected both Marxism and capitalism. This operation would ideally have been carried out through a revolution that was gradually implemented and led by an elite avant-garde. Initially the group was strongly influenced by the ideas of Julius Evola. It manifested the co-existence of apparent extreme left within the radical right. In the 1970s, the TP fought side-by-side with Roman squatters in Palmarola (a suburb in the north west of the city) against the left-led local administration that sought to evict them. These types of actions are remarkably similar to what the *UltraS* identify as 'social campaigns'. Marco (of the *Boys*) explains their involvement in such actions: 'One time, we protested against the inefficiency of the management of the electricity supply company (ACEA) for Rome's working-class districts. This problem did not touch the affluent middle class districts, so we displayed banners stressing this problem at a demonstration following the death of a person due to electric cables

---

[7] The group originated in Rome via an alliance of five high school student groups who had become detached from the influence of the MSI. Two years of activity focused on educational issues, but evolved as the members grew up and moved towards more adult political issues. Eventually the three leaders, Roberto Fiore, Gabriele Adinolfi and Giuseppe Dimitri, founded *Terza Posizione*.

being left without maintenance by the ACEA. We support, although are not involved directly with, the Social Mortgage initiative led by the guys of *Casa Pound* (see below) and of the rock group *ZetaZeroAlfa* (*see* chapter 7). Many people have realised that a banner publicising their cause and hosted by us in the stadium is more effective that making a CD. The banner is often shown for 30 seconds on national TV and can have a big impact.'

The political actions of TP were based on two strategies. The first was to target youth to 'educate' them on the idea of revolution and, if necessary, the use of violence to achieve political changes. The second strategy was to create a strong hierarchy-led structure; from this, an elite group would form who would manage power. Propaganda, cultural programmes and violence against political opponents would work hand-in-hand to achieve the ultimate aim of erasing the dominant Italian political system. At the same time, TP declared its solidarity with international 'liberation' movements ranging from the Basque separatists to the Republican movement of Northern Ireland and even the openly 'communist' struggles of the Nicaraguan Sandinistas. Their ideology had four crucial elements: tradition, national independence, anti-imperialism and militancy. The concept of tradition focused on the identity of the 'new' Italians – the *popolo* – who manifested positive and enduring neo-fascist values, and were inclined to militancy, revolution and radical transformation. This explains the inclination of TP to support the inhabitants of poor Roman districts in their socio-political struggles. National independence was anti-imperialist, and sought to detach Italy from any international alliance and thus retain its autonomy in national and international decision making. Their publication, *Terza Posizione*, explained that revolution meant not only seeking radical change in the Italian social system (as a substitute for old political establishment) but also sought to destroy the current 'mentality'; to promote the value of personal sacrifice to achieve a social and political uprising.

The ideas of TP have not been lost over time; 30 years later, they are currently alive in *Forza Nuova* (FN), a party that has its origins in an internal faction of the MSFT. In 1997, the AN (and former ON) leader, Pino Rauti, decided to expel *Forza Nuova* from the MSFT, believing that it was becoming too powerful and the catalyst of internal dissent. The ideology of FN is well known within the Roman (and Italian) *curve* and was regularly mentioned by both the *Irriducibili* and the *Boys* during interviews for this book. They are also known to have the support of a number of well-known AS Roma players, such as Daniele de Rossi and Alberto Aquilani (now at Liverpool). The party is led by Roberto Fiore, a former member of the European parliament. Between 2003 and 2006, FN collaborated in the creation of a political cartel called *Alternativa Sociale* led by Alessandra Mussolini (a niece of Benito Mussolini) and which included the *Fronte Nazionale*, *Azione Sociale* and *Forza Nuova*. The cartel aimed to make alliances with the centre-right coalition of Prime Minister Silvio Berlusconi while stressing their autonomy. Berlusconi, however, rejected their advances because he did not wish to endorse their neo-fascist leanings. Determined to operate in the legitimate theatre of the Italian democracy, *Alternativa Sociale* ran for the European Union elections of 2004, the Regional elections of 2005 and the national elections of 2006. The coalition, however, did not produce the hoped-for results and subsequently crumbled. More recently, however, FN has started a political crusade with more revolutionary overtones and, as a consequence, has obtained an increase in membership and has opened a number of new offices around the country.

If a man isn't willing to take some risk for his opinions, either his opinions are no good or he's no good. (Ezra Pound)

Not all Italian neo-fascist groups have as their primary purpose the pursuit of pan-European unity or even the pursuit of a supra-national policy. Some seek to address local issues. Such activism leads them to assist those whom they perceive as helpless to the injustices of the powerful. The recently formed organisation *Casa Pound Italia* (CPI) demonstrates this tendency.

According to media coverage in the new millennium, FN and the MSFT (with its strong ideological ties to ON) were considered the most popular groups within the Olimpico; but this was not the case. The above quotation represents one of the most explicit slogans of the CPI, one that encapsulates their action-based ideology. While CPI is a rival to FN for the hegemony on Italian youth, they share the same Movimentist foundation; the Third Positionist Gabriele Adinolfi[8] is the most respected intellectual among members of CPI. In one interview, Todde repeatedly mentioned this group, explaining its popularity among neo-fascist Roman youth. It was a link that had not been made before.

Before becoming a national association, CPI was a building in Rome squatted in 2003 by youth of the *Occupazioni Non Conformi* (ONC), whose aim was to reclaim social spaces in the city by occupying houses or other buildings left vacant by local councils. The name 'Pound' was chosen in honour of the American poet Ezra Pound. He argued that by promoting money as the crucial ethos of Western civilisation and charging high interest rates on the money they lend, the banks are guilty of usury. The squatting spread to various Roman neighbourhoods and eventually led to the formation of the CPI with 35-year-old Gianluca Iannone as its leader. The association now organises events and activities of a counter-cultural ethos; it manages libraries throughout Italy, and organises conferences and meetings that are often attended by 'left' leaning intellectuals and writers. The peculiarity of this youth group is the inclusion of many female militants who have the same status, dignity and opportunities as the men. CPI also ran an Irish-type bar called the Cutty Sark in the Colle Oppio district near the historic centre of Rome, which was notorious for neo-fascism in the 1970s and was the location of a fundamentalist faction of the MSI's youth front.

CPI believes in the right to private property, but not as a reason to exploit others. CPI promote campaigns on social issues, such as disability rights, and collect medicines for the impoverished in countries such as Iraq. The housing campaigns claim to have obtained homes for hundreds of formerly homeless Roman families. They support

---

[8] Adinolfi's ideas, which were popular on the terraces at the Olimpico, can be summarised in the following statements: re-affirm the concept of national sovereignty; give the nation a role and a destiny; defuse the globalisation 'bomb' and overcome capitalism; build social economies based on the three concepts of work, solidarity and commitment; reject servility to money; pursue the spirit of justice and cultivate common sense; realise the people's lobby that will fight and oppose political and economic oligarchies; form the 'elite' (leadership) in spiritual, cultural economic and organisational spheres; make a [counter] cultural revolution.

orphanages and solidarity projects for the Afghans and the Karen population.[9] CPI numbers 300 militants and 200,000 sympathisers throughout Italy. The most famous slogan of CPI is to promote the 'fascism of the third millennium', which signifies an attachment to tradition, but at the same time a revision of fascism to address current societal issues and problems.

One of its most popular projects is the *Mutuo Sociale* – a regional organisation that uses public money to build a public infrastructure, but which takes into consideration the quality of life of the individuals. The organisation seeks to sell properties via mortgages – at discount rates – to families who do not own houses. Such sales are to be arranged without interest and in instalments that do not go beyond one-fifth of the family income, payments that would stop if the members of the family become unemployed, thereby excluding profit-making specu-lation from banks. The project is supported by both the *Boys* and the *Irriducibili,* who have advertised it via banners and in their fanzines.

In 2007, the CPI allied itself with the MSFT, but Iannone was not happy with what he considered to be the party's 'hunger for power' and its lack of internal debate as to its make-up. To make matters even worse, in the build-up to the 2007 elections the MSFT leadership suggested co-operation with the centre-right coalition of Silvio Berlusconi. Iannone objected and was expelled from the party, creating a schism in the neo-fascist world and the creation of the CPI as a political group.

> *CONSTRUIREMO IL MONDO CHE VOGLIAMO!*
> *La vita, cosi' come ci 'e stata confezionata, la gettiamo volentieri nel cesso*
> LET'S BUILD THE WORLD THAT WE WANT!
> This life, in the way that it has been shaped, is only worthy of being thrown down the toilet (CPI).

In 2005, AT met the representatives of CPI together with four Roma and Lazio *UltraS* in the *UltraS* favourite bar, the Cutty Sark. For others

---

[9] One of the longest lasting political struggles in the world has seen the Karen ethnic group claim its independence from Burma since 1949.

it is known as 'the most hated bar in Italy'. The Cutty Sark is both a bar and a cultural association. A visitor needs to be invited before he or she can enter. Located near one of the most historic Roman streets, the black armoured door displays the symbol of Captain Harlock, a Japanese cartoon character created by Leiji Matsumoto (a former member of the Japanese Communist Party) in 1978.

This cartoon strip has become a sort of heroic narrative for neo-fascist Roman youth. Harlock's story depicts the 'warrior spirit' proposed by Julius Evola. Harlock lives in the future, in the year 2977, a time of peace due to the welfare state created by technological development. Machines are working while people relax in front of the television in a state of apathy. Matsumoto deemed the growing link between the media and human beings as dangerous and this is reflected in his cartoon. In Harlock's world, television rules individuals' lives and eliminates any positive impulse or motivation to improve the human race. Humans are unable to make decisions and are fed on fake happiness by the media. In such a state of lethargy, humans are incapable of feeling emotion or believing in ideals or values. The hero, Harlock, is the only man who understands the decline of the human race. He escapes from this human degeneration aboard his galactic vessel *Arcadia*. He tries to isolate himself in outer space, taking only the few necessities he needs to survive. Nevertheless, 'Captain Harlock', as he is named by the authorities, is considered a pirate and seen as a danger to society.

This contempt for cultural conformism is a common neo-fascist theme. Captain Harlock represents the ideal type of neo-fascist hero. He is called on to save people from an empty and superficial state of being. The Italian neo-fascist youth perceive today's world to be in a progressive process of moral ruin; civilisation has created a post-industrial society that, while highly technological, erases cultural individuality to produce emotionally sterile humanity. Harlock is a rebel, a 'national revolutionary' combatant who is willing to resist any hegemonic and politically correct societal discourses. For many *UltraS*, cartoon characters are figurative heroes (*see* chapter 8). They are part of the *UltraS* culture and a means for the groups to represent their lifeworld and logic and to set behavioural examples in a setting, such as the *curva*, with which they are familiar.

Once inside the Cutty Sark, there are many artefacts to look at. Its walls are adorned with pirate flags, English and European football scarves, and stickers from global extreme right groups alongside similar stickers produced by Irish nationalists, one of which states, 'England out of Ireland'. For some Italian neo-fascists, England is still considered an enemy by virtue of the Second World War and its dominant Christian creed of Protestantism. Inside the bar there are men and a few women, mostly aged in their 20s and 30s. Some of the former sport military style trousers and T-shirts, with slogans celebrating *Casa Pound* or mottos such as 'The fascism of the third millennium starts with squatting', proclaiming a commitment to the *Casa Pound* housing strategy.

That said, the pub's customers were diverse in their dress code, ranging in style from ska-inspired pork pie hats, to skinheads and people such as Todde, dressed in elegant casual clothing. Almost everyone had tattoos, mainly runes[10] or other designs that come under the genre of 'Celtic'. The visit to the pub coincided with a bout of tension between *Casa Pound* and local extreme left-wing groups that centred on advertising space used to promote their contrasting initiatives. Every evening, *Casa Pound* propaganda leaflets that had been placed in strategic parts of the city were removed by the extreme left groups. It was an 'underground' propaganda war that the city largely ignored, but one that was always more evident during elections. The Cutty Sark had been attacked several times by left-wing militants and was once hit by a bomb in 2001, though it caused only structural damage. People in the pub explained that danger came their way, not only by virtue of them drinking in the pub, but also when outside the venue for their spreading of propaganda, most notably leafleting political statements on the city advertisement boards. Security for the pub and its customers is thus paramount. Members volunteer to undertake security shifts both at the door and along the nearby streets

---

[10] Symbols from the runic alphabet have been used for centuries as tools of divination. They emerged during the time of the Third Reich because the head of the SS, Heinrich Himmler, was interested in occultism and in the esoteric meanings of the runes. The symbol of the SS was formed by the union of two *Siegs*, the rune of victory that has the shape of a thunderbolt.

in order to spot potential trouble. In expectation of the inevitability of having to fight for their cause, nearly every member of the pub staff is a practitioner of boxing or *Muay Thai*.[11]

After an hour of drinking Dublin-brewed Guinness, Todde introduced AT to three men in their early 20s, all members of *Casa Pound*. One, Paolo, was a university student and a SS Lazio *UltraS*. The other two, Carlo and Luigi, were members of the *Boys*. Asked to explain why they engaged in violence, the resounding answer was a determination to test themselves in physical confrontation. They spoke specifically about fights at the most recent Rome derby. When asked how they could put aside often violent rivalries to cease hostilities and drink in the same space, one answered and the rest agreed, 'We are all *camerati*, we believe in the same ideals, that's why!' This unusual answer provoked a question about what they would do if they saw a fight involving friends from the other group. 'We would not get involved. We have loyalty to our group, so we have to fight even if we see friends from the other side of the barricades. So [to avoid this moral dilemma], we prefer not to be present in the situation.'

Asked what he would do if he saw one of his *camerati* from Lazio being beaten up by Roma fans, Todde answered that he would fight side-by-side with the Lazio *camerati*. This was further evidence that being fascist was more important to be either *Laziale* or *Romanista*; for the *UltraS* ideology tends to overcome any football-related rivalries. All four *UltraS* explained this behaviour by arguing for a substantial difference between 'ordinary' fans and them; the love for the team was important, but their ideology and being a comrade (and hence sharing a way of life) was more significant. It is, therefore, possible to understand why many *UltraS* groups, even if football rivals, are united against those whom they perceive as the common political enemy. Asked if there was a specific *UltraS* group that was particularly hated, they replied that such status was accorded to their equivalents in Naples. They recounted an unspecified recent match between Napoli and Roma during which a fan of the former group, supposedly the son of a *Camorra* (Neapolitan

---

[11] *Muay Thai* (Thai Boxing) is a full contact martial art that originated in Thailand. It is often called the 'Art of the Eight Limbs' in recognition of the permitted use, while fighting, of the four limbs plus hands, shins, elbows and knees.

mafia) boss, was stabbed. This event created tension between the two sets of fans and rumours of revenge had been sent from the notorious crime 'family' when Roma next visited Naples. On the day of the return fixture, the *Boys* (and other AS Roma fans) were indeed attacked with Molotov cocktail incendiaries at a motorway service outside Naples. This episode, while extreme and probably unprecedented, indicates the risks that are evident in *UltraS* life.

Gianluca Iannone, leader of the CPI, joined the conversation. An articulate politician, he is highly respected in neo-fascist circles for his ability to explain ideas and strategies. He is also a keen martial artist and a Thai boxing instructor. Explaining that he had a busy few days ahead because *Casa Pound* was hosting comrades from England, Greece, the former Yugoslavia and Spain, he listened to the conversation, but interrupted to condemn *UltraS* football-related violence. Those present listened with great deference; a 'sage' was speaking. The *UltraS* violence was to him unnecessary and of poor judgement; violence was an extreme political tool to be used only when needed, not wasted on a 'fucking football team' and, most of all, not when families were watching the match at the stadium, hence putting them in danger. Everyone agreed that the use of a knife in a fight was the act of a coward. Iannone's strong condemnation of the *UltraS* violent behaviour supported the argument that the *UltraS* could not be manipulated by anyone – including their more respected comrades in the neo-fascist movement. They were non-conformist; in their words *non omologati* (*see* chapter 7).

He also spoke briefly about the dangers of globalisation, which he saw as promoting the problem of illegal immigration and the evil of the capitalist system. The system was destroying Italian society, he said, because it made people slaves to the banks and unable to control their own lives. He saw the banks as hoovering up people's life savings and increasing their debts, instead of helping them to build their lives. For him, the CIP was a spiritual and ethical expression of a community that was needed to supersede superficial individualism.

Iannone left the pub and the conversation about the *UltraS* continued. In response to the question of why so many young people dedicated themselves to an ideology that was so extreme and one therefore that could never succeed in assuming power in contemporary Italy, Paolo replied, 'We know we have chosen an ideology that will make us lose most of the time, but we believe in it and what we want to do via our battles is to live our belief and values and most importantly set an example of how to live.' The others agreed.

This rhetoric, a common neo-fascist theme, is powerful because it offers a solution to a problem that many cultures have not been able to solve: how to live with death, defeat and failure. In the seemingly 'tired' Italian democracy, extremism and immobility have coexisted since its constitution. Nothing ever seems normal. For instance, the alternative state in the south of Italy provided by the Mafia and other criminal fraternities also exists within the north-south divide, which sits in a society that has a seeming absence of ethics in public administration with overarching chronic governmental instability. Nothing of significance is really accomplished in this region; any change is cosmetic.

Since the 2008 schism from the MSFT, CPI has started to cultivate political ambitions. In 2009, the emblem of *Casa Pound* first appeared on a wall in a street in the centre of Rome. Todde explained what he saw as the significance of the symbol of a turtle in its shell. He claimed that it was the emblem of the *patria*, which is based on the concept of a strong and closed community in which individuals find their self-realisation. But in reality the symbol has greater meaning. The CPI website explains its origins. It is based on a well-known occult symbol, which represents Chaos Magic, a form of magic that originated in England in the 1970s. Through a variety of rituals, Chaos Magic practitioners believe that they can change both their subjective experience and objective reality. It is a form of magic that exalts individualism, as shown by the eight outward pointing arrows, the opposite of what CPI preaches, which is unity against hardship. For this reason the eight arrows of CPI symbol have been reversed and converge at the centre, signifying unity. This connection with the occult highlights one of the other fascinating lines of enquiry related to Italian neo-fascism: the link to esotericism and the occult, which found an authoritative exponent in Evola.

Speaking about CPI and more importantly the *Boys*, Todde underlined the value of symbols for those sympathetic to fascism. The *Boys* have, as their most significant symbol, the double-bladed axe, symbolising the affinity of the group's ideas with the Italian tradition of neo-fascism (in this case, *Ordine Nuovo*). Such symbols, as well as those evident on the clothing, in the music and the rituals, provide a sense of commitment among the members that endures, even in the face of social marginalisation. And so an evaluation of the *UltraS* cannot discount the powerful role that culture has in promoting the existence of extreme ideological groups, such as the *Irriducibili* and the *Boys*.

Rival fans fight on the terraces – violence is a significant part of the *UltraS* lifestyle

08

UltraS SOCIETY

The *Irriducibili* and the *Boys* exist through organised gatherings; they are also driven by a series of shared rules, or norms, values, standards, behaviours and collective hierarchies shaped by political ideology. The *UltraS* find self-preservation of the group to be more important – contrary to the 'ordinary' hardcore football fans – than the football club that they support. The group must be defended in all circumstances and in all contexts. This sense of self-preservation was best expressed by the Boxer, who argued, 'We wish to create a strong group based on militancy, which is represented by dedication. We strongly support our social campaigns and rebut the media's false information. We will always fight back against the repression of the police.'

The use of the term 'we' in the above statement illustrates the *UltraS* collective perception of not being treated fairly. When they speak of the 'others', they mean the Italian state, the football institutions, the police and the media that perpetrate their perceived discriminations. In response to this, the *direttivo* of each group functions to reinforce collective identity and, more specifically, the consciousness of belonging to a 'respected' group.

Although it is easy to characterise the two groups as communities of like-minded individuals, they are actually more than that. They are what some social commentators term a *communitas*. The two groupings differ. A community is made up of people committed to and supporting one another. Members of a *communitas*, however, are part of a group that is undergoing 'a never-ending shared ordeal'. Society functions to define the differences between individuals, by limiting their interactions and dividing them, while a *communitas* serves to unify, bond and transcend structural relationships. A *communitas* occurs in situations where individuals are driven together by a common experience of trial; it involves intense feelings of belonging that originate from having to rely on others in order to survive. In a *communitas* such as the *UltraS*, identity is strengthened when individuals emphasise group similarities over individual peculiarities.[1]

In the case of the *UltraS communitas*, shared ordeals constantly serve to test the members. Such ordeals range from the constant worry of being banned from their *curve* by the Italian authorities to the sense of stigma (and discrimination) that they perceive from mainstream society. Of course, this sense of stigma is real. The *UltraS* are labelled by the Italian media as mindless hardcore thugs – a dysfunctional element in both Italian football and society. They are labelled as such, stereotyped and socially excluded. To make matters worse, they are alto devalued in the eyes of various 'others' for their adherence to fascism.

---

[1] For more on the concept of *communitas*, the reader is directed to the work of Victor Turner, 1969, 1974.

Sara, a member of the *Boys*, explains their predicament. 'It is not a secret that the *Boys* were one of the first groups that brought ideology to the stadium. The stadium remains a place where we can be ourselves; so our ideology at least can be manifested albeit with difficulty. If we articulate our ideology in society it is difficult to find a job – who wants to give a job to a 'fascist'?[2]

This type of discrimination is consistent with those of other Italian youth neo-fascist movements who, over the years, have developed a strong rhetoric of marginalisation. But those labelled as 'fascist' do not seem to be put off by the negative treatment they receive. In 2009, when asked if he felt marginalised for his beliefs and if this feeling would lead him to abandon his neo-fascist convictions and live a more socially acceptable way of life, Todde answered, 'Being openly fascist is very hard for me because it might prevent me from finding a job; this is the reason why I asked my father to help me in starting my bed and breakfast business in Rome. I can be independent and continue being myself. However, I do not care what they think about me; I will remain an *UltraS* and a fascist.'

Todde's attitude was shared by other members of the *UltraS direttivo*. They were, at times, discouraged, but also strongly moti-vated to continue being part of the group. The *UltraS communitas* thus constitutes an efficient coping strategy for members in dealing with this stigma. To those sharing an ideology and way of life, the *UltraS* offers both emotional and practical support (in some instances even providing money to pay for the lawyers of those who are arrested for the cause or banned from the stadium). One might then understand why, on numerous Italian football terraces, there are many aspiring 'Captain Harlocks' with their politically incorrect ideas. With this frame of mind, the arrests of the *UltraS* and others are perceived as attacks by the State. But such attacks do not push the *communitas* to a crisis or force their disintegration. By contrast, such attacks reinforce their myths and rhetoric, giving them strength and enhancing their power of social identification and ultimately finding new recruits among like-minded youth.

---

[2] After the constitution of the Italian Republic a strong stigma was attached to anyone who was a member or sympathiser of a neo-fascist group.

However, it seems likely that recruits mainly come from those already marginalised from society in some way. It might be through political persuasion, it might be through culture, but this estrangement from society is crucial in bridging the gap between 'others' and *camerata*. This belonging which the groups provide is essential and strong. Once you belong, you are a *camerata* and must be helped when in difficulty. This philosophy of mutual help is most obvious when the *UltraS* clash with rival supporters, particularly those manifesting a different ideology, and when confronting the riot police or the media. Todde explains this feeling of brotherhood: 'All the members of the group are *camerati*; you are willing to put everything on the line for them, even your life. If a comrade dies or is banned from the stadium or is in prison at Regina Coeli [in Rome], he still remains in our heart, he never disappears from his group, he is always present. The group has a strong identity, of which we are proud.'

Recruitment to the ideology, to the *communitas* and the *curva*, can occur at an early age. For the adolescent, attending a football match is an exciting experience. Aside from the game there is the charisma of the colours, the banners and the chants. There is an immediate sense of belonging. A good example of this is the son of the leader of the *Boys* who often attended the *curva*. When in the *curva sud*, he was taken care of and treated with great love by the *UltraS*. In the same way that a 'normal' family can play a crucial socialisation role, so in the *UltraS* family youths learn not only to love their teams but are socialised and learn, for example, to oppose the 'system'.

For the *UltraS*, recruitment is important. They need people to join to guarantee survival of their group. But they don't only need fighters, they also need people who are skilled at drawing banners, at selling merchandise and others with computer skills. To be a 'true' member of the *Boys* or the *Irriducibili*, though, is not just a case of turning up each week. There are two types of activism – the 'sympathisers' and the 'elite'. To be a 'sympathiser' is relatively easy and entry is for anyone who buys a membership card. People join for different reasons, some for real political reasons, some simply to 'show-off', others because they see being an *UltraS* (and hence a neo-fascist) as the Italian 21st century rebellion of choice. Some join because they are attracted by the traditional aspects of fan culture – instantaneous intimacy, faith, loyalty, courage, and the myths and legends of the hero or the warrior – others because it's fashionable.

The 'elite' (which includes the *direttivo*) are by contrast the 'true' *UltraS*, those who are present at every match – home and away – no matter what. It is here that we find the most extreme shades of *UltraS* ideology. To become a member of the elite, of course, requires a rite of passage. A prospective member of the elite must enjoy the complete trust of the *direttivo* and must believe firmly in the *communitas* ideology and its way of life. Outsiders are distrusted and not tolerated.

Gino, in his 20s, worked on the *Irriducibili* magazine and was allowed to participate in 'elite' activities. He explained that at first it was difficult to bond with the top members. The phase during which an aspirant takes his place at the headquarters of the group and becomes involved in as many activities as possible is complicated. This phase is difficult for the newcomer because every member seems to know each other and the novice feels excluded. On the other hand, if the newcomer shows he or she really wants to belong, shows 'balls', there is a strong chance that that person will be accepted and one day become part of the 'elite'. Showing that one has 'balls' means many things, ranging from not being intimidated by the police and rival fans to always being there when needed by the leaders. What Gino describes is the process of separating yourself from 'normality' and crossing over what might best be termed the 'liminal' phase to the *communitas*. An individual has to really want it, because it might mean separating themselves from friends with whom they normally attend matches.

The next phase in the transition is a kind of trial. The newcomer has to show all the necessary qualities and belief in the group's ideology and in return discovers the depth and meaning of being part of the *communitas*. If the trial or test is passed then the newcomer is integrated into the elite. So it was in Gino's case.

The *communitas* of the *Boys* and the *Irriducibili* allow an individual to construct meanings and be part of a gathering that provides a sense of refuge and of being in the 'right place'. The self is refocused from the individual to the 'elite'. As mentioned earlier, to become a 'true' member, the individual must demonstrate a series of attributes (or at least an absolute willingness to accept them as directed by the leaders) that allow them to be considered trustworthy. Furthermore, when the occasion requires it, the members must use violence against those perceived to be the enemy and thus must be prepared to suffer violence enacted on them in the course of such hostilities. Leaders share a sense of presence; they articulate their ideology by standing up for what they believe is socially 'just' and for the cause of their football teams, but most importantly they are prepared to fight for the *communitas* causes. This strong sense of unity promotes in both the *Irriducibili* and the *Boys* an unusual, autonomous vision of the world and of justice, fairness and respect that drive the members' lives and make them loyal and consistent in their membership in the *communitas*. Giorgio explained this vision of life:

> *Irriducibili* means 'our way of life', our way 'to be' in everyday life not only at the stadium. For example, for two years now we have been involved in a battle against the president of Lazio, Claudio Lotito, which only those who share our 'mentality' could endure. He is tormenting Lazio and its supporters; many have thrown in the towel and do not come to the stadium because of him. For this reason, we are resisting and fight. The system [media, police, politicians] think that *Irriducibili* is synonymous with 'no-brains', and there are indeed some like this in the *UltraS*; but we speak about our mentality, we fight this monster [the system] that has 30 heads and we try every now and then to cut one of the heads off. As far as the values of the *Irriducibili* are concerned, we do not want to be associated with people that go to matches and carry out gratuitous violence. We are the *Irriducibili* of Lazio; we think about the team and its future and we do what we consider just. Friendship and respect are the things that we have gained a reputation for over the years. In the beginning, we were *feccia* [scum] to many and we are still considered so to some, but in life, there is *feccia* that can teach even the *respettabili signori* [respectable gentlemen] how to live.

For 24-year-old Paolo, the *Irriducibili* logic was beyond personal interests and could never be corrupted and compromised. The logic to which Paolo and Giorgio refer involves a set of symbolic and behavioural codes that lead the collective and individual actions of the *Irriducibili* and *Boys* members. The *UltraS* celebrate and are convinced of the validity of their deviance, based as it is on ethical belief; *their* logic supports them in any situation providing 'ethical' justifications to their actions, including violence.

While few wish to join such *communitas*, many are fascinated by it. The *UltraS*, consequently, provoke both consternation and fascination because they are perceived to be different from the norm. The difference is founded in their separation from 'normality' and the *communitas* they display. To many this is a deeply human pursuit.

The *Irriducibili* and the *Boys* have rituals that they carry out regularly in the *curve* on matchdays – these are visible to all in the singing, chanting and choreography of the crowd. These are mannered and stylised such that they contain elements of role, script, audience and stage. Behind the scenes are darker actions, violence, and evidence of fascist ideology that focus on the celebration of masculinity, youth and strength, the regenerative power of violence and notions of mystical unity. But they go further than this. In 2005, the *Irriducibili* 'elite' devised a test to socialise members to the rules of their *communitas*. The test was presented with irony but, behind the humour, were manifestations of the most important norms of the *Irriducibili*, considered the real *Laziali*. The test was also intended to show the public that the *Irriducibili*, while a *communitas* inclined to violence, still lived by a code of conduct.

The test featured different scenarios in which prospective members were asked to choose what they would do in a specific situation. The more points the newcomer accumulated, the less they were considered a 'real *Laziale*' and *Irriducibile*. For instance, 100 points would be awarded to those who said they would insult an elderly lady on a train; 50 points would be awarded to those who perform the Roman salute with a joint in their hands (an *Irriducibile*, or indeed any fascist, is against any kind of drug use); 50 points would be awarded to someone who'd steal a drink from the stadium vendor. Those who gained 0 points would be regarded as a 'real' *Laziale*; those who gained more than 200 would be regarded as a 'fake' and no longer accepted in the group.

There are even rules concerning violence – the *UltraS* trait that most upsets 'others'. Both groups condemn the use of knives as an act of cowardice; Federico of the *Irriducibili* preferred the use of fists but also used belts and batons if necessary. He also affirmed that an attack was 'gutless' if one group clearly outnumbered another. Moreover, Federico considered ambushes as cowardly as they might involve unsuspecting women and children. Todde agreed and explained his concept of violence and the socio-historical tradition in which Roman knife violence exists:

There is a big tradition of knife carrying in Rome, since the times of the Popes and the Rome of the *bulli* [local gangsters], when someone would say 'hey you have looked at me bad' and a fight would start, but it was done with a sense of equality and both parties were armed. Traditionally in football rivalries, the 'rule' was *famo a calci a cazzotti* [let's use punches and kicks]. The knife problem began again in 1995 when Vincenze Spagnolo, a *tifo* of Genoa, without any provocation, was stabbed in the heart and killed by rival Milan fans when he was speaking to his girl-friend in a phone booth! This provoked a reaction in the *UltraS*, who drew up an agreement that has lasted for 10 years.

Then came a group of Roma *UltraS* – BISL [a group that fights using blades] who changed the slogan *basta lama basta infami* [stop blades stop scum] into *basta infami solo lame* [only blades will stop the scum], who wanted the scum – police informers – to be punished with knives if necessary. I don't even know if they are in the *curve* anymore. For them, real *UltraS* only enter a police station when arrested. They argued that a man needed courage to stab a person and face the consequences. I am personally against it because such actions destroy the real values and codes of the street, namely, fight without dirty tricks. We fight with fists and sometimes with batons or chains, tables, bottles, but we remain in limits that are not sadistic. Of course, you hit opponents to cause harm, but it is very different from inflicting stab-wounds.

Here in Rome, there is not one football Sunday where someone is not stabbed, often by youngsters – but not from our group. Now, during a fight involving 10 or 15 people when someone

falls or turns his back, he risks being stabbed. The stab is given
90 per cent of the time in the backside because, if the perpetrator
is arrested, he will not be charged with attempted murder.
Wounding from the waist down sees the lesser charge of bodily
harm. The purpose of such a wound is meant to signify that you
have been hit from behind as you ran like a coward.

Todde's account is informative on many levels. It stresses that a code exists
among the *Boys*, but that this code is not uniformly shared by all the *curva
sud*. This underlines the *curva sud*'s fragmentation in comparison with the
hegemony of the *Irriducibili*'s *curva nord*. It also shows that they are
unwilling to enforce moral codes on other Roma *UltraS* and that the *UltraS*
ideology is not very persuasive in some circles. His assertion that using a
knife was within the rules of old Rome, but that it was done in such a way
as to avoid the possibility of serious criminal charges and to humiliate
rather than kill, are hardly the actions of warriors 'brave and true'.

The concept of *non-omologazione* (non-conformism) is one of the four
core elements of the *UltraS* logic and a crucial part of the strong alienation the *UltraS* felt from wider Italian society. Both the *Irriducibili* and
the *Boys* despise who they consider to be *omologati* (conformists).
Giorgio explains the concept of being *omologati*:

> *Omologati* means 'under control' of the current political system
> – in line with the rules of the game. A simple citizen who works
> in an office is *omologato*; their system of life is imposed by
> dominant power and values and they conform. It does not break
> the balls of the powerful. We are as politically incorrect as our
> symbol – Mr Enrich; we do not answer to any political parties
> regardless of ideologies; we have members who can be supporters
> of political parties but they never speak in that setting for the
> *Irriducibili* – neither will they try to exploit our name. We dislike
> Italian politics; it is a farce! We are not like the so-called *disobbe-
> dienti sociali*[3] – extreme communists that state their rebellion to

---

[3] The term applied to radical left-wing militants who do not recognise the authority
of the State.

society but are comfortably helped by their parties. It is easy to be a *disobbediente sociale*, blocking the train containing our soldiers going to Iraq. Actually we agree with them and would have done it with them, but, unfortunately, if we attempt something similar, the police would have shot us; we would have the DIGOS (the Italian police's anti-terrorist unit) in our homes. We fight the system without political protection; we risk our skins.

Remember, however, that we are an opinion-making force. Last week, we advised supporters not to go the stadium in protest against the Lazio President and 15,000 accepted our suggestion.[4] We scare political power because if, hypothetically, we leave our *UltraS* identity and move into politics, we could do some damage.'

Giorgio's explanation illustrates the wider platform on which the *UltraS* make their stand. They are profoundly anti-system. This system, of course, includes football and the Italian state but also has an international element, one which features the rhetoric of anti-capitalism, anti-Anglo-American politics and anti-globalisation. Perhaps the ultimate personification of this philosophy can be found in the character of Paolo Zappavigna, once leader of the *Boys* and a figure once feared by many in the Italian hardcore football supporters movement, who said, 'Our motto is always oppositional and never conformist, never together the force of disorder,' [a clever play on words that targets the police who, in Italy, are forever identified with the term *forze dell'ordine* (forces of order)].

Zappavigna's loathing for the *omologazione* and for the 'system' is a powerful and appealing message central to Italian neo-fascism inside and outside the stadium. The *UltraS* concept of being always against institutions is illustrated in a statement made by the AS Roma *Opposta Fazione* group (*see* chapter 4) in the early 1990s:

---

[4] Giorgio explained that President Lotito's management was guilty in the eyes of the *Irriducibili* of managing Lazio ineffectively and specifically of not spending enough money to reinforce the team. Such a policy was creating disenchantment among the fans and, as consequence, fewer of them attended the stadium. At the same time, from a more prosaic perspective, one consequence was a decrease in the sales of the *Irriducibili's* merchandise.

... The *Opposta* mentality emerges in opposition to the modern [supporter]; rebellious to the rules imposed by a life and a system lacking ideals. The *opposto* does not have [football] myths, neither does he make the game [of football] his reason for living; instead he exploits the stage of the stadium to show rebel spirit, to shout to the world that he will not compromise. The *UltraS* is *opposto* because 'against' is the way of life for those who lead: slave of nothing and no one; fight the arrogance of those who wear a uniform [the police] and the hypocrisy of certain media.

The *Irriducibili* and the *Boys'* anti-democratic sentiments are ever-evident. But it is not only neo-fascist *UltraS* that believe in this revolutionary ideology. Left-wing supporters express similar sentiments. When Livorno FC were promoted to Serie A (in season 2003–04) after 55 years in lower divisions, the attention of the national media focused on the politicisation of their *curve*; the Livorno *Brigate Autonome Livornesi* (BAL) is the most extreme left-wing group in Italian football. They would praise Stalin and Lenin, and regularly sing the *Bandiera Rossa* (the 'Red Flag'). The BAL are also respected abroad; in 2009 Livorno played a friendly against the Turkish team Adana Demirispor. The match was organised by the supporters of the Turkish team because of their love for Livorno and its BAL, who are considered the only ones in Italy to challenge the capitalistic and bourgeois football system. For their politicisation, the BAL came under the scrutiny of the *DIGOS*, who consider them similar to the *Irriducibili* and the *Boys* as a revolutionary political group.

Being *non-omologati* means more than just being anti-system. The *non-omologazione* principle is reflected in the *UltraS* relationship with political parties that share their ideology. Giovanni explained the link between the revolutionary message of the *UltraS* and the Italian political system:

Q: Are the *Irriducibili* linked to any Italian political parties?

G: If people want to call us politicised, yes we are but, and this is crucial for us, we are politically incorrect. We do not worship any parties even if we have some political roots in common. We never bring symbols of political parties into the *curva*. We do not manifest deference in favour of anyone be they the Pope or the President of the Republic. The media speak about politics only when we use the stadium to send our messages, but they forget or pretend to forget very important national and international football matches where the big names of Italian politics are present to show that they follow football for opportunistic reasons – namely to gain votes.

The media sometimes claims that the *Irriducibili* and the *Boys* are subordinate sections of various neo-fascist parties who do little but spread the word among the youth of the *curve*. But this view is simplistic and shows no understanding. In reality, both groups should be considered as authentic extra-parliamentary groups, who – along with a love of their football team – express a political ideology and, with it, visions of how society should be shaped autonomous from any political parties or pressure groups. They refuse to be subordinate to any political groups, even if they share similar values. Their autonomy from formal politics was stressed by Marco (a member of the *Boys*) when he said, 'although I attend meetings with people from *Forza Nuova* or MSFT, I do not have a membership card… we are completely autonomous.'

Perhaps the most striking example of the autonomy of these groups occurred at the 2006 regional elections in Lazio. The list of *Alleanza Nazionale* candidates included Giulio Gargano, a Christian Democrat, who had little in common with the neo-fascists. However, Gargano received support from both *UltraS* groups because he was willing to lobby for the reform of *diffide* (football stadium banning orders) alongside the left-leaning Green MP, Paolo Cento. Similarly, Cento was championing the rights of the *UltraS* while having little or nothing in common with their political ideology.[5]

---

[5] When politicians and the *UltraS* come up against each other, the latter can use the elected individual in their pursuit of self-preservation; the former will deny that the group will influence them in any way. Career moves from the *curve* to parliament have been tried and achieved by some who have used their ability to create consensus and procure the youth vote. The *curva* of Reggina once had in its midst Giuseppe Scopelliti who was Mayor of Reggio Calabria – one of the biggest cities in the south of Italy – from 2002 to 2007.

The *communitas* of the *Boys* and *Irriducibili* are territorial; no one, not even a group linked to a party that they support, can enter their social space and dictate. Aware that they can move votes and opinions among sections of Roman youth, they do not want to lose this potential by being subsumed by any neo-fascist groups or parties. At the same time, both gatherings have relationships with politicians whom they consider useful in the defence of their interests as *UltraS*. From this perspective, they might be considered a political and pragmatic lobby aimed at ensuring self-preservation.

The stadium provides the *UltraS* with an arena for action that they are normally denied by both public order policing and the banalities of everyday life, with its requirements of the workplace, neighbourhood and the pursuit of individuality. Inside the stadium, in 'their' territory, the neo-fascist *UltraS* are able to push their ideology using slogans, banners and violence. A neo-fascist outside the stadium watches almost inertly what they perceive as the decadence of the Italian society; however, inside the stadium, passivity changes into action. Such men and women believe that their only choice lies in opposing the decadent present to both make them feel alive and superior to the rest of their fellow citizens. For the protagonists of neo-fascism the project of Italian democracy has proved to be a failure. They see the nation state as a failure in permitting both corruption and in being unable to control those things considered alien to Italian life. The football system is similarly decadent, the 'beautiful game' aesthetic is tarnished by the hideous realities of individual venality and corporate finance. In this setting, fascist ideology plays a crucial role in facilitating interaction with others and, consequently, serves to help the individual pass from theory to action; the unthinkable becomes thinkable. Ideology provides a consistent structured system of symbols, values and beliefs by which the groups interpret society and football. The *UltraS* logic operates as a selection tool and helps the 'elite' discern who is part of their world and who is not.

The *Irriducibili* display banners, including an image of their mascot, Mr Enrich

09

'TRUE' *UltraS* AND THE MODERN WORLD

I am proud to be a Boys – a 'true' UltraS group that is part of the history of the curva sud.

This quote from Todde illustrates the importance of authenticity to members of the Roman *UltraS*. The crucial aim for members of both the *Irriducibili* and the *Boys* is to become accepted and considered 'true' *UltraS*. What they want is a sense that their lives, both public and private, reflect their real selves. This attitude is a strong affirmation of the *UltraS communitas* and strengthens the 'us' versus the 'others' dynamic of their ideology. Those who do not express this logic are not 'true' *UltraS* and do not deserve to be respected.

One example of this 'us and them' philosophy is the *UltraS* attitude to recreational drug use. Giovanni (of the *Irriducibili*) says, 'if I see anyone smoking pot or taking drugs in the *curva* or near me, outside the stadium, I will slap him.' The *UltraS* feel that drugs are one example of the shallowness of contemporary youth whom they consider are products of a mediocre and valueless society. This is not a view shared by others on the terraces or in wider Italian society where drugs are an integral part of youth culture. 'True' *UltraS* are anti-drugs – an aversion to any type of drug use is one of the norms, or rules, of the *communitas*.

This need for authenticity is also expressed by the *UltraS* in their support for social causes. Giorgio explains, 'One of our beliefs is against paedophiles; one of our banners at the stadium advertised the *Telefono Azzurro*[1] because we consider the stadium and our *curva* an extraordinary *palcoscenico* [stage] on which we fight social battles. With our battle against paedophiles, we had also the support of the *tifosi* who, while distant from our ideology, are willing to collaborate with us on the issue. Not even an organised demonstration at Piazza Venezia [the piazza famous for Mussolini's fascist celebrations] compares to the power of expressing our ideas in the *curva nord*; *la curva* is our piazza; our powerful piazza!'

Giorgio's statement not only shows the will of the *UltraS* to campaign for issues that they consider 'just', it also demonstrates the radical nature of the 'true' *UltraS*. The *Boys* and *Irriducibili* are extreme in everything they do. Opposition to the imposed social standards and expectations enables the *UltraS* to forcefully follow their path in life, which is guided by their ideology. They speak the unspeakable and, in

---

[1] *Il Telefono Azzurro* is a non-profit-making association founded in 1987 which aims to protect children from abuse; it operates a free telephone line to report any crimes against children.

so doing, further isolate themselves from mainstream society.

But the concept of the 'true' *UltraS* is not only constructed around ideology, it is also based on cultural practices. The *UltraS* use culture to shape a sense of 'similarity' among themselves and, just as important, a sense of 'difference' from others. An understanding of their culture helps in understanding how the groups survive and recruit new members.

UltraS culture is visible in four areas: symbols, heroes, rituals and values. Among the *UltraS*, all four elements combine to create a sense of ideology. Symbols are the most readily available manifestation of the *UltraS* culture. They advance – and advertise – ideas and make those ideas appear to be tangible. These symbols, often connected with the idea of tradition, can comprise words, gestures and objects that have particular significance, recognisable only to those who share their specific culture and logic. For the *Boys* and the *Irriducibili*, recurrent symbols are short sentences that are used to end a dialogue, such as *In alto I cuori* (keep high our hearts) or gestures such as *Saluti Romani* (Roman salutes). Other regularly used symbols include the Celtic cross, the eagle (for the *Irriducibili*) and the sword. Symbols are also found in their taste in clothes and music.

The importance of symbols and, most importantly, their connection to the 'glorious' Roman past is explained by Marco (of the *Boys*):

Symbols are very important! Not just how they are used, but most of all in what they represent. Sometimes we see *le rune* [the runes] in neo-fascist groups; however, they do not belong just to our tradition or culture, but more to a northern European one. We use the *fascio littorio*, which was a symbol of authority during the Roman Empire. Mussolini used it to signify both a will to regain the territories that once belonged to the Roman Empire and the pursuit of national unity overcoming the North-South tensions that are always evident in Italy. The Celtic cross, linked to the Roman Emperor Constantius is part of our heritage, but, in Italy, it is forbidden by law to display because it is considered neo-fascist! [He then revealed tattoos depicting the Celtic cross]. The sun is the most important theme for us; if you listen to the old song of the youth movement of the MSI ('Tomorrow Belongs

121

to Us'), the sun is always present; we use it because strangely enough it is not infamous as an extreme right anthem.

For the *UltraS*, symbols constitute repertoires of action that signpost the importance of past events – whether real or imagined – thereby providing popularly accessible 'points of entry' for individuals to locate and contextualise their own personal experiences within the broader collective. Antonio (of the *Boys)* elaborates on this theme, 'The Celtic cross, one of our symbols, is forbidden in the stadium, so we substitute this with the arrow, another type of *runa* that symbolises a certain political [but also religious] identity.'

The Celtic cross is one of the most widely used symbols among members of the *Irriducibili* and the *Boys*. When asked why, both groups based their explanations on the link of the symbol to traditional Roman Catholicism and to the history of the Celts. The link between this symbol and the politics of the extreme right originated in the organisation *Jeune Europe* (1960). *Jeune Europe* was founded by Jean Thiriart (1922–92) and manifested anti-American and anti-Semitic sentiments. The Belgian politician tried to create a European Revolutionary Party – an anti-imperialist party based in the ideology of the extreme right. The *Jeune Europe* exported the Celtic cross to Italy, where it was adopted by the *Fronte della Gioventú* under the influence of Pino Rauti in the 1970s. In Italy, the Celtic cross was banned by Law No. 205 (approved in June 1993) because it was associated with neo-fascists and those who supported racial, national, ethnic and religious discrimination.

The relationships between symbols, meanings and tradition for the *UltraS* are not casual. Symbols (connected to the past), legendary tales and myths not only serve to unite them but also to provide inspiration for their actions. The motto of the *Irriducibili* – 'Dare, Believe, Be Reckless' – is symbolised by the Imperial Eagle. The eagle symbol possesses dual meaning. First, it represents SS Lazio, although the Lazio Eagle is quite different in shape from the *Irriducibili* Eagle; secondly, it is very similar to the fascist Imperial Eagle. The Imperial Eagle represents many aspects of tradition for the Italian neo-fascists. Julius Evola explained that the eagle has both Olympic and heroic meanings. It was sacred to Zeus, a divinity who was represented in the Aryan-Roman tradition by Jupiter. Zeus/Jupiter was the god of light and power. For the Ancient Romans, the appearance of an eagle was a good omen, a divine sign of impending victory against the barbarians.

Symbols serve as a sword to the *UltraS* that may be used in 'battles', primarily against the modern world, which neglects traditions. Confined by ideas of modernity, rationality and technology and a world in which cultural practices are increasingly commodified, the absence of a sense of 'soul' results in disenchantment. 'Traditional values', in the *UltraS'* eyes, celebrate a sense of pride in the Roman, fascist and national historical roots. Such values are, together with myth, articulated to oppose the dominant and 'politically correct' societal values. They are consciously used by the *UltraS* to reinforce members' motivation to shape their logic, knowledge and behaviour.

For their heroes, the *UltraS* choose both real and imaginary people, individuals and groups. Benito Mussolini is high on the list, as are their deceased comrades of the *Fronte della Gioventú*, who were killed by the hated communists during the political turmoil in Italy in the late 1970s and early 1980s. There are heroes among their own groups too, leaders such as Paolo Zappavigna and the Boxer, and the *diffidati* (*UltraS* who are banned from the Olimpico by order), who are held up as examples of 'true' *UltraS*. They also have imaginary heroes, such as Mr Enrich for the *Irriducibili* and Lupin III[2] for the *Boys*. These are figurative heroes and are sometimes used by the *UltraS* to socialise the youth of the *curve* to their lifeworld. A sort of Robin Hood figure, Lupin III represents an anti-system hero, a 'gentleman thief' who steals from the rich, not only for himself, but also to help the needy.

The *UltraS* also use rituals to distinguish themselves from the 'non believers'. One such ritual is using the 'gladiator salute' by way of a greeting. This practice, widely shared among the Italian neo-fascist community, is also considered as a 'hidden' way to profess their ideological identity.

One of the most important rituals practised by both groups is in the preparation of banners and choreographies for matchday. Every 'elite' member of each group has a role in such activities; other trusted

---

[2] Lupin III is a character from Japanese manga comics, created by French writer Maurice Leblanc.

members too are called on to help. The leaders generally choose the slogans for the banners, leaving others to construct and paint them. If the banners are to feature important ideological statements then only a member of the 'elite', such as Giovanni for the *Irriducibili* or Todde or Lele for the *Boys*, will actually paint the words onto the cloth. Perhaps the leader most famous for his slogans was Paolo Zappavigna (former leader of the *Boys*), who always favoured an ironic tone. The organisation for such activities is surprising. For regular matches, banners are normally prepared at the groups' headquarters, but for big games, such as the Roman derby, warehouses outside the city are rented to provide enough space for the work to be done. The parading of banners and displays of graffiti are hugely significant for the 'true' *UltraS*; such words and slogans not only promote the values and logic of the *communitas*, but also serve to warn 'outsiders' of their territory and the danger faced if they trespassed beyond the boundaries.

While symbols, heroes and shared rituals may be the most visible parts of a culture, values are fundamental. For the *UltraS*, values are broad tenets that raise certain types of behaviours over others. The spirit of the 'warrior' encapsulates all of the values that the 'true' *UltraS* should follow – honour, faith, the sense of duty and fairness – which should be expressed in both 'battles' and daily interactions (*see* chapter 9).

One way of expressing their values to others is via the concept of 'style'. Marco (of the *Boys*) explains, 'We wear elegant casual clothing in contrast to many of the *curva sud* supporters. We dress casual. We take care of the aesthetic, we want to show off our ideals and hence we want to present ourselves in a decent way – with "style". This way of dressing and thinking has to be a daily choice, not one reserved only for the stadium.'

UltraS 'style' is a collective presence that is associated with symbolism, image and identity. It exists beyond notions of social class. 'Style' is manifest most obviously in their clothes, posture and gait. In the above statement, Marco connects their clothing with a way of being and, most importantly, with the function of promoting the group. Such a casual 'style' is very popular among both the *UltraS* and the Italian neo-fascist youth. Instead of the black bomber jacket or the Doc

Martens boots of the stereotypical European extreme right groups, the *UltraS* wear expensive jackets, such as those made by the English company, Stone Island, or Aquascutum labels or the Italian CP Company. The *UltraS* not only adopt and appropriate a 'style'; they also create their own. One of the *Boys'* more popular items of merchandise is the Diabolik sweatshirt taken from the eponymous Italian cartoon character.[3] As well as expressing an ideological belief, these shirts are worn by 'true' *UltraS* involved in actions on the terraces to avoid identification by the police CCTV cameras; thus linking 'style' with something more practical.

The *UltraS* also use their style to give the impression of toughness, exalting the power of their *communitas*. Crucial to the groups are notions of the body, in what they wear, the symbols and brands that they sport, but also in other items of consumption, notably in music.

Music helps to mark the *UltraS* distinction from the 'ordinary'. Of course members' tastes vary. For example, Giovanni's favourite band is *270 bis*. For him, the songs of their leader Massimo Morsello[4], are enjoyable for the beauty of the lyrics and for the messages they contain. This music was also popular among the *Boys;* it was often played in their *sede*. Another band popular among the *UltraS* is ZetaZeroAlfa (ZZA). In 2005, during a visit to meet the *Boys* in their headquarters, the stereo was playing their music, and the CD cover was placed beside a statue of Benito Mussolini and shelves displaying their merchandise. A 'hard punk' band, they share the *UltraS* disgust of the *omologazione* of Italian youth, blaming it on the nation's political and cultural 'system'. They began playing live in Rome in 1997 and perform regularly

---

[3] The cartoon character, Diabolik, was created by Angela and Luciana Giussani in 1962 and appears in a publication titled *Casa Editrice Astorima*. He is a ruthless robber who, accompanied by the beautiful Eva Kant, uses sophisticated technologies to steal money and jewels from rich families, banks and from people who have obtained money via illegal means.

[4] Massimo Morsello, a talented songwriter, popular in radical right political circles, was also co-founder – with Roberto Fiore – of *Forza Nuova*. He described himself at various times as a fascist, a Catholic, a fugitive and a politically incorrect songwriter. Certainly Morsello had many strands to his bow; he was also a member of the *Nuclei Armati Rivoluzionari* (NAR – Revolutionary Armed Nucleus) a terrorist group that operated in Italy between 1978 and 1981. He died of a tumour in 2001 (Cf. http://massimomorsello.it).

throughout Italy and abroad. Their most detailed tour, called 'European Revolution' included concerts in Eindhoven, Marseille, Stuttgart, Paris and Madrid. The band encourages their followers to engage in political and cultural matters and to use their sense of style to disseminate oppositional messages. Much of their merchandise, especially the T-shirts, are popular among the neo-fascist movement, including the *UltraS,* and the messages contained in these garments promote their philosophy of action; one of the most popular mottoes is 'Beauty is in Acting!' Their lead singer is Gianluca Iannone, also leader of *Casa Pound Italia.*

The ZZA CD *Dictatorship of the Smile* contains the songs '*Il Grande Fratello*' (Big Brother) and '*Indipendenza*' (Independence), which focus on the negative role played by the media in society. According to the lyrics, television rules individuals' lives, eliminating any positive impulse or motivation to improve the human race. The pessimistic message states that humans are unable to make decisions when fed fake happiness by the media. In living in such a state of lethargy created by this artificial welfare, people are unable to feel emotions and to believe in ideals and values. The suggested tool of resistance to this society is culture. Such an idea is not new; Italian communist Antonio Gramsci similarly argued for the power of culture in his theory of hegemony (complete political or cultural dominance). The novelty of these songs is in the use of hegemony by a neo-fascist group, a concept that had long been thought of as the preserve of the extreme left.

A key area of expression of *UltraS* values can be found in the fanzines the two groups produce. The *Boys* title *l'Onore di Roma* (the Honour of Rome) and that of the *Irriducibili, La Voce della Nord* (the Voice of the North) are important. They feature articles and opinion pieces through which their sympathisers can understand their vision of life, but they also help to interest others, curious to find out what they stand for. These are key tools for the recruitment of new members.

A famous cartoon that appeared in *La Voce della Nord* encapsulates the 'true' *UltraS* philosophy of never conceding defeat against the Italian State. The cartoon features a young man in a Stone Island T-shirt, with a Lazio armband. He's sitting down in a police cell in handcuffs. The casual style of clothing is emphasised. The title of the cartoon is 'Never

Defeated'. The accompanying text explains, 'It is not true that a lion in a cage does not change! He has only two paths, either he breaks the cage and resists till he dies or he becomes old, lives and dies in ways the others have decided for him!!!' This description, like so many others in the groups' fanzines, also serves another essential function: it emphasises the epic vision of the life of the *Irriducibili*. It aims to establish the norms that the 'true' *UltraS* should follow by creating images that highlight the *communitas* struggles and, at the same time, express a sense of pride at the magnificence of their resistance.

Distant heroes are also celebrated in the fanzines. One such character is the Last Samurai. In the eyes of the *Irriducibili*, the Samurai present admirable self-confidence in making life's decisions and in their rejection of superficial values in the *Bushido* (the Samurai way of life). For the Samurai the path that leads to honour is the most important one to travel. In another article, the writer explains, 'if something is missing from the Samurai, it is fear.' The implication is that fear – not the police – is the number one enemy of the 'true' *UltraS*.

The same concept can be found on the cover of one edition of the *Boys'* fanzine, which features a muscular hero astride his horse, swinging an axe as he fights against a many-headed snake, the universal symbol of evil. The lack of fear, shown in the hero's ability to commit himself to fighting for the common good, underscores the will of those gathered in the *UltraS* name not to bow before authority in their fight for survival. The serpent can represent many things: the State, the police or Italian society. Another edition features a cover that uses the symbols of the Roman Empire to criticise the AS Roma players who are considered to be mercenaries, interested only in money and not in making the Roma club great and worthy of representing the greatness of their Roman ancestors.

Both fanzines have similar internal layouts; both contain information and comments on the teams' results and other club matters. In addition, they feature anti-Italian State 'editorials' as well as articles on issues outside football. The *Irriducibili* call these editorials *Non Solo UltraS* (Not Just *UltraS*), and use them to demonstrate their commitment to their current 'social campaigns'. These range from international politics (the Iraq war, the Middle East conflict) to domestic problems, such as housing shortages, illegal immigration and political malpractice.

Regardless of stylistic and symbolic differences between the two groups, the fanzines both promote the *UltraS* commitment to the sense of *communitas*. Both present the social and the logical world of the *UltraS* – a world which is based on a sense of hostility toward those who do not share their logic, and manifest a contest between a celebration of the past and the condemnation of a decadent present.

Being part of the *Boys* or *Irriducibili* clearly goes beyond football. The *curva* stands as the locale where being part of the *communitas* is appreciated without social class, and where the myth of Rome as the glorious capital of the Roman Empire is celebrated. As Marco details, 'I do not believe in Roma as a football team, it would be limiting and superficial; I believe in what it represents. AS Roma represents the capital city with its glorious traditions. It is sufficient to walk around Rome to breathe this ideal – not Rome today with Veltroni [a former centre-left mayor] with the smog and the traffic – walk along the *Fori Imperiali* and feel the power of ancient times. We need to be proud of living in this city.'

The *UltraS* see the Rome of the Empire and the Italy of the fascist era as ideal models of society, another preference that links them to other neo-fascist groups. Images and ideas from these societies are often based on legendary tales about 'origins' and 'roots' and around them an oral tradition has been founded through which ancient lore and legends are passed on.

Of course, the most important person in Italian fascist history is Benito Mussolini. Giovanni explains this in simple terms, '... in the first 13–14 years of his regime, he built a national identity and gave pride to the country, especially at the international level, for the only time in Italian history. The professional politicians of today are petty bureaucrats who think only about a good salary. Who is the most negative politician at world level? That is easy! The President of the USA; the *Irriducibili* believe that if many nations today have to live with the fear of terrorism, this is due to America.'

The traditional and symbolic universe of the *UltraS* revolves – as illustrated in Giovanni's statement and in others collected from both groups – around the myth of Benito Mussolini. The glorification of the figure of *Il Duce* is a dominant aspect of the culture of both the *Irriducibili* and the *Boys*, in which he is regarded as the greatest man in Italian history. Mussolini is seen as the only Italian politician who has ever been able to represent the interests of his people and, most importantly, to restore to the country the prestige of its glorious past. His status as the nation's hero is continually fostered by the *UltraS* 'elite' through narratives and symbols. They promote fascist ideals as vastly preferable to the politics of contemporary Italy where political principles are used to bolster individual egos and not for the benefit of the people. This is a populist principle but fits their elitist nature. After all, the *UltraS* originated on the *curve* where they are part of a crowd united in support of their football team.

It is essential for the 'true' *UltraS* to know about and honour the glorious history of the Roman Empire and the fascist era but it is also essential for them to understand and celebrate the history of their own *communitas*, not only their actions against the 'system' and the State but also against *le zecche* (ticks – communists in neo-fascist slang) of Livorno FC. Through this knowledge they can learn about the roots and traditions of their neo-fascist ideology.

Behind the rhetoric of the *UltraS*, of course, there is the common theme of cultural memory. Memory is a phenomenon related to the present; our perception of the past is influenced by the present. Memory is also forever changing. The past is reinterpreted or reinvented to give new meaning to the present. For those who embrace fascism (and its modern ideological manifestations), the myth of the 'golden age', a glorious past, is constantly compared to an uncertain and worrying present. The myth expressed by fascism, and adapted by the *UltraS* to their everyday experience inside and outside the football stadium, is transformed into accomplishment. Myth is a projection that is different from a utopian vision. It is a logical representation that could be rationally examined. It is not important that the myth is realisable; its purpose is to be the engine of human action in its appeal to those seeking radical change and to stress the moral legitimacy of the *communitas* of the neo-fascist collective.

The concept of tradition also has a decisive influence on how the *UltraS* conceive 'modern' football. The *Boys* have a slogan that states they are 'against a football system that, in the name of modernity, promotes impunity from its own mistakes and has debts of millions of Euros.' To its critics, 'modern' football manifests a total lack of values and is synonymous with corrupt politics, mismanagement and hyper-commercialisation, which treats fans as consumers and not as one of the most important elements of *calcio* – the spectacle. The *Boys direttivo* explains it in this way in a document in their collection:

> In this *calcio* bought by money – where Buffon [the Juventus and national team goalkeeper] is worth more than all the Chievo football team – there is no longer any space for values. The *tifoso* has been replaced by the spectator, the manager-fan by professionals; the football fan-players have disappeared, replaced by mercenaries ready to change their teams every year. The *UltraS* mentality is to fight this to ensure that football passion can defeat money; to give the stadium back to their legitimate owners [the supporters]. To fight such repression is not violence; it is the will to conquer what has been sacrificed in the name of business. *UltraS* follow the team anywhere. The television is for spectators [not *UltraS*]; the *UltraS* refuse compromises with anyone. *UltraS* honour the team shirt regardless of who wears it. *UltraS* fight *il calcio moderno*.

The lamented changes of Italian football mostly occurred during the 1980s and 1990s, most notably with the auctioning of the game's broadcasting rights and the rise of pay TV.

Practical changes were made to make the game more dramatic, such as the introduction of three points for a win and a change in the offside rule to encourage more goals. There were changes too in match scheduling – to suit satellite TV programming. Suddenly the supporter became a consumer, who was exploited for maximum financial profit. While Italian football has always been in pursuit of the lira, club presidents and owners also had a sense of personal prestige in their desire for success. However, new commercial influences in the past 20 years have changed things. Vast amounts of money are now paid for global broadcasting rights, and similar sums are laid out to persuade the world's greatest players to play for clubs like AS Roma and SS Lazio. In this capitalist (and potentially highly profitable) football milieu, many thousands of paying supporters have lost their sense of importance. Their financial investment in buying tickets cannot compare with that of the paying TV viewer. The long-time supporters are marginalised, alienated from their clubs despite remaining loyal. The Boxer argues that the *UltraS* are the only opposition against such profit-making logic. According to him, in this 'new worst' *calcio*, football traditions, and the values that have sustained the game for more than 70 years, do not count anymore. Similarly, Giorgio condemns both modern football and modern politics. To him, the two issues are congruent:

> The football system and the political one are the same – both are corrupt; look at where we watch football. In the Olympic Stadium, the fire brigade can only enter to a certain point because of the wrong design for the 1990 Italian World Cup. It is a stadium that is the safest in Italy [stated ironically], so safe that, every Sunday, they need to ask the provincial authority [the Prefect] for permission to use it. They use us as a smoke screen to distract the media instead of focusing on problems that are more serious. They accuse us of being the cause of families moving away from the stadium but, in reality, it is because of the ridiculous cost of the tickets. The day before yesterday, at Treviso [in Serie B], because they were playing Milan, tickets were selling at 130 Euros! We are considered trouble, but that is only because we annoy the 'palace of power'.

In April 2003 the *UltraS* organised a public demonstration against the state of contemporary Italian football. They wanted to unify Italian hardcore football fans of different loyalties to let the authorities know what they felt about escalating prices and the effects of TV as well as police repression and the criminalisation of hardcore supporters. The *Boys* and the *Irriducibili* were the main organisers, but other groups such as the *UltraS Romana*, the *Boys San* from Internazionale, the *Fighters* from Juventus and *UltraS* of Verona, Brescia and Milan also attended. However, the ever-present political divisions within the hardcore movement meant that left-wing fan groups from Livorno, Ternana, Perugia and Cosenza decided not to attend. The demonstration saw 6,000 *UltraS* shout slogans such as, '*UltraS*-free', 'We hate pay TV and Sky', 'No to police repression' and 'No to your *calcio*'.

The *Irriducibili* set out their case in a series of slogans: *Per una legge più equa e contro la criminalizzazione indiscriminata degli UltraS* (In favour of a fairer law and against the indiscriminate criminalisation of the *UltraS*) and *Per un calcio più a misura di tifoso e contro il calcio moderno* (In favour of a football more focused on the supporter and against modern football).

In March 2005, following the departure in July 2004 of the food tycoon Sergio Cragnotti, SS Lazio was hit by the Italian tax authorities with a bill for unpaid taxes of E107 million (£90 million). The club was faced with bankruptcy. New president Claudio Lotito (according to the *Irriducibili*, linked politically to FI and AN) opened negotiations with the government. However, the *Irriducibili* took their own action and organised a sit-in outside the Italian Ministry of the Economy in Rome. Violence erupted and 10 Lazio supporters and four police officers were injured. Fortunately for SS Lazio, and thanks to public activism, after 10 months of negotiations with the leaders of the *UltraS* group, the club reached an agreement with the government and agreed to pay E140 million (£120 million) over a period of 23 years.

Today football produces more wealth for its employees (the players) than its employers. This has pushed the game into crisis. The trouble began in the mid-1990s when clubs began to realise that they did not generate enough income. For decades their projected budgets had included future profits based on the presumed income from the transfer of players at the end of their contracts. But December 1995 saw the revolutionary Bosman ruling, which gave footballers in the EU greater freedom (and power). At the end of their contracts, players could ask their clubs for money to stay. In order to avoid losing the players, clubs were forced to renew the contract, paying huge amounts of money in some cases. A few months later a new Italian law was passed, Law No. 586, which confirmed the transformation of Italian professional football into a business-orientated system. The new law allowed for the distribution of profits among football clubs' shareholders. Shareholders wanted dividends and so the clubs went in search of more money. The sport of football became part of Italian business, which was owned and controlled by those in search of profits.

Italian clubs risked financial disaster.

To minimise the effects of the Bosman ruling on the financial status of Italian football, Prime Minister Romano Prodi's centre-left government (from 1996 to 1998) introduced an amendment to Law No. 586. This allowed football clubs to itemise in their budgets the credit (i.e. losses) accrued by the players and, crucially, allowed the clubs to pay off the losses over a three-year period. It was an ad hoc law aimed solely at helping to resolve the debts of the elite clubs. However, this law did not stop the crisis. In July 2002, eight clubs failed the financial scrutiny of the COVISOC – the committee tasked with controlling the financial propriety of Italian football clubs and to guarantee the regular procedures of the Italian Football Championships. Among these were SS Lazio and AS Roma. Faced with this economic crisis, the Italian football authorities, in the shape of *Lega Calcio*, who controlled *Serie A* and *B*, asked the then Italian Prime Minister Silvio Berlusconi for assistance. His centre-right government responded in February 2003. Parliament modified Law No. 91, thereby allowing *Serie A* and *B* clubs to devalue 50 per cent of their assets, as represented by the players, and to pay the debts accrued in the purchase of players in 10 yearly instalments.

This has not really helped and the situation is likely to worsen because of today's worldwide economic crisis. Many Italian football club presidents need to cover the yearly debts of the club with their own money, for example, the oil tycoon Massimo Moratti – president of Internazionale. Even the 'wealthy' AC Milan has debts of E30 million, while Juventus' debts are E20 million. The Italian Football Union has forecast a 20 per cent cut in players' salaries and complains about this 'injustice'. On the other side of the 'barricade', the president of Fiorentina and fashion tycoon, Diego Della Valle, argues, 'I and my brother feel uneasy paying all that money to players, knowing that there are people who come to the stadium earning a thousand Euros a month, struggling to make ends meet'.

For the *UltraS* the events in football during the last 20 years have been hateful. Marco explains how the two sides have moved apart:

The *UltraS* logic no longer acclaims the football player. They are not like a Giannini or Conti[5] of long ago; they do not care about the supporters anymore, so we do not support them as individuals. Before, when a player was injured, he was frequently with us watching the match from the terrace: not anymore. They do not give emotional contact to us, so they do not merit anything in return. They are mercenaries out for the money; we leave this silliness to the normal *ultrá* supporters who think Totti is the King of Rome [laughs]. Our banners are more about Roma the club and its traditions or about the social issues that affect Rome and Italy.

In essence, the *UltraS* were (and are) prepared to fight symbolically against what they dismissively refer to as *calcio moderno* (modern football), and its highly commercialised – but ultimately disastrous – economic performance and occasionally scandalous mismanagement. If they don't do it, they argue, then who will? For them, the mass of fellow supporters are too compromised to care or to protest, and for the *UltraS*, to oppose, to promote and to resist is a duty. However, although they are dismissive of the game's materialistic pursuits of efficiency, profit and productivity, the *UltraS* still search for and appreciate the abstract qualities of the game, and especially those players who embody the 'warrior spirit'.

---

[5] Giuseppe Giannini (nicknamed 'The Prince' on account of his good looks) is a former captain of AS Roma. He gave the best years of his career to AS Roma, playing for the club he loved from 1983 to 1996, though he finished his career in Austria at Sturm Graz. Bruno Conti is another example of a player attached to the AS Roma colours, playing from 1973 until 1991 and winning a Serie A *scudetto* in 1982–83 and the World Cup with the *Azzurri* in Spain in 1982.

A fan sets off a flare – such incediaries are ostensibly banned from the Italian football stadiums

10

THE 'WARRIOR SPIRIT'

Nessuna notte è così lunga da impedire al sole di risorgere.
(No night is ever so long as to stop the sun rising)

Slogan of the Boys Roma

For the *UltraS*, honour provides a code for both interpretation and action on two levels. One is as a 'system of symbols, values, and definitions' to think about and interpret as a phenomenon. On a second level, honour embodies the *UltraS* acts, which are organised into 'categories, rules, and processes ... that may be specific to the given culture.'[1] Being an *UltraS* warrior does not only mean being able to fight, it also requires that the individual pays the price for their convictions, and this, in the *Boys* and *Irriducibili's* case, is inseparable from their fight against the 'system'. For instance, among the *Boys*, everyone who was *diffidato* (banned from the football stadium) displayed a gold double-blade axe pendant given by the *direttivo* and symbolising, not only political identity, but also the respect of the 'elite' for the way the member behaved in challenging the authorities. The member received the pendant as recognition of his or her warrior status.

The 'warrior spirit' directs not only the *UltraS* actions and the value of honour but also encapsulates faith. Values need to be fulfilled to become part of the moral duty of an *UltraS*. For the *Boys*, faith has nothing to do with the AS Roma team (contrary to 'ordinary' fans) because it has ideological connotations. Faith means stressing the glorious traditions of Rome and the Empire. Faith for Giorgio (of the *Irriducibili*) has the same purpose; it means being consistent in what you believe and not renouncing your chosen way of life, even if it comes to violence. Both football support at its most extreme and neo-fascist ideology share a similar sense of piety and excessiveness; they contain belief systems that result in the traits stressed and admired by the *UltraS*. Honour and faith, in the case of the *UltraS*, are inseparable from the sense of duty – the *UltraS* must do what they consider to be 'right'. This attitude emerged from Giorgio's explanation of why the *Irriducibili* are so respected by other *UltraS*:

> After the death of 'Paparelli'[2] we decided to make the *Laziali* more respected. Over the years, the *Irriducibili* have faced all *UltraS* groups in all possible ways, even the less orthodox ones. We are the elite of the *UltraS*. Check the newspapers since 1987; those were different years, there was less police repression. We used to leave Rome to see Lazio play away sometimes a day early to be in

---

[1] An idea inspired by the work of the anthropologist Friedrich, 1977
[2] On 28 October, 1979 an incendiary device fired from the *curva sud* by Roma supporters during the Rome derby killed a Lazio supporter by the name of Vincenzo Paparelli.

front of the rivals' end in the morning. We challenged them in their homes! Nevertheless, at the same time, we have never done malicious and infamous actions and perhaps this is the reason why we are respected. We are always fair.

Doing what was ideologically right was an issue also stressed by Marco (of the *Boys*). In the following statement, he gave one reason why there is so much hostility toward the fans of Livorno FC. 'When Livorno were relegated to *Serie B*, their supporters produced a banner which said: *Tito ce lo ha insegnato le foibe non sono un reato* [Tito has taught us: the foiba is not a crime].[3] The police did not seize the banner; this is something very shameful. We would never tell the police to go and seize it because we are against the *infami* [informers]; we deliver our own justice instead.'

Doing 'the right thing' justifies fighting rival fans *per se*. However, the assault is more enjoyable when rival fans manifest politics that are diametrically opposed to those of the *UltraS*. In these cases, opponents are insulted, denied the accolade of being 'true' and, at worse, labelled as communist. Todde is scathing about the communist fans of Siena and Bologna, whom he regards as cowards and police informers:

Historically, we have never had difficulties in small cities like Siena. They know we Romans travel in big numbers. In a big city, like Milan – with Inter and Milan – we can have a fight with 5,000–6,000 Romans. However, places like Empoli and Perugia only have about a thousand supporters and do not have the numbers to give us trouble. They know that if they 'break our balls' [annoy us], the *Boys* will destroy their stadium, so they are not hostile.

---

[3] A *foiba* is a deep, natural cavity. But the term is also used to describe a tragic era in Italian history. Between 1943 and 1946 the communist Yugoslavian militia of General Tito took advantage of the chaos in Italy to revenge themselves on the fascists. In the region of Istria, Trieste and most of Venezia, Tito eliminated Italian fascists as well as civilians of all political creeds, guilty in his eyes of being Italian. Thrown into the *foiba*, men and women were then robbed of their houses and possessions. Women were raped and men tortured. The number of Italians killed has never been formally established. On 10 February 2007, the President of the Italian Republic, Giorgio Napolitano (a former leader of the Italian Communist Party and later the Democratic Party) gave medals to the relatives of 30 Italians massacred by Tito's militia. (http://tgcom.mediaset.it/cronaca/articoli/articolo169293.shtm)

At Siena, however, once there were 30 or 40 fans who were desperately looking to fight Roma fans; they did not want to face us all together but were looking for families and 'ordinary' fans to pick on. In Siena, five or six Roma *UltraS* saw this aggression against these families and tried to defend them. They received lots of *botte* [Roman slang for beatings]; however, two Sienesi were stabbed during these fights. These Sienesi went to the police. This is very bad because the *UltraS* code is to 'wash dirty linen' within the family and not be an *infame* [informer]. They have not followed the rules; they used the police to defend themselves. They have behaved like the *Bolognesi* [fans of Bologna FC] that are deemed throughout the *UltraS* movement as cowards and spies because they report their fights to the police.

This 'sense of right' among the *UltraS* is complicated by a number of factors. Firstly, in Italy the plethora of masculinities have their own set of rules around violent confrontations, and these are further contorted by the *UltraS* political ideology. This bewildering number of 'rules of engagement' means the *UltraS* carry a heavy burden as to what is right. Within this framework, the confrontations that the *Boys* and the *Irriducibili* enter into might best be considered as 'competitions', which they have to win as part of their obligation to both protect and save their world. It is a concept that could equally be applied to politicians.

Within the *UltraS* actions – in this case we mean violent actions – members have a choice. There are general guidelines for this conduct that allow for 'right' or 'wrong' judgements that can justify their behaviour. Within that, of course, there is a moral question, because there are accepted ways of winning without actually cheating, and ways of cheating without being found out. But politics and the *UltraS* world do differ. For politicians, the rules are open and public, and if they are broken then the politician will usually be removed from office. For the *UltraS* the rules come from the inside. It is important that they win their competitions – fights – but they must win them properly, through 'fair play' and with honour. This is the 'warrior spirit'.

Of course, the warrior has more to do than fight. As Todde explains, 'the *Boys* are more than this, our most important commitment is about social campaigns, and it is important not to forget the *diffidati* or those who are not with us anymore, such as Gabriele [Sandri].' A warrior like Todde does not forget his *camerati*. For the *UltraS* warriors in death, the *camerati* are remembered. This duty of memory also extends to matters outside the football stadium.

Lele (a 23-year-old member of the *Boys*) recalled the events of 7 January, 1978. After a meeting of the MSI Youth Front, two members of the group – Franco Bigonzetti and Francesco Ciavatti – were attacked and killed by a six-strong commando unit of the communist terrorist group *Nuclei Armati*. Another militant neo-fascist, Stefano Recchioni, died in subsequent clashes with the police:

> After a few hours, the news of the event became known by many *camerati* who arrived in Via Acca Larentia. The tension was high; a journalist from RAI [the Italian state-owned broadcasting company] and a cameraman filmed the street where the shooting occurred and stopped in front of Francesco's bloodstain on the street... One of them threw a cigarette butt down next to it; the crowd reacted immediately. The police charged; Captain Sivori took his gun and shot into the crowd, but the weapon jammed; so he asked for another and targeted Stefano Recchioni, who died on 9 January at the San Giovanni's hospital. After many years, their memory makes them immortal and frees our eyes from squalid boundaries! Honour to the fallen of Acca Larentia.

This attitude clearly shows that respect for their dead heroes is integral to the *UltraS* logic. It seems that commemoration can be added to the other factors – symbols, myths and heroes – as something that defines their ideological boundaries with society and, at the same time, incites the group members to hate the 'enemy'. This account also illustrates Lele's contempt for the police, which is just as strong as for the murderers; it is clear that the police are among the *UltraS* most hated enemies.

The Boxer is the living embodiment of the 'warrior spirit', which is a combination of thought and action. Meeting the Boxer was always a difficult task; he was busy leading the group and running his own business. At the time he was sought, he had a clothes shop in Rome. But a meeting was eventually arranged. When arriving at the *sede* of the *Irriducibili*, located in a pleasant district of Rome, the first thing that the visitor notices is the security, with big gates and a tall fence surrounding the premises. Inside the building, the foyer leads onto a series of corridors with furnished offices with adjacent waiting rooms. Beyond the offices is a large warehouse with shelves full of merchandise – hats, sweatshirts, T-shirts, jackets, pictures of the SS Lazio team and a large imperial Eagle emblazoned with the motto 'Dare, Believe, Be Reckless'. The radio broadcast heard through the building was tuned to *La Voce della Nord* radio station.

Conversation with the Boxer was preceded by chat about a mutual enthusiasm for boxing and martial arts. The Boxer's friend, Alessio Sakara, known as *Il Legionario* (the Roman Legionnaire), is a successful professional fighter in the Ultimate Fighting Championship (UFC).[4]

Physicality is important to the Boxer. A well-known regional boxing coach and a former semi-professional boxer, his pugilistic skills are renowned among the *UltraS* – if the Boxer fights, he rarely loses. He is a complex figure; his comportment suggests a very tough character, which tends to scare people. Upon talking with him and gaining mutual trust, his various qualities emerged. Like all members of the *UltraS* 'elite', the Boxer has a strict code of honour that typifies those who practise combat sports at a high level. The first few questions he was asked were about politics and the state of Italian society. His view was that the First and Second Republics were the same. The cards of politics have been shuffled, but the people in power remained the same. He felt great pride in being Italian, despite what he considers the major problem of Rome, namely illegal immigration from Eastern European countries, 'At times I do not like to be Italian; too many things are wrong, especially in Rome. The situation with immigration is crazy. I am proud to be Italian when I am abroad. I hate it when Italians go abroad and badmouth our country. Every country has its own defects, but few people *sputtanano* (slander) their own country like the Italians. It is impossible to walk in Rome during the night without seeing young prostitutes, most from Eastern

---

[4] The UFC is a full contact no-holds-barred tournament in which fighters compete against each other regardless of their fighting style. This practice is also known as Mixed Martial Arts.

Europe. The "Albanian and Romanian plague" is responsible for this unacceptable condition.[5] It is not politics that exploits the *UltraS*, but the *UltraS* that use politics to resist the State.'

A number of 'modern' changes inform his politics. For the Boxer, the practice of football spectatorship had changed for the worst. He considers that, whilst fandom has always been overtly political, the ideological and political statements now needed to be disguised because the police and the State did not like to hear the 'truth' from the *curva*. Beneath his calm and muscular exterior, the Boxer manifested an anger and incredulity towards the Italian State. But regardless of what the Italian authorities and its representatives have brought to his door, he remains undeterred. He carries the strength of political conviction and is willing to pay the price for what he deems to be the 'right' way.

'Warriors' among the players wearing team colours on the pitch are more evident at SS Lazio that at AS Roma. Over the years a number of Lazio players have openly declared their sympathy with fascist ideology. Consequently, the *UltraS* of SS Lazio have more role models to identify with than their AS Roma counterparts. One ex-player, Giorgio Chinaglia, is currently 'exiled' in the USA and is sought by the Italian authorities for his part in a proposed 'illegal' takeover of SS Lazio in 2005. Born in Carrara, Chinaglia moved with his family to Cardiff in Wales at the age of nine. His football career began with Swansea City. Two years later, he moved to Italy and joined Massese, in *Serie C*. He was later to move to Internapoli, also in *Serie C*, and then to Lazio in 1969. In the 1971–72 season (when SS Lazio were in *Serie B*), *Giorgione* Chinaglia (Big Giorgio) topped the goalscorers table with 21 goals. He was the force behind SS Lazio's return to the top level at the end of that campaign. The following season, SS Lazio played great football and were contenders for the *scudetto*. Managed by Tommaso Maestrelli, Lazio were one of Italy's leading clubs at the time. The fans remember the great players of the era, including Giuseppe Wilson, Luciano Re Cecconi, Felice Pulici, Renzo Garlaschelli, Vincenzo D'Amico, Luigi 'Gigi' Martini, Mario Frustalupi and Giancarlo Oddi. But Chinaglia was the undisputed

---

[5] The Albanian link with European prostitution is well known in Rome as it is in London and other major European cities.

leader; he was rewarded for his efforts at club level and given his debut for the Italian national team in 1972. In the 1973–74 season, SS Lazio won the *scudetto* for the first time in the club's history; Chinaglia scored 24 goals. The following season, he scored 14 goals, but realised his adventure with SS Lazio was about to end, particularly when his friend Maestrelli became terminally ill.

At the end of the 1975–76 season, Chinaglia accepted an offer to play for the New York Cosmos, where he joined Pelé, Franz Beckenbauer, Carlos Alberto and Johan Cruyff. He also established residency in the USA. Chinaglia proved to be the best striker in the history of the North American Soccer League (NASL). In seven seasons, he scored 193 goals in 213 matches. He was voted best striker in the NASL in 1976, 1978, 1980, 1981 and 1982. He was considered the best player of the tournament in 1981, and was part of the team that scooped four Soccer Bowls in 1977, 1978, 1980 and 1982. When he retired from playing, SS Lazio supporters asked him to return to Italy to become Chairman of SS Lazio, a position he held from 1983 to 1986. Always controversial, Chinaglia was issued with an arrest warrant in 2006 by the Guardia di Finanza for alleged extortion and insider trading due to irregularities concerning ownership of the SS Lazio. Chinaglia fled back to the USA, where he remains as a fugitive from Italian justice. In his absence, in November 2007, Chinaglia was fined E4.2 million for financial irregularities during an alleged attempt of a foreign-registered chemical-pharmaceutical group to acquire control of SS Lazio.

Regardless of such dealings, the side that won the *scudetto* in 1973–74 is remembered by SS Lazio *UltraS* as a team of 'true' warriors. The team of Chinaglia and Maestrelli was the answer to the prayers of SS Lazio fans, who hitherto had known only disappointment. At the same time, the team caused great controversy in a period characterised by the politicisation of all realms of Italian society. The fans not only watched a good team, but saw a group of men with whom they could identify politically. The players did not fit the cliché of the 'modern footballer' and were inclined to controversial gestures. They trained with passion; at times they brawled with their opponents. One famous incident occurred in the 1970–71 season. After a 2–2 draw in a Fairs Cup tie between Arsenal and SS Lazio in Rome (Chinaglia scored both goals), the players, while eating in the same restaurant but at different tables, exchanged pleasantries. A gift of leather bags from the hosts to the visiting players was little appreciated by the British, who considered the item effeminate. A brawl between the two tables ensued and ended well for the SS Lazio players who were very experienced in such matters.

This macho (warrior) passion among the players was reinforced by a passion for parachuting, which at the time was considered synonymous with militaristic sympathies and thus an inclination to be ideologically on the right. Chinaglia and three of his teammates regularly went shooting in their leisure time. The squad terrified newly-signed players via initiation ceremonies by firing pistols loaded with blank cartridges. Public statements made by a number of players told of their intentions to vote for the MSI. This was enough to identify the players as fascists in the eyes of political opponents; but the players were keen to stress that they did not want to influence Roman voters. Years later, however, a number of players took up political office: Luigi Martini became an MP of *Alleanza Nazionale*; Franco Nanni stood for election in support of the mayoral candidate Gianni Alemanno. Felice Pulici was a candidate with Francesco Storace, a former senator of *Alleanza Nazionale* and now leader of the right-wing *La Destra* party. Giorgio Chinaglia was a fan of Giorgio Almirante, the one-time leader of the MSI. Many Lazio players wore the Celtic cross and on returning to the Olimpico in later years members of the *scudetto* winning team were greeted with the Roman salute. For the *Irriducibili,* Chinaglia and his men are heroes and 'true' warriors.

In the *curva nord*, one does not need to be Italian to be a warrior. In 2000 during the SS Lazio v Arsenal Champions League match, Lazio's Serbian-born Sinisa Mihajlovic called Arsenal's Senegal-born captain Patrick Vieira *scimmia di merda* (shit monkey). Despite verbal spats between the two that followed the incident, the referee took no action. The SS Lazio player later confirmed that he had indeed called Vieira a 'shit monkey', but only in response to Vieira calling him a 'gypsy shit'. The next Champions League match saw SS Lazio play the Ukrainian team of Shakhtar Donetsk; Mihajlovic made a pre-match on-pitch announcement stating his sorrow for expressing such an insult to Vieira and asking supporters to cease their monkey grunting noises, directed towards black opposition players. The Boxer dismissed Mihajlovic's gesture, which he and others thought was not spontaneous but rather imposed by the SS Lazio management in the face of threats from UEFA. He further argued that Vieira should have also apologised to Mihajlovic. Many SS Lazio fans shared this sentiment.

The Serbian player had arrived at SS Lazio from Red Star Belgrade where he was popular with the hardcore supporters. He was also a personal friend of the *Tigers*, a hooligan group turned paramilitary, and its leader Zelijko Raznatovic, better known as 'Arkan'. When the civil war began in Yugoslavia in 1991 – put sharply in focus by rioting during a match between Croatian Dinamo Zagreb and Serbian Red Star supporters – the first militias were drawn from the football terraces. Arkan's *Tigers* militia was notorious for its brutality and mass murders. In 2000, during a home game in Rome, the *Irriducibili* produced a banner depicting the Serbian paramilitary leader, which caused huge controversy among the media and Italian politicians, who interpreted it as a tribute to the notorious paramilitary commander. Motions at the Chamber of the Deputies were written in condemnation; politicians promised to stop future *UltraS* displays.

The outcome was a stadium full of police for the next month. Federico (of the *Irriducibili)* strongly denied that there were any political links or sympathies attached to the banner. According to him, the banner was made and displayed out of admiration for their tough player Sinisa Mihajlovic, who was Arkan's friend. However, it is difficult to believe that this gesture was not done out of admiration for Arkan, who was never shy about having his image circulated, particularly the one of him in military fatigues holding a tiger cub. Uncompromising in his pursuits, he was considered a hero by many Serbians and a symbol of Serbian Nationalism. Arkan's personality fits all the warrior-like qualities so admired by the *UltraS*. Following the Arkan episode, tension between police and *UltraS* worsened. At a SS Lazio-Udinese game, plastic bottles were thrown at nearby carabinieri in protest against their repression. The police responded by charging at the *UltraS* at the exit to the stadium injuring, according to the *Irriducibili,* the elderly and children alike. The *Irriducibili* declared that some innocents, beaten indiscriminately by the police, had left the stadium in ambulances.

Another 'true' *UltraS* hero is former SS Lazio player Paolo di Canio. A brilliant player, Di Canio is also someone who has publically declared his fascist ideology. A member of the *Irriducibli* in his youth, he has tattooed on his arm the Roman numerals DVX – a Latin appellation for *Il Duce*. Throughout his successful professional career, which started at SS Lazio in 1985, Di Canio has embodied the *Irriducibili* values par excellence. A winner of the UEFA Cup with Juventus in 1993 and the *Scudetto* with Milan in 1995–96, he moved to Celtic in 1996 and on to Premier League side Sheffield Wednesday the following year. An inclination towards violence was first seen in 1998 during a match between Sheffield Wednesday and Arsenal at Hillsborough. Angry at a decision made by referee Paul Alcock, Di Canio pushed him to the ground. The official left the pitch on a stretcher; Di Canio was sent off. He was fined £10,000 by the FA and banned for 11 matches. He went back to Italy and refused to return to his club. In response, Wednesday sold him for a bargain £1.7 million to West Ham United in January 1999. During a four-year stay in East London, he scored 48 goals and became the hero of the Hammers fans. In 2000, he also won the BBC Goal of the Season Award for a magnificent volley against Wimbledon.

The tough but 'honourable' code of the *Irriducibili* was well illustrated in two important gestures made by Di Canio during his career. The first occurred in 2000, during a match between West Ham and Everton on Merseyside. The match was level at 1-1. The Everton goalkeeper, Paul Gerrard, was prostrate as a consequence of an injury sustained seconds earlier. The ball was passed to Di Canio in a goalscoring position. Instead of exploiting the situation and scoring what would have been an easy goal, Di Canio caught the ball and stopped the match, pointing to the prostrate keeper. The home fans understood the chivalrous gesture and gave him a standing ovation. Di Canio received an official letter of commendation from FIFA President Sepp Blatter and was later awarded the FIFA Fair Play award.

The second significant public display came during the 2004–05 season by which time he had returned to SS Lazio. Following the SS Lazio-Roma derby in January (won 3-1 by SS Lazio), Di Canio performed the Roman salute towards the joyful throngs of the *Irriducibili*. A photograph of this moment created worldwide controversy. Di Canio repeated the gesture during a SS Lazio-Livorno fixture (a highly political match due to the Livorno supporters extreme left-wing sympathies) and received a fine of E10,000 and a one-match suspension from the Italian Football Association. Later, during a SS Lazio-Juventus fixture, he performed the salute yet again, signifying to the *Irriducibili* the indomitable 'warrior spirit' never to bow in the face of authority. He received another fine and another suspension. When questioned, Di Canio explained that his salutes arose out of a sense of belonging to 'my people', adding 'when you have values, you're always in the right'. One of Di Canio's defenders was Italian Premier Silvio Berlusconi, who explained that the salute 'did not have any meaning, [Di Canio] is an exhibitionist, but a good lad.' Di Canio's Lazio contract was not renewed in the summer of 2006 following disagreements with, and his dislike of, the club president and majority shareholder, Claudio Lotito. He left SS Lazio in July 2006 to finish his career at the Cisco Roma club in *Serie C2*.

Di Canio's relationship with the *Irriducibili* was well illustrated in 2005 when AT met him at Formello (the club's training ground outside Rome), together with the Boxer and another youth called Daniele. Di Canio was good friends with Giorgio of the *Irriducibili*, and the group loved the player because, despite his fame, he did not forget his roots or the 'guys'. Meeting the *Irriducibili* delegation in the room where the SS Lazio players sign autographs or speak to the *tifosi* after training, Di Canio was friendly and happy to pose for photos for their website in a new *Irriducibili* T-shirt. He was perfectly willing to promote their merchandise without asking for a fee.

The connection between Di Canio and the leaders of the *Irriducibili* was so strong that when the four leaders were arrested in 2007 over the Lotito-Lazio affair and were waiting for the judicial process to begin, Di Canio met Giorgio to pledge his support. Even in such difficult moments he always defended the *UltraS* against allegations that they knew Chinaglia's attempt to facilitate the purchase of the club by a group of foreign investors to be a fraud.

Although firmly masculine as a group, the *UltraS communitas* also includes a number of women. In 2005, AT was invited to watch the Lazio-Milan match with the Boxer at the Olimpico and allowed into their 'territory' down beside the pitch. The Boxer was at one point on the pitch, walking towards the *curva nord* in the company of Paolo Di Canio. Upon arrival, both stood by the perimeter fence and acknowledged the thousands of *Irriducibili*. During the match, AT spoke to another member of the 'elite' – Giuseppe (a law university student aged in his late 20s) who was curious about the research into the *Boys*. He introduced his ex-girlfriend Monica (of similar age and a university student in communication science), who explained her status as one of the group's veterans, having been present among them for more than five years. She spoke of her admiration for the Boxer, who in the meantime was busy holding the megaphone and leading the *curva*'s chants.

During the conversation she explained that for her the attraction of the group was friendship. She complained that such elementary values were not publicised in the media coverage that they received, which was only interested in reporting violence, saying, 'We have been persecuted by journalists and police who take any opportunity to call us thugs.' When asked about the nature of her relationship with others in the group, Monica responded that, while respect was given by the *direttivo* to every member in the past, the situation had gradually changed. Despite this change, the four leaders were able to keep order, but there were 'kids' emerging – what she called the 'new generation' – who were difficult to handle. She indicated that the Boxer had had to 'deal' with them quite a few times. They were around 16–18 years of age and did not have respect for seniority. She implied that they likewise did not give her the respect due to her as a female. They were trouble for the *Irriducibili*. She did not want to speak about them any further because they were standing near her. In the tumult of a goal celebration, she looked scared and uneasy until the veterans moved down the stand and hugged each other.

The 'female' dimension of the *UltraS* did not exist as warriors. In general, the female element of the group was more task-orientated, but definitely not ornamental. They had roles to play (in organising the matchday event and banners) and, while not counted on to partake in any brawls, could be relied upon to watch the back of a *camerata* and not reveal information to the police. They were similarly expected to show duty and honour to those they lived among. Their presence may shock observers who study hardcore football fandom.

The *Boys* also had female *camerati,* but their roles differed from those in the *Irriducibili.* Influenced by ideology of the *Casa Pound Italia,* women naturally played a more active role in their *communitas.* One such member is Sara, 20 years old in 2005 and in her first year of a political science degree at the University of Rome. Sara gave some details about her involvement with the *Boys:*

Q: How many times do you visit the group's headquarters?

S: Every day at the moment. But soon I will start my university lectures again, so I will come depending on the lecture schedule.

Q: What do you do in your free time?

S: Most of my free time I spend with my friends here.

Q: Do they (the *Boys*) pay you to be here?

S: At the end of the month, they give me money for expenses because I am a student and students, as you know, are not rich.

Q: How long have you been a member of the *Boys*?

S: Five years. One year ago I started working in the headquarters. I have been an active member for two years now. This means that I follow the group to all away matches.

Q: In a group such as the *Boys,* with a neo-fascist ideology, the common consensus is that women do not count. What do you think about that?

S: The *Boys* have two women who take part in any decision concerning the group and then we have many women members who come to the stadium to follow the team and sympathise without holding a membership card.

Q: Is your relationship with the guys 'equal'?

S: Group decisions are taken by six people; they are the 'vets' [the status of veteran is established through loyalty to the groups and courage in 'action']. I am not part of that because I am young, but there is a girl who is one of the vets. I show my attachment to the group and to the team. I am part of them with the same rights and duties. I belong to the *direttivo*. We have 30 members of the *direttivo* that do security at the stadium. We share resources for the good of the group. For instance, tomorrow we have to go to Florence to get some materials, so someone has made their car available to me.

Women such as Sara and Francesca (*see* chapter 2) are fully integrated into the *Boys* grouping. This is positive in a society where appreciation for the female is often based simply on aesthetic attraction. Female members are publically involved in spreading the *communitas*' values in the *curva sud*. Further questions attempted to find out about the female perspective of *UltraS* membership:

Q: So what does it mean for you to be one of the *Boys*?

S: It is an elite group of *UltraS*. The group has, since 1972, shown great attachment to the team of Roma and its tradition. I am with them first because of a love of football. I want to share this with guys and girls that have the same passion and life vision as me. With them, I also travel a lot, so it is good fun! When you travel by train around Italy and abroad, emotional attachment to the group is built up. I do not find this at university. I have many more friends here in the *Boys* and this friendship is real; it lasts.

Q: What are the group's main values?

S: We are not only the *Boys* inside the stadium, we are the same outside too. Members of the group lead by example in their lifestyles. They are faithful to the team. We always say friendship is one of the most important values. If something happens to one of us, it is as if it happens to all of us. A good example is the *diffidati*, you know, the ones banned from the stadium. They are remembered at the stadium during matches with banners or, if our members have been arrested, the *Boys* share the cost of their legal representation.

There was no difference in Sara's thinking to that of the other male members. She was keen to stress the unity of UltraS purpose both inside and outside the stadium. In contrast to 'ordinary' supporters, the use of symbols, banners and chants are not just part of the stadium ritual but intimately intertwined with the group's values and ideology.

The interview continued:

Q: What do you say to the people that negatively judge the *Boys* and the *UltraS*?

S: The *UltraS* is a movement; we are united against the common enemy, which is State repression and the police.

Q: Why is the bust of Benito Mussolini in the headquarters of a football fan group?

S: It is an important symbol to show our political ideology.

Q: What does Mussolini mean for you?

S: I see Mussolini as an influential man; he had charisma and the first thing that comes to my mind is 'order'. Italy needs order even if I would not like to see a dictatorship of the right.

The cult of Mussolini provides a strong link between the older members of the *Boys* group, and the younger ones, like Sara. He cuts a striking figure in many of the fascist icons that still exist around the city of Rome. For many, these icons with their highly spiritualised visions of violence have turned the fascists who died during their turbulent era in to martyrs for the fatherland. They and he have attained a kind of quasi-religious divinity. This provoked the following questions:

Q: I hear that some of the *Boys* have friendships with members of *Forza Nuova*.

S: These are personal friendships. We are completely autonomous of the parties and they never influence us. We have similar ideals with *Forza Nuova*, but we are completely independent. No political groups or party would dare to say they represent the *Boys*. If there are official political manifestations of parties, we do not attend them; members can, if they wish, attend rallies for personal reasons too, but never as representatives of the *Boys*.

Q: What about the symbols that the group uses on merchandise?

S: We do not put unmarketable symbols in our materials; how can a person wear a swastika? We use marketable symbols that are 'cool' such as the double axe of *Ordine Nuovo*.

Ultimately, of course, Sara belongs to a group that supports a football club. The way Italian football was going was the pertinent issue:

Q: What is your assessment of Italian football today?

S: Too many people 'eat' from the Italian football table. Exceptions exist, but many players are not attached to the colours of the team as in the past. Loyalty does not exist anymore. The *Boys* have zero contact with the team management. We are very independent, so when we think that they are doing something wrong, we have the freedom to voice our dissatisfaction.

The *Boys* fanzine often features articles written by women and on women's subjects. Perhaps the most famous article written by a woman was Katia's report that defended the *Boys* for their actions during the notorious Roma-Lazio derby in 2004 (*see* chapter 12). In the article, she accused the police of using hardcore repressive tactics; she affirmed that her nine-year-old son was, like others, made ill because of the tear gas fired by the police in the stadium. Katia also exhorted the media to use more objectivity in their reports of the *UltraS* and, most of all, to ascertain the facts before reporting.

Another notable article, written by Lele, was intended to make sense of 8 March, International Woman's Day (IWD) – a celebration of women supported in Italy by leftist groups and feminists. The article concerned the mimosa flower (customarily given to women on that day), describing it as perfumed and delicate, but at the same time, resilient – a symbol of strength and femininity; this analogy represents the ideal of the females of the group.

Willing to accommodate women, open to men of a wide age range, and not concerned about occupational status or social origins, the *Boys* and the *Irriducibili* might therefore be considered as all-inclusive gatherings with few parallels in Italian society. However, inclusion is always restricted and confined by a shared orthodoxy in political opinion. To join the *UltraS* means to adhere to certain ideological concepts, of which *Patria* (fatherland) and 'Race' are essential.

The Italian flag flies among the banners and flags of the *UltraS*

11

RACE AND THE FATHERLAND

The ideologies of nationalism and racism are closely related because of their shared historical origins. Both concepts are of interest to the *UltraS*, as Giovanni (of the *Irriducibili*) points out in the following statement:

> The Italian radical right still represents the two fundamental values of Italian society – the family and the concept of the *Patria* [Fatherland]. When the family is substituted by single parents or

'natural unions', or when people will no longer be proud to be part of the Italian nation and when those who arrive from abroad have more rights than Italians, then our society will dissolve.

Patria and family are two fundamental elements of the longed for neo-fascist society. They have a long pedigree. In 1926, the PNF constituted a youth organisation, the *Opera Nazionale Balilla* (ONB), comprising children from six to 18 years. They were told: *Ama la Patria come i genitori; ama i genitori come la Patria* (Love your Fatherland as you love your parents; love your parents as you love your Fatherland). But such love comes at a price – some had to be excluded. Exclusion was mainly based on a sense of common self. Giovanni explained:

> It is useless to speak about 'multi-ethnic' models of co-existence or even 'European' models. To have social peace, every nation has its own identity that needs to be respected. We can see the English situation where social peace is forever disturbed by the multi-ethnic society imposed by the UK government and championed by Tony Blair. We are not 'racists'; we support the concept of tolerance, but this exists only when there is reciprocity, otherwise it is all bollocks. For example, when a Muslim wants to build 10 mosques here in Italy, he has to allow us Christians to build 10 churches in his country. It would be more equal if they allow us to put a crucifix in Muslim schools just for the principle of reciprocity.

Hence, in the *UltraS* reasoning, the exaltation of the *Patria* does not necessarily translate to the exaltation of a 'race' over and above all others. The exaltation of *Patria* is underlined by differences founded mainly in cultural and religious identity, which constitute for the *UltraS* barriers to immigration and are the crucial factors in their favoured policy of the exclusion of immigrants. In this context, racism and nationalism intertwine. This discourse is the expression of what can be termed as 'neo-racism', which is increasingly emerging in Europe. In simple terms, prejudice is normalised mainly via cultural and religious differences and not through notions of racial superiority.

The significance of symbolism, once again, helps the *UltraS* to communicate and promote their beliefs around the idea of nation. Marco (of the *Boys*) explains, 'Our symbols are the *sole nascente* [rising sun] and *l'ascia bipenne* [double-blade axe]. The *sole nascente* has a political value; the sunrise represents a new era for our nation – a rebirth – the symbol of the sun is also found in the Celtic cross.' The 'elite' of the *Boys* demonstrated their collective heroic identity by being the only ones to wear hats displaying the *sole nascente* insignia, which is also a lesser-known symbol of nationalistic neo-fascism. It symbolises the re-birth of fascist ideology.

However, where and when will this re-birth of the nation appear, and where does such a belief originate? The answer, of course, lies in the roots of Mussolini's fascism. Among the most important elements of *UltraS*-nationalism are the uniqueness of national culture and an ever-growing awareness of shared history, ethnicity and language. Italian neo-fascism draws on such elements, but adds new dimensions, most notably the concept of Revolutionary Nationalism, which, in 21st century Italy, is represented by *Casa Pound Italia*. Revolutionary Nationalism should be interpreted as a 'Third Way' between those who champion (at any cost) the processes of globalisation, which the neo-fascists believe homogenise and erase national identities, and 'fake patriots'. According to the Italian neo-fascists, 'fake patriots' make decisions on behalf of the nation based on capitalism and selfishness, which neglect regional identities and the expression of glorious local traditions. They believe the current political class in Italy denies the country a significant political and moral role at the international level by accepting a servile position in relation to Britain and America. Contempt is therefore shown towards those servile to Anglo-American ideas and ways of life that champion consumerism. This Anglo-American opposition shares common traits with the French *Nouvelle Droite* (New Right) and its guru Alain de Benoist. Anti-Americanism and the fight against globalisation, which is considered a domain of international finance controlled by Jews and Freemasons, are the main themes of this new party and can be seen in *UltraS* banners and graffiti around the Olimpico. As an example of this, the following piece appeared in the *Boys* fanzine in 2002–03 under the heading 'The Anglo-American Arrogance in Iraq'.

The reasons [for this war] as advertised by Bush are about international justice and terrorism, but do not have any real basis. Iraq has not respected the UN resolution, but what about Israel that has not respected 200 UN resolutions, or the USA, which often bypasses the UN resolutions? ...No proof exists or episode confirms the involvement of Saddam Hussein in terrorist actions. Furthermore the States that have weapons of mass destruction are numerous and either pro-American or are visited by VIP tourism or have less petrol than Iraq [the writer is being ironic] ...We need also to consider that in moments such as this when the economic system, led by the West, is in a crisis, American economists are pushed to use new imperialist ideologies to renew the economic-industrial process via a war economy to conquer a monopolistic position in the world energy-petrol industry. Everyone knows this, even our politicians – always servants of the American power – influenced by the restrictive and tedious presence on ITALIAN land of American military bases ready always to forget with great infamy our history.

Anti-USA sentiment has drawn sympathy of sorts for the most unlikely of captives. The *Irriducibili*'s 2006 statement on their website about Saddam Hussein proclaimed the following:

While I am writing, many images of Saddam Hussein, the former president of Iraq, are flooding the websites of major online newspapers. As a group, we cannot comment on the judicial part of the matter because we did not read any judicial document but, as people with brains, we can express an opinion on what such a process in Iraq means today.

As *Irriducibili* we well understand, unfortunately for us, the inefficiencies and injustices of our judicial system. Many times because of this, we were convinced that perhaps in no other country in the world existed a judicial system worse than the Italian one. Actually we have found one in Iraq; we laugh at a tribunal that by its nature should be impartial ... is it possible for a tribunal to be impartial when composed of judges appointed by a 'joke' government in a 'joke' state that does not have any national sovereignty? Can it be considered impartial when those who have arrested him appoint the judges? What will be the likely outcome of the process?

… Saddam Hussein will be condemned to death (a vice that the Americans imported into Iraq in 2006 from their 'civilised' land and continue to assassinate people using the electric chair as did the French with the guillotine two hundred years ago) with all his advisers who, like him, would prefer to die in prison than collaborate with the Americans. We hope that the same justice that will kill Saddam Hussein one day (hopefully soon) will punish those who committed crimes such as the slaughters of Sabra and Shatila, the massacres in Iraq by Anglo-American troops using white phosphorus; the civilians killed during the invasion of the country, the Palestinian population who no longer have houses destroyed by bulldozers, the torture in the concentration camps of Abu Ghraib and Guantanamo Bay. For past crimes (Vietnam, Dresden, Roma, Berlin, Hiroshima, Nagasaki, Baghdad, Kabul and Belgrade) and so on … We are full of hope, but we also know that it will be difficult because the tribunals that will judge these *signori* are designated by those themselves![1]

UltraS nationalism is, consequently, conceived around the idea of a *Patria*, sharing a sense of common participation with a collective destiny. Such a society has to be fought for and, with battles to be won, warriors are needed. It is this representation of 'remote traditions' that gives the *UltraS* a sense of moral and cultural authority and, most importantly, authenticity that produces a direct link to the past.

This pride in the *Patria* and the sense of 'people' expressed by our two *UltraS communitas* provoke both prejudice and admiration. The most unlikely of groups can be offered the plaudits. Realism and contradiction are evident. The *UltraS* celebrate the symbols of defiance manifest by both Palestinians and Irish Republicans, which form the basis of their anti-Israeli and anti-British sentiments. The anti-Israeli stance is evident

---

[1] The prophecy of the *Irriducibili* was fulfilled on 30 December 2006, when the former Iraq president was executed by hanging, having been judged – and found guilty – by a special tribunal on charges of crimes against humanity.

in the frequent display by the *Irriducibili* in the *curva nord* of the Palestinian flag and their chants in praise of the repressed: 'Palestine: Never Give Up'. Some of these sentiments are genuine; many are pragmatic.

Using the Palestinian issue, the *Boys* express their opinions against what they negatively define 'Zionism'. The following document titled '*Libertá per La Palestina*' was published in the *Boys* fanzine in 2001–02[2]:

It is right to dedicate a space on what is happening in the Middle East, about the aggression of Israel against the Palestinian people, about the invasion of a land that rightly belongs to another population, also a land that for Christians represents a Holy ground. Ten days ago, the Cis-Jordan [West Bank] invasion began with the Israel army deployed by Sharon, using Palestinian terrorism as an excuse. The reality is different. The war has always been an option since the PLO leader Arafat was confined to his office and kept under surveillance 24 hours a day. They forbade him to see people from the international community. This is already a despicable act in itself because Arafat was elected democratically by the Palestinian people and the Israelis have no right to deprive him of power by the use of force. In the meantime, in the rest of Palestine the war 'against terrorism' runs wild. Entire cities are bombed 'to drive out terrorists', curfews are imposed; houses are either destroyed or occupied. The world seems initially surprised; no one [however] condemns the Israeli aggression.

In Europe, we have news about ambulances used as targets by Israeli soldiers because they carry injured Palestinians. This is documented by reporters always looking for sensational news even if it means risking their lives. In fact, to demonstrate once more that the witnesses of wars are always tedious observers, the soldiers decide to shoot the press. Among them, an Italian journalist died after being hit by a tank while documenting the assaults of Israelis troops upon Palestinians.

[2] This article was written in April 2002 at the time the Palestinian Authority Chairman Yasser Arafat was confined to his office compound in the West Bank city of Ramallah by Israeli troops during an escalation of the Israel-Palestinian conflict. Arafat died in 2004.

This article demonstrates once more that the *UltraS* include individuals in tune with current national and international political affairs. The journalist they are referring to is Italian photo-journalist Raffaele Ciriello, killed by Israeli Defence Force gunfire in the West Bank city of Ramallah in March 2002. Ciriello was working for the well-known Italian newspaper *Corriere della Sera*. According to press reports and eyewitness testimony, he died during an Israeli offensive. The article finishes as follows:

> All the world continues to show its disapproval against Sharon, who disregards international protests and continues his path enforcing the siege of the Palestine, continuing to keep Arafat in forced exile and threatening to kick him out of his own country. During these last days, even Bush has demonstrated in a timid way his disapproval. Because the Americans are always ready to run and help every nation and then deceitfully colonise them, in this case they just intervened lightly [again, the writer takes an ironic tone here].

At other times, contempt for Israel is combined with similar hatred for the global capitalism of the USA. For the *UltraS*, the only bulwark against this seems to be Roman Catholicism:

> Firstly, the Israeli army has been armed – and probably still is – by American firms. All their weapons are made in USA. Secondly, the Israelis are one of the strongest minorities in the world, their power comes from an almost total control of the economy especially in industrialised countries. Aggression against Israel could cause a reaction of the world's dominant class [linked to the world economy] and bring economic reprisals. Only the Pope has tried to oppose this slaughter because this war is fought on the Holy Land and in these times the fighting involved the Church of the Nativity in Bethlehem; the church dedicated to the nativity of Jesus!! Israeli soldiers have surrounded it, bombed it, occupied it and they are continuing to shoot inside the walls. This demonstrates that the Israelis intend [not] to respect the friendship that our Pope has so

strongly wished. It is useless to continue justifying this war as a reaction against terrorism because, as senator Andreotti said, who would not in the current conditions fear to be confined in an Israeli concentration camp; who would not have considered [been pushed] stuffing themselves with TNT to promote his/her cause? SOLIDARITY FOR THE PALESTINIAN PEOPLE.

In a country with a proud and famous footballing tradition the stadium in Rome (and throughout Italy) is a place to articulate the legacy of a nation. The Olimpico is the embodiment of this function. The main street along which spectators access the stadium is dominated by the *Obelix*, bearing the dedication to *Mussolini Dux* and adorned by a sequence of symbols and mottos from the most important stages of the fascist regime. This connection to the past is so strong that, around the stadium on matchday it is possible to find stands selling not only merchandise of the teams of AS Roma and SS Lazio, but also busts of Mussolini and other fascist regalia. The authorities appear to ignore such enterprise; the merchandise is sold in defiance of the Mancino Law passed in 1993, which prohibited the use of political symbols linked to fascism. Such artefacts are also to be found on sale on stalls in the north-eastern town of Predappio where Mussolini was born and buried. In Rome, the same artefacts are on sale in the popular Via Sannio market and in Via Conca d'Oro. Badges in praise of Mussolini can also be found sold by entrepreneurs outside the Colosseum. There is no shortage of buyers.

The Italian football stadium is not dissimilar to those in other countries in that it is a site of racism and xenophobic intolerance. A study (2007) conducted by the Italian Observatory on Racism and Anti-racism in Football underlined a phenomenon of 'normalisation' in the Italian media and football organisations around the issue of racism; although the media focuses on the *UltraS* societal 'threats'. In analysing the 2005–06 and 2006–07 football seasons, the study identified 134 episodes of racism around the game, which were categorised into two types: 'indirect' racism (or propaganda), which were shown regardless of what was occurring in the pitch, and 'direct' racism, which was defined as targeting players of different skin colour, religion or ethnic origin.

Racism, normally, has two strands: 'foreigners' are regarded either as 'inferior', or 'different'. If they are inferior then they are isolated in social and economic domains. Those who are different might be so because of cultural differences or the fact that they do not share the same nationalistic distinctiveness. This poem, written by the *Boys direttivo*, sheds light on the matter:

> *I walk along the streets bold and proud.*
> *I am the son of an ancient EMPIRE*
> *I serve my Fatherland, I am Italian*
> *I am proud to make the Roman SALUTE*
> *Attached to affections and to religion [Catholicism]*
> *Never will I bend my will in front of the 'master' [Italian authorities]*
> *The motto that I follow is*
> *Will, Power and Freedom*
> *I do not love the weak and promiscuous*
> *I am not violent*
> *I do not wish to repress*
> *Nevertheless, I wish that everyone remains in his or her nations*
> *People respect me*
> *Because they know, I am a perfect citizen*
> *I wait for the Celtic Sun to rise*
> *In the hope that everything will improve*

For the *Boys* then, it is the variable of 'difference' that is central to the issue of race, based on a generalised sense of shared kinship and expressed in their proclamation of a Fatherland united by a common religion, Christianity. To complicate matters further, racist activity among the *UltraS* takes a number of different forms, and behaviours in the *curve* that fit the description of being 'racist' can be ambiguous and contradictory. The first type of insult originates from Italy's North/South divide; such chants and insults are mainly spontaneous and ritualised. In 2006, during the Rome derby, the *Boys* started chanting, '*Paolo di Canio – Napoletano! Paolo di Canio – Napoletano!*' even though Di Canio was not born in Southern Italy. Opposition players and rival fans often face the accusation of being a 'southerner'; in other words someone who does not wash, nor work, but lives to exploit State welfare. The term can be synonymous with *Napoletano* [from the southern city of Naples]. This light-hearted spontaneous banter had little significance. It was from the heart, during a match between two teams that have a fierce rivalry. But Di Canio was respected by the *Boys* who regarded him as a *camerata*. Besides which he is an Italian, and both the *Boys* and the *Irriducibili* are unlikely to racially abuse other Italians.

The second and more insidious type of insult is ethnic, which comprises different dimensions that focus on skin colour, religious difference and the perceived danger of irregular immigration, mostly from Eastern Europe. In 2007, at the SS Lazio-Dynamo Bucharest Champions League qualifying match, monkey grunting erupted from the *curva nord* against the Ghanaian-born Bucharest player George Blay. Seeking explanation for the motivation behind the monkey chants, Federico (of the *Irriducibili)* justified the noise by claiming it was a means to distract opposition players and should not necessarily be regarded as an expression of racial contempt. To complicate the issue, as anyone who knows about Italian football is well aware, insults like this can be spontaneous, involving the whole stadium, not only the *curve*. These dynamics are also present in other football stadia in Europe.[3]

Ignorance concerning race and ethnicity can be manifest in the stadium, not only among the *UltraS,* but also among the 'ordinary' and respectable fans. This behaviour illustrates that racial bigotry is present not only in the football stadium, but also in wider society and thus beyond ideological explanations. Moreover, behaviours that fit the description 'racist' manifest ambiguous and contradictory forms in the Roman *curve*. It is not uncommon in the *curva nord* to hear racist insults directed towards black opposition players, while the same supporters laud black SS Lazio players. However, sometimes in the pursuit of offending an opponent, pragmatism and self-censorship are evident. At times, supporters who might use racially inspired insults

[3] For example, during Spain's friendly against England in November 2004 several England players were subject to prolong racial abuse and chanting. Whilst many Spanish journalists argued that such sentiment was provoked by a right-wing *UltraS* group, witnesses claimed that at least 80 per cent of the crowd joined in.

realise that they would not be able to offend the black players of other teams without offending their own team.

The connection between ideology and racism produced one of the most compelling *UltraS* statements about race displayed on the *Lazio UltraS* website, a site with strong links to the *Irriducibili:*

> The concept of race is influenced by the vision that one has of the human being ... I have a traditional conception as a strong base of my ideas; this recognises in the human being three elements: the body, the soul and the spirit. A complete theory of the race needs to consider all these three elements.
>
> Julius Evola

The sayings of Julius Evola are crucial for defining the *UltraS* thoughts concerning race and ethnicity. For Evola, the term 'race' is synonymous with quality; a person having values is a person of race. Evola rejected Hitler's biological ideas of racism, a distance from Hitler's racism also stressed by the *UltraS*. For instance, when Todde was asked about the issue of race in 2008, he replied: 'We are against immigration, but not against the immigrants; the biological racism of the Nazis is not part of our tradition and beliefs.' Of the three elements in Evola's notion the spirit is crucial, as it manifests the metaphysical element worn down by centuries of secularisation and modernisation. The element of body is based on a specific appearance. Evola believed there are two types of Aryans: Ario-Germans and Ario-Romans. The latter were considered superior in soul and spirit to the former and provided the raw material required for a national cultural rebirth. For Evola, 'mixed races' and racial degeneration were negative consequences of modernity. Consequently, Evola's philosophy argues that, in the fight against modernity, society must return to the traditional differences of the races; resistance against modernity is resistance against racial mixing. The struggle against modernity implies a process of renewed differentiation and a hierarchy of races. However, even if Evola's racism is quite distant from the biological racism of the Nazi – it contains instead cultural and esoteric elements – the potential consequences of this conception are the same.

Media accusations of racist (and especially anti-Semitist) attitudes are strongly challenged by both *UltraS* groups. One notable instance concerned SS Lazio player Fabio Liverani, who is of Italian-African heritage and became the first player with such a background to play for the Italian national team. In 2001, the *Irriducibili* were accused by the Italian media of being responsible for spreading racist slogans around the city of Rome against Liverani, who was newly arrived from Perugia. According to the graffiti, the player was 'guilty' of having a black Somalian mother. The *Irriducibili* were immediately blamed even though Giorgio declared in a statement to the newspaper *La Repubblica*, 'The *Irriducibili* disagree and dissociate from the writings and symbols used against Liverani. We invite Lazio fans to show solidarity with the player and the team today during training.'

At times, the *UltraS* have also challenged other belief systems; they have aimed actions and words at 'others' whose faiths are at odds with Christianity. Giorgio (of the *Irriducibili*) deliberated upon such 'others':

> The organisation of today's society causes crimes because, in some cases, stealing is the only way of surviving. It also favours intolerance towards others. Let's take an example, in Rome's Parioli district (a very affluent area), instead of building and funding a park (perhaps it would have been even better to spend this money in the peripheral districts), they have allowed the building of a mosque. They allowed people who are against our way of life and our religion to build their sanctuary, their symbols, which have stated for centuries their tradition against ours. I cannot accept this! We Italians are not owners of our land any more. I cannot accept that, in our schools, for instance, someone spoke about taking away the crucifix to avoid offending people belonging to other religions! I have never been interested in religion, but I am ready to participate in a religious war against this idea. That crucifix symbolises not only Catholicism, but also Italy and its history. To the 'beggar' [Muslim] with the daughter with the veils who does not like it, I would say 'go away to your country with your daughter and make her wear however many veils you want.' If you want to stay in Italy, accept our way of life or leave.

While the ideology of the neo-fascists can celebrate the struggle of Muslim groups (such as the Palestinians or Iraqis) against what they consider to be Anglo-American and Zionist imperialism, this celebration should not be seen as support for their religion, especially if such a religion tries to establish itself in Italian cities. The majority of Italian neo-fascist sentiment is linked to Catholicism with a minority related to paganism. The *UltraS* support this claim; they see themselves as champions of Catholicism. One such example is provided by an editorial written in the *Boys* fanzine in 2003, which invites fellow believers to act against the 'sinister' forces of globalisation, modernity and liberalism and reminds readers of the pride that they should manifest in Italian Catholic identity against Islam:

> I would have preferred to speak about other things but my conscience leads my hand. Adel Smith – President of the Italian Muslim Union[4] – has appealed to the Tribunal of L'Aquila [an Italian city] to eliminate the cross from all the Italian schools, which your sons attend. The Deputy Prime Minister Fini needs to think well before giving the immigrants the votes proposed. Many other threats of this kind are around the corner and can get out of our control. Guys, we live in a world where the sacred is not important anymore; where all is sacrificed to the rhythms of production and mass consumerism disregarding sentiments and values. These people act out of revenge and not feeling. Instead of fighting with honour, they fight with infamy. Their eternal dissatisfaction is about to bring horrifying imbalances... Should we not act and see the decadence that surrounds us? I ask you *UltraS*, you warriors of the new millennium, defenders of the ancient values; they are attacking our identity and we will not allow it! Those who do not respect our culture do not deserve our respect. First on the list: Adel Smith!'

The same sentiment was expressed a few weeks later on a banner produced by the *Irriducibili* , which proclaimed: *Adel Smith buffone – fuori dalla nostra nazione* (Adel Smith clown – out of our nation).

---

[4] The *Unione dei Musulmani d'Italia*, located in Ofena (in L'Aquila), seeks political representation for Muslims in the Italian Parliament.

The minority ethnic group that has provoked particular resentment among the *UltraS*, however, is that of white Eastern Europeans. The problems thrown up by illegal immigration to Italy, particularly from Romania and Albania, are strongly felt by the *UltraS*, due to the perceived correlation between this ethnic group and crime in Rome, along with the apparent inability of the authorities to deal with the problem. Given this context, one of the Boxer's typical statements that: 'you can look at the *curva* and understand your city' can be explained. These words are (potentially) profound. People in the Roman *curve* have, for many years, articulated what the Roman population, as a whole, thinks about things. The fear of crime, however, provokes prejudicial attitudes and seeks simplistic solutions.

It should be noted, though, that the perception of an ever-increasing influx of Romanians (and specifically Romanian gypsies) into Italy is supported by state-compiled data. Romanian immigrants have doubled in number in three years based on data compiled by the ISTAT annual survey on the presence of foreigners in Italy. Residents in Italy classified as 'immigrants' on 1 January 2007 numbered just short of three million, an increase of 10 per cent over the previous year. As the Italian population is shrinking due to a very low birth-rate, the increase in the number of foreigners entering Italy is even more significant. The Boxer is dismissive of the newly arrived citizens, considering Albanians and Romanians responsible for the unacceptable level of street prostitution in Rome. Although some will claim that this is a generalisation, and therefore not a helpful opinion, it is important to remember that the stereotype of the Romanian petty criminal in Italy is supported by official crime data. In 2007, Romanian citizens were involved in 14 episodes of serious violence in Italy, which resulted in 13 deaths. A 2008 report on crime published by the Ministry of the Interior argued that Romanian organised crime was gaining strength and visibility in Italy. The document reported that an astonishing 90 per cent of crimes committed in Milan involved Romanians, which placed them at the top of the 'crime ranking' of foreigners residing in Italy. In Rome, Romanian-related offences accounted for 31 per cent of recorded crimes.

One event that caused a national outcry – and a singular *UltraS* reaction – occurred in October 2007 when Giovanna Reggiani, the 47 year-old wife of a high ranking naval officer, was murdered at *Tor di Quinto* (an area in the north of Rome) while returning home from shopping. She was attacked by a 24-year-old Romanian, raped and thrown into a nearby street. She died shortly afterwards. Following this tragedy, the former Mayor of Rome, Walter Veltroni, rounded on the Romanian government, telling them, 'You cannot open the hatch to the entry of Romania into the EU'. He stressed that, before the arrival of Romanian immigrants, Rome was one of the safest cities in the world. The former Italian centre-left Prime Minister, Romano Prodi, called his Romanian equivalent to express the anger of the Italian government. Giorgio Napolitano, President of the Italian Republic, spoke of the act as one of 'barbaric aggression'. For the *Serie A* matches the following Sunday, the players of AS Roma and SS Lazio wore black armbands in respect for the deceased. Gianni Gumiero, the victim's husband, declared, 'I am desperate. If I was not a devoted citizen, I would do justice by myself.'

Some vigilantes did seek justice beyond the courts of law. A punitive blitz against Romanians in the Roman working-class area of *Tor Bella Monaca* followed. This high-density immigrant area was subjected to attacks by groups of young men clad in motorcycle helmets or balaclavas. They attacked four Romanians in a parking lot. The assailants were not 'unknown' to the Lazio *UltraS*. The four Romanians were hospitalised. Journalists of *La Repubblica* interviewed the local Italian population and asked their opinion about the attacks. Some answered that Romanians were lazy, indolent and regularly and publicly drunk. They made the public areas, be it park benches or public transport, potentially dangerous places for decent citizens.

Not all attacks on Romanians should be considered as provoked by vengeance. In August 2007, just two months before the death of Giovanna Reggiani, during the SS Lazio-Dynamo Bucharest Champions League fixture in the Olympic stadium, the Bucharest team and their fans were the subject of hostile chants. Among other insults, the Lazio *UltraS* chanted, 'Gypsies, go away'. Outside the stadium, five Romanian supporters were stabbed; none sustained life-threatening injuries.

Lacking a significant colonial history, Italy was not prepared for the massive immigration from Albania and the former Eastern Europe from 1990 onwards. The Italian election of April 2008 changed the government's policies concerning illegal immigration. Silvio Berlusconi and Walter Veltroni created two large parties, one of the centre-right and one of the centre-left, ostensibly to simplify and give stability to the Italian government. A dominant cause – for both opposing parties – was the worry over illegal immigrants – in particular those from Eastern Europe – and the associated crime they brought with them. The centre-left mayors in many cities, from Parma to Bologna, initiated voluntary groups to act as 'city angels' and provide security and public reassurance in parts of the city that were notorious for drug use and violence. Such citizens did not have the power to arrest or seek to engage directly with suspects, but their presence was considered an attempt to discourage criminality. But the election saw Berlusconi and his *Partito Delle Libertá* victorious based on a policy of 'zero tolerance' against crime, especially those committed by non-nationals. He also promised greater severity in custodial sentences.

The politics of fear played a large part in the outcome of the election. The roll-call of those allied with Berlusconi reminded observers of the electorate's recent right-wing tendencies. His campaign team included *Il Duce's* granddaughter, Alessandra Mussolini, and Roberto Calderoli, a senior member of the Northern League, who was once tipped to become Deputy Prime Minister. Minister of Reform in Berlusconi's previous government in 2006, at the height of controversy over the publication in a Danish newspaper of a cartoon considered blasphemous by Islam, Calderoli had taken his shirt off live on television to reveal the same cartoon printed on his vest. In articulating his opposition to the building of a mosque in Italy, the same man organised a 'Pig Day' in 2007 in an attempt to offend Muslim sentiments.

Another major significance of the election of 2008 saw small parties, which were characteristic of Italian politics since 1948, erased. The Communists, the Greens and the Socialists are no longer represented in Parliament, as they did not acquire the 4 per cent necessary to obtain representation. However, the anti-immigrant rhetoric of the Northern League allowed its representatives to gain 60 MPs and 25 Senators – a significant result for the far right.

Today, the neo-fascists, who since 1948 were represented in parliament by the MSI, have no elected representatives. But information gleaned from polling data at the election showed strong support for *La Destra* (the Right), a small party originating from the radical faction of AN in 2007, the MSFT and *Forza Nuova*, who all fell just short of the 4 per cent required for representation. For example, in the Lazio electoral region, *La Destra* polled 3.8 per cent of the vote. In the Lazio 1 electoral district, the percentage vote for the Chamber of Deputies was the highest in the region. Such data support two arguments. First, that the Lazio region is once again confirmed as the historical bulwark of neo-fascism, a fact also evident in the subsequent Mayoral election in Rome. Second, even if the majority of neo-fascist parties did not gain representatives, the ideas of neo-fascism are alive in this region (as in the whole of Italy). There is further proof of this in that Berlusconi offered Alessandra Mussolini, the leader of *Azione Sociale*, the elected deputy of the Campania region and a national board member of *the Popolo delle Libertá* (PdL), a place in his government.

The ideology of fascism still holds appeal in Italy. The extreme right is now more central to the Italian State than at any time since the demise of Mussolini. Italy has shifted to the right since Berlusconi's first electoral victory in 1994 (the left's 2006 victory is regarded as an anomaly). The Italian people's disillusionment with politics has ushered in the new far right anti-politicians, such as Umberto Bossi, Alessandra Mussolini and Roberto Calderoli. The people seek out variations of authoritarian populism. They are enraged by Italy's economic declines and find in the criminal acts of some immigrants a wider but vague opposition to globalisation. In April 2008, Gianni Alemanno defeated the Democratic Party's candidate Francesco Rutelli in the race to be Mayor of Rome. Alemanno was elected for his intransigent approach to the 'problem' of illegal immigration. Alemanno's 16-point 'pact for Rome' promised to 'immediately activate procedures for the expulsion of 20,000 nomads and immigrants who have broken the law in Rome'. He also promised to eliminate illegal Romanian gypsy camps. The mood and protest of the Romans against the failing management of illegal immigration in the capital, which had been expressed for at least a decade by the *UltraS* of Roma and Lazio (speaking in their 'piazza' freely and without the filters of political correctness), may now have found an institutional and political outlet. Football plays many roles, both obvious and subtle, recognised and unrecognised, and often highlights historical reasons for such discourses.

Roma captain Francesco Totti is surrounded by *UltraS*

12

THE ITALIAN MEDIA AND THE *UltraS*

The link between football and the media is very strong the world over and particularly relevant in Italy. The Italian media, for instance, have greatly contributed to the popularity of the game. The media have a tremendous influence on supplying publicity and in creating the need for advertisements. Equally, football influences the media: it is the reason why many Italian newspapers exist. However, not everything in this relationship is constructive; the saturation coverage of football by the Italian media has created some dysfunctions, for example, the triviality of many sport talk shows that in content resemble bar room 'debates'. Heated arguments (and even brawls) among sports journalists frequently occur on such shows. On some channels this kind of behaviour is promoted to improve audience ratings. One sports talk show, hosted by journalist Aldo Biscardi, exemplifies this trend.[1] The tone of the commentators and conversations has progressively worsened in recent years with intellectual debate now virtually absent as commentators adopt simplifications often bordering on vulgarity.

Three Italian newspapers give extensive coverage to sports (especially football): *La Gazzetta dello Sport*, *Il Corriere dello Sport* and *Tutto Sport*. Moreover, on Monday, all Italian newspapers focus on the Sunday football league results. Many national and satellite TV channels dedicate entire programmes to the games, their tactics, results analyses and trivia. One can also find regional and local television focusing on their local teams and fans; these broadcasts are often presented by hardcore football supporters. It is in this context that radio programmes such as the *Irriducibili's La Voce della Nord* (the Voice of the North) and the *Boys' Giallorossi si diventa* (Become a Yellow-Red) also emerged and became popular in the Lazio region in the late 1990s.[2]

The media have extraordinary power in today's society, not only to make things 'visible' but also to manipulate what people think. They provide definitions and explanations; present both problem and solutions. Over the years the *UltraS* have been portrayed in a very negative way by most media outlets, so how do the various groups feel about the press? Among the *Boys* and the *Irriducibili,* the media provoked strong sentiments, though these were not without ambiguity. Generally, the *UltraS* have a policy of avoiding media representatives. A spokesman for the *Boys* said, 'We avoid speaking to the press. The group has its hierarchy and needs to have only one public voice. The only one who has media contacts is the "big boss".' Giorgio (of the *Irriducibili)* never

---

[1] The television broadcast title *Il processo di Biscardi* (The Trial of Biscardi) is broadcasted every Monday after the Sunday football matches and since 2006 has been hosted by Channel 7 Gold.

[2] The broadcasts were and still are used to advertise the *UltraS pensiero* (i.e. values, opinions) about football but also about political and social issues.

fails to stress his and the group's dislike of the Italian media; for him the media have discriminated against the *UltraS* and specifically against the *Irriducibili*. Considering them hypocrites, Giorgio could not comprehend why they focused on the *Irriducibili's* display of the Celtic crosses (which he admitted were not only a Christian symbol but also a neo-fascist one) but at the same time failed to criticise footballers (such as Livorno striker Cristiano Lucarelli) for displaying tattoos of communist icons like Che Guevara, or groups that openly supported communism. For Giorgio communism has committed as many crimes against humanity as fascism.

The *UltraS* also consider the media as an ally of the forces of their repression, acting as a tool to serve the interests of the 'system'. They also believe that media money is the main reason why Italian football is lacking in values. This is a common feeling, not only among the *UltraS*, but also by a large part of the Italian hardcore supporters groups regardless of ideology. This attitude, of course, is a contradiction. On the one hand they claim at best to ignore the media, while on the other they use the media and its coverage of matches to get their messages publicised.

Three well-known Italian sport journalists were interviewed to find out their views on the *UltraS* phenomenon and the relationship between the *UltraS* and the media: Franco Arturi (deputy director of *La Gazzetta dello Sport*); Giuseppe Tassi (sports journalist and deputy director of *Quotidiano.net*); and Gabriele Marcotti (of *The Times* and the Rome-based *Il Corriere dello Sport*). From these interviews, two reactions emerged around the media-*UltraS* dynamics; one we might term 'alarmist and interventionist' (Arturi and Tassi), the other 'sceptical' (Marcotti).

Asked what he thought about the hardcore football supporters and more specifically the *UltraS* phenomenon, Arturi answered in these terms:

We should not be afraid of words such as 'terrorism' and 'terrorists'; for example when a person commits a crime, he/she is a criminal. In Italy we tend to be tolerant and to use meaningless formulae... we in fact seem not to criminalise... I argue that if anyone imposes fear in a *curva* and masterminds a strategy of terror then he is a terrorist. The *curve* enjoy territorial immunity;

the police do not enter these locations because they are strong-holds of these groups.

Tassi took a similar line and called the *UltraS* 'young thugs disguised as football supporters'. Arturi, more than Tassi and in agreement with most of the national press, identified the groups (often without any distinctions between them and 'ordinary' supporters) as 'outcasts' from Italian 'civil' society, requiring strong state intervention to control them. In addition and in defending his hypothesis of associating the *UltraS* with terrorism, Arturi argued that ordinary people in the *curve* were often not allowed to sit in their seats because they are in *UltraS* territory and the stewards or the police could do nothing about it. In his opinion, many Italian stadiums events resembled anarchy: there were no rules and the *curve* were dominated by groups who chanted horrible slogans and exposed disgusting symbols. This accusation shows little knowledge of the *curva* and the logic of the *UltraS*. There are indeed words spoken and chanted that many would not agree with; but as we have seen this behaviour has precedent and is logical for the *UltraS*. In the *curva* the principle of seniority is strictly respected by the groups, regardless of ideology. Such seniority highlights the supporter-team connection, and is considered by fans as a badge of loyalty. If an individual has occupied a seat for many years, then that seat, regardless of its number, is considered 'reserved'. This process does not follow the dominant reason of the wider society, but it is perfectly logical to both the 'ordinary' *curva* supporter and the *UltraS*.

Another source of contention between the *UltraS* and the media is the groups' involvement in social campaigns. During his years of lead-ership of the *Boys*, Paolo Zappavigna was the main promoter of these campaigns. The first such project was focused around agitation for a national referendum to abrogate Law No. 40 (2004), which regulated assisted procreation. The law banned testing on human embryos and prohibited more than three embryos from being implanted in a womb simultaneously. The law also forbade fertilisation by the use of semen or ova provided by persons other than the couple. Zappavigna collected signatures proposing a referendum to repeal the law. He did this in the *curva sud* and convinced groups therein to create a huge banner urging people to sign the referendum. These actions helped the protagonists reaching the necessary target signatures for a referendum to proceed. However, due to pressure from the Catholic Church, technical confusion around the issue and the effectiveness of the oppositional campaigners convincing people not to vote (only 25.9 per cent voted), the law remained unchanged. The second cause Zappavigna supported was that of the Argentinian Desaparecidos.[3] In doing so, he invited Estella Carlotto, a representative of the *Abuelas de Plaza de Mayo* (Grand-mothers of *Plaza de Mayo*) into the *curva sud* where he collected money for their cause.

The *Irriducibili,* vociferous in their campaigns against paedophilia and against drugs, also aimed to raise public awareness on other issues, as Giorgio outlined:

We help a dog refuge near Rome for mistreated and abandoned dogs; we got involved five years ago because they did not have funds and the refuge was about to be closed and the dogs killed. Now the place is a safe haven supported by *Laziali*. We also help an association in the fight against tumours in children; we donated a machine called the 'Retcam Photography System' to the Bambin Gesú hospital [in Rome] to help diagnose tumours and complex eye diseases. We also collaborate with the Italian Anti-Tumour Association. We are involved in the fight against vivisection; we have considered going to the university/drugs companies' labs and freeing the animals as they do in the UK. We are against vivi-section, especially when testing for cosmetics; we have also finan-cially supported people who lost their homes when their building collapsed in Rome [he did not remember the date during the

---

[3] The term literally means 'disappeared' in Spanish and is applied to people arrested ostensibly for political reasons by the police of the Argentine Junta of the 1970s and early 1980s. It is estimated that between 1976 and 1983, up to 30,000 dissidents went 'missing'. The *Abuelas de Plaza de Mayo* (Grandmothers of Plaza de Mayo) are mothers and grandmothers of the 'disappeared'. Since its foundation in 1977, the organisation has also been searching for over 200 'disappeared' children, some born in clandestine detention centres during the captivity of their mothers or 'disappeared' with their parents after being taken into custody by members of the police or the security forces.

interview]; on that occasion, Lazio supporters lost their lives. We are available for any socially worthwhile battle; we have a radio and a television programme that is open to any cause if we can help. Just to have one of us on the radio speaking about the initiative is helpful.

The response of *La Gazzetta dello Sport*'s journalist to such projects was dismissive; Arturi compared such gatherings to the Mafia and dismissed the campaigns as 'ordinary' good actions any citizen would undertake. He rejected the accusation from the groups that the media did not advertise their social campaigns but only their violence, and affirmed that when such groups were involved in social campaigns his newspaper informed the public. Nonetheless, he dismissed the campaigns as a publicity stunt conducted to 'buy' a sort of immunity for the groups' violent acts. Arturi maintained that the press had to fight the *UltraS*. Tassi spoke from a more moderate stance and tried to differentiate between supporters. He argued that the press had the right to denounce strongly the violence of mindless thugs like the *UltraS* and the degeneration of the *tifo,* but needed not to dismiss the good side of the hardcore supporters' movement. Tassi believed that their choreographies are an integral part of the footballing show and contributed to the 'good' atmosphere of the stadium.

Of course, there are two sides to every argument. Just as it would be incorrect and naive to consider the media as 'evil', as many *UltraS* and other hardcore supporters would argue, the Italian media coverage of events connected with these 21st-century 'folk devils' has often been poorly researched, populist and without foundation. As Todde argues, with some justification: 'they [the media] seldom write the real facts; they do not understand the *UltraS* phenomenon in its entirety and most of all are superficial and lazy in researching and understanding.'

The reporting of two events helps illustrate the faults in Italian press coverage of the *UltraS*. The first episode occurred at the final game of the 2003–04 *Serie A* season between AS Roma and SS Lazio. The match saw the normal pre-match mingling, accusations and boasting between the rival fan groups, augmented by mutual chants of abuse and occasional missile throwing in the stadium. What was unprecedented was the mass confrontation between the forces of the law, clad in their riot gear, and the momentarily united ranks of AS Roma and SS Lazio supporters some 60 minutes later. This Roman fan alliance, which Arturi defined as 'unnatural', was unique in terms of the numbers and anger involved but not unusual to the participants. The uniqueness originated from the nature of the event. The dynamics around this fixture were bizarre. In the second half, a rumour circulated in both *curve* that, in the pre-match mêlée between fans and police outside the stadium, a police vehicle had struck and killed a young boy. This rumour had the effect of transforming the vociferous antagonism between both sets of supporters and the police into open conflict. The police subsequently faced attacks from angry *UltraS* throughout the stadium. The police responded with baton charges.

The two teams, clearly shocked by what was happening on the terraces, stopped playing shortly after the beginning of the second half when smoke bombs were let off, making it difficult to see events on the pitch. In the hiatus, three men in their 30s – AS Roma *UltraS* – ran onto the pitch. One put his arm on AS Roma captain Francesco Totti's shoulder and demanded that he lead the players off the pitch (thereby suspending the match) both out of respect for the dead boy and in a show of protest against the supposed police brutality. The next 20 minutes made for global debate. Totti discussed matters with SS Lazio's Serbian-born enforcer, Sinisa Mihajlovic. The referee encouraged the two captains to continue the match. Meanwhile the public address system broadcasted denials that a child had been killed. In the chaos, Totti spoke to Roma coach, Fabio Capello. He is recorded as saying, 'If we play on now… they'll kill us'. The majority of the players wanted to stop the game. However, a representative of the *Prefetto di Roma* (the highest provincial authority of public security) then appeared on the pitch demanding the referee and players restart the game in the interests of public order. The referee then took a call on a mobile phone from Adriano Galliani, the President of the Italian League. After a short conversation, the game was abandoned. The police were powerless in this football context. By the end of the night, 15 fans and 60 police were reported to have sustained injuries and some 36 fans had been arrested.

The abandonment of the match brought global notoriety to the city of Rome and Italian football. Several Italian newspapers ran headlines the day after, which compared the *UltraS* to the Mafia. The following article published by the Italian magazine *Panorama* reported the *tifosi* invasion in the following impressionistic fashion:

> They approached Totti threateningly and spoke agitatedly to the captain. Sky's [Murdoch's television channel] camera operators were sent away as if they were spying (which is an unacceptable violation of the right of information). The players' faces are perturbed and frightened; it is not possible to hear it but the scene suggests that they have been threatened.

The three *UltraS*, Stefano Carriero, Roberto Maria Morelli and Stefano Sordini, who had got onto the pitch from the terraces, were arrested as they left it. Days later, the Roman magistrate Giorgio Maria Rossi released the three from police custody arguing that they had not threatened Totti. The supporters had entered the pitch to inform him of the (false) death of the boy and asked him to abandon the game so that fans could go home and stop the angry reprisals against the police. While entering the field of play is not permitted under the regulations of the Italian Football Federation, the circumstances at the Olimpico did not belong to the realm of normality. The *UltraS* had shown the nation watching TV on a Sunday evening that in some situations they had enormous power, but at the same time they strongly denied the media's theory that they had organised the episode to show it off. Francesca (of the *Boys*) dismissed the allegations of a plot as silly, arguing that she would have know if they were planning anything and in that case would not have gone to the game. The Boxer instead accused the media in this occasion of being *infami* (awful):

> They just wrote what they wanted without even asking us what we thought and our version of the story. They think if the *Irriducibili* are involved there is surely something 'dark' behind it. Almost every journalist behaves in the same way; when we plan a nice show in the *curva* with banners and choreographies, either

they will not cover it or will minimise our work; if instead there are problems at the stadium, it is our fault, we are the mindless thugs, the fascists, the delusional; I say instead they are the scum.

A few years later, in 2007, an article in *La Repubblica* contained an epilogue to the episode:

The magistrates' beliefs after nearly three years of investigations were crucial to the fate of the seven Roman fans suspected. All the serious criminal charges (among these conspiracy to violence and incitement to disobey the laws of the State) were dropped, while they still faced minor charges of violations of the law on the safety of the stadiums and creation of panic, which will carry only a small fine.

In this instance the press had clearly reported the episode incorrectly, and without establishing the facts of the matter. It was a similar situation when reports emerged about incidents before the first match of the 2008–09 season between AS Roma and Napoli. Media reports stated that 1,500 Napoli fans had attacked a train in Naples, forcing 300 passengers to get off, attacking four guards, looting supplies and damaging the train. On arrival at the Roma Termini station, they were said to have thrown smoke bombs and tear gas. Trenitalia (the Italian State railway company) estimated the damage at E500,000. Newspaper headlines were savage: 'Naples *UltraS*, Owners of the Railway', '*UltraS* – Out of their Minds', 'Trains and Stations Destroyed'.

One respected Italian journalist Oliviero Beha reported the episode on his popular blog. He included an account of the incident by German journalist and chief editor of *Ballesterer FM Radio*, Reinhard Krennhuber, and his colleague Jacob Rosenberg, who had travelled to Rome for the match on the train with the Napoli fans. His report differed wildly from those in the Italian national press:

Firstly, it is incorrect to say that the Napoli fans threatened and pushed 300 passengers to get off the train; we also did not see any train controllers attacked. The train should have left at 9.24 a.m.

but after 11 a.m. *Trenitalia* representatives came aboard to advise the passengers to leave the train and take another one. We left at 12.30 p.m. with the train completely full. When we arrived, the match had already started, in fact they had already played 52 minutes; it is a shame the fans had paid for their train and stadium tickets. The frustrated fans started to demolish the toilets but I am unsure how such damage reached E500,000 ... I cannot imagine why a person should loot a train; what is there so important to loot? I also find it strange to hear the news about the tear gas at Termini.

Krennhuber was also asked if he had been scared at all during the journey to Rome:

We were not scared by the Napoli fans, they did not attack the police in the train station nor at the stadium, because they knew what was at stake... The allegations that the incidents were planned and orchestrated by the fans or even by the *Camorra* (organised crime organisation of Naples) seem totally absurd.

Krennhuber concluded:

In the future, I will believe even less Italian media reports about clashes involving fans. There is an enormous discrepancy between what we experienced that day and what the media reported. All that day we did not meet a fellow journalist. The media had not done any research on the spot; they are collecting information from the local authorities. In addition, in their coverage the fans' version is not taken into account or only minimally. Rai Uno [the main television channel of the Italian state broadcaster] was the only broadcaster to permit the fans and ordinary people to speak, instead of just politicians and representatives of various authorities. The versions of the facts from the ordinary people and the fans are similar to ours.

In his reaction to the incident, Krennhuber portrayed the Italian media as too lazy to find out what really occurred and too reliant on the 'spin' of authority. It is difficult not to notice that Krennhuber's argument is similar to many *UltraS* opinions about the media. While it is tempting to think of the national newspapers' coverage of the incident as lazy, it might be much worse than that. Journalists have easy access to the versions of events given by individuals or institutions in positions of power and as such become the 'primary definers' of crucial issues because they have privileged access to information out of the sight of the public. Deviant actions and their coverage are often shaped around their perspectives of the 'primary definers'. The primary definers interpret the event creating an interpretation discursively powerful and extremely difficult to challenge. So whether they got it wrong through laziness, or simply wanted to use the news to back up pre-conceived opinions of the *UltraS*, once they had their angle they stuck to it.

But in analysing the media in this way it is important not to characterise them all as passive recipients. Once the journalists receive the primary definers' versions, they act to select and shape these viewpoints; as a result, they are not merely passive tools in the hands of the powerful. Events are 'coded' into each paper's own mode of address and into its public idiom; the media often adapt stories by using versions of reality that fit into the common language used by the 'average Joe', giving further strength to discourses characterised by popular force and resonance and 'naturalising' these views for the audience. Moreover, both examples mentioned earlier underline the role of the Italian media as agents of moral resentment. The dynamic between the media and the *UltraS* (and more widely the whole of the hardcore football fans), however, cannot be completely understood using just this hypotheses; it is complex and multi-dimensional. An excess of media coverage is also another issue in this highly complex media-*UltraS* relationship; dense coverage is a dysfunction that may become dangerous. The excess focuses mainly, but not exclusively, on negative actions, real or perceived. This trend appears to be rooted in two factors; the first is economic, namely the need to sell news. The other is specific to the *UltraS* identity, notably their oppositional stance.

Two different opinions on the amount of coverage given to the *UltraS* emerged from the interviews with the Italian sports journalists.

From one side, Arturi did not mention any problems related to an excess of coverage even if he rightly underlined the difference in quality of the coverage according to the skills of the journalist:

> The press – I would add the 'good' press, because as always in life there are the average journalists, good journalists and bad journalists – is one of the pillars that underpin a democratic country, these 'Mafiosi' see the police and the media as an obstacle to their criminal business. If the press intervene strongly it is due to living in a state of emergency.

The third journalist, Gabriele Marcotti, though, held a different view:

> Violent acts from hardcore fans receive less coverage in the UK media than in Italy. For example, two years ago, Chelsea and Tottenham fans fought and 13 Tottenham fans were hurt and ended up in hospital; if you search, you will find only brief reports on the incident. I do not remember any Italian match ending with 13 fans wounded but I imagine that if this episode had occurred in Italy, the press would have covered the event for ages. If we want to be cynical we could say that broadcasting channels such as BBC and Sky do not cover the phenomenon so much to avoid damaging football as a product and business. We can also say that they do not want to encourage an emulation process. When the Italian inspector of police – Raciti[4] – tragically died, the Italian TV channels showed the episode millions of times; I am not sure how necessary this obsessive coverage is; can this instead have an opposite effect?

While Arturi's statement argued for the supposed 'emergency' situation that justifies an excess of media coverage, Marcotti pointed out an

---

[4] Filippo Raciti was an Italian police officer who died in violence between Calcio Catania supporters and police officers in February 2007. A week before his death, Raciti gave evidence at the trial of a football hooligan, who was then freed by the local magistrate. According to one of his colleagues, the hooligan laughed in his face as he left the court. Raciti died after the end of the local derby between Catania and Palermo, due to liver damage caused when he was hit by a blunt object (see page 4).

'obsessive' coverage of negative episodes involving not only *UltraS* but also any hardcore football fans gives their actions the 'oxygen of publicity'. The first, apparent, justification of the Italian media coverage of the *UltraS* phenomenon might be best explained by the statement 'bad news is good news'. Fights between rival fans are more likely to be reported than the *UltraS* campaigns against paedophilia, for example. A more articulate explanation might be that, according to some sociologists, the pleasure that audiences draw from crime stories comes from the eternal battle between good and evil. Such stories ideally contain, as protagonists, heroes (the state, the police and the media) and villains (the 'mindless' football thugs). This representation is a constant feature of news about crime. The media increase the tension/drama between the two forces, which is 'good' news but hardly 'fair' coverage.

The other possible explanation focuses on the *UltraS* having a dual vested interest, not only as hardcore football fans but also as 'genuine' neo-fascist extra-parliamentary groups, motivated by a logic of 'action' and opposition against the Italian authorities. The militant nature of the *UltraS* encourages the media to represent any aspect of their protest as dangerous. Their symbolism, ideology and warrior/rebellion spirit does not provoke inquiry but seems only to help the media in portraying them as a threat to the social order. Commenting on the *UltraS*, Arturi considered them, 'more than terrorism, this is Mafia! Within the stadium, there are Mafiosi attitudes. The contempt shown for journalists can only be understood in this context.' Therefore, groups of militants, such as the *UltraS*, increase the media discourses of fear and terror, and serve to justify a strong repression that at times involves not only the *UltraS* but also 'ordinary' supporters. This type of coverage, on the other hand, can strengthen the very phenomenon, especially considering the nature of *communitas* of the *UltraS* where there is a strong group identification based on 'a shared ordeal'. As Marco (of the *Boys*) argues:

We tend to defend the young guys of 17 or 18 from the control and labelling of the state; you must understand that being an *UltraS* and being a neo-fascist can be devastating for the future of these guys. In Italy, there is not a democracy; we are guarded and herded by the police. We do not expose these youngsters to this danger even if we fight; the *direttivo* is in the first row and the young follow. We do not want to expose them – when they will have the maturity they will choose. We do not want to let them become labelled, otherwise they will be discriminated against like many of us are.

The risk of reinforcing their discourses of persecution and discrimination is real.

A study of Italian neo-fascist militants, published in 2006, stressed that the crucial element that motivated the participants to join the 'action', was the discrimination suffered by those who embraced this ideology. Similar to the *UltraS,* the young participants suffered discrimination during their adolescence or early adulthood at high school and university. The study explained that such discrimination did not discourage them from identifying themselves in public as fascist. In fact, it had the opposite effect, reinforcing such identification. In the past, these perceptions have brought the *UltraS* to act together against oppressive institutions. This type of coverage might reinforce the claims of marginalisation made by the *UltraS,* and supports their vision of being the righteous victims of persecution perpetrated by a system-wide conspiracy. The sense of 'being against' creates tension, anger and hate that could develop into new forms of attack against the State. At the same time, this type of coverage also contributes to promoting the underdog and helps recruitment in the *curve.*

It seems most likely that current Italian media coverage does nothing but stoke the fires of opposition and that a more balanced use of media coverage is a strategy that would help contain the *UltraS* violence. This opinion is backed up by experience in Austria, for example, where an experiment to give less publicity to football violence was met with a decrease in activity. Perhaps the British attitude towards this phenomenon, which is similar to that experiment and which the journalist Gabriele Marcotti supports, could be exported to Italy.

Violence between opposing fans is common, but confrontations with the police can often have far more serious consequences

13

THE ENEMY

Le squadre ferme nel centrocampo, sulle gradinate scoppia l'inferno,
le squadre ferme nel centrocampo, sulle gradinate scoppia l'inferno.

[The teams stop at the centre of the pitch, on the terraces there is hell].

*FRA**NA** LA CURVA, FRA**NA** SULLA POLIZIA ITALIA**NA**,*
*FRA**NA** LA CURVA FRA**NA** SU QUEI FIGLI DI PUTTA**NA***
[The terrace collapses on the Italian Police, the terrace collapses
on those sons of bitches]

*Volano calci, pugni e spint**oni**, macchie di sangue sugli strisci**oni**!*
*Volano calci,pugni e spint**oni**,macchie di sangue sugli strisci**oni**!*
[Kicks, punches, shoves fly; bloodstains on the banners!]

*FRA**NA** LA CURVA FRA**NA** SULLA POLIZIA ITALIA**NA**,*
*FRA**NA** LA CURVA FRA**NA** SU QUEI FIGLI DI PUTTA**NA**.*

*Se deve esserci violenza che violenza, **sia**, ma che sia contro la*
*POLI**ZIA**!*
*Se deve esserci violenza che violenza, **sia** ma che sia contro la*
*POLI**ZIA**!*
[If there must be violence, OK, but against the Police].

*FRA**NA** LA CURVA FRA**NA** SULLA POLIZIA ITALIA**NA**,*
*FRA**NA** LA CURVA FRA**NA** SU QUEI FIGLI DI PUTTA**NA**.*

DIGOS – BOIA
DIGOS – BOIA
DIGOS-DIGOS-DIGOS – BOIA-BOIA-BOIA
[DIGOS – SHIT]

This song, sung by *Gli Hobbit* – one of the best-known Italian neo-fascist rock bands – is popular among the *UltraS*. The song's words depict their level of anger against the Italian police. Giorgio (of the *Irriducibili*) articulates this rage:

Football is based on business and people like us have become trouble. They have tried to sterilise the environment; they try to make the experience of watching a football match like going to the cinema. We live with passion, feelings, with ideals – this is our way of watching football. We are not against the police who punish those who throw bottles on the pitch or who create violence but this has to be proven; justice cannot be discretionary. People get banning orders without being proven guilty.

The Italian police forces have, for decades, found themselves as the bulwark against football-related disorders. They have paid a high price both in terms of resources and the deployment of manpower. In this spiral of violence, involving reactions and counter-reactions, the police have increasingly become the focus of the anger of the *UltraS*. In return, the police have sought to enact increasingly repressive legislation created to combat their attackers. Over a five-year period (2003–2008), 1114 incidents involving fans and police were documented, equating to 222 per year. Resulting from these incidents, 5388 injuries were recorded (of which 574 were to police officers); 6000 people were arrested and 2000 were charged.[1]

Following the May 1985 Heysel stadium tragedy, when 39 people were crushed to death before the European Cup Final between Liverpool and Juventus, a permanent multi-disciplinary commission was established by the Italian Ministry of Interior. The commission was composed of the Chief of Police, the President of the Italian National Olympic Committee (CONI), the Director-General of National Professional League, the Secretary General of the Federation Football (FIGC) and a representative of the *Serie C* league. This commission was a crisis unit established to address football fan violence. The Italian Parliament had to take into account the post-Heysel framework of pan-European policing cooperation. Consequently, on 1 November 1985, the Convention on Violence and Disorders of Spectators at Sporting Events came into force.[2] In 1988 (again at the Ministry of the Interior), a joint

---

[1] Source: Il Sole24.com, *Diritto e società*. http://professionisti24.ilsole24ore.com/art/AreaProfessionisti/Diritto/DIR_VIOLENZA%20STADI.shtml?uuid=822462e6-b75d-11db-ae4c-00000e251029&type=Libero. Readers are also directed to the following texts: D.Mariottini (2004). *Ultraviolenza, Storie di sangue del tifo Italiano*. Torino: Bradipolibri. http://osservatoriosport.interno.com/dati.html

[2] The first pan-European awareness about the cross-border dimension of football violence goes back to the Council of Europe's 1984 *Resolution on Violence Associated with Spectator Sport*. In August 1985, the *European Convention on Spectator Violence and Misbehaviour at Sports Events and in Particular at Football*

commission was formed – with the participation of the Ministry of Tourism and the FIGC – for the preparation of legislative proposals against violence related to sporting events. It is in these contexts that later laws against the *UltraS* (and other neo-fascist groups in the Italian *curve*) should be understood.

In June 2006, the Ministry of the Interior presented an intelligence document compiled by the *Squadre Tifoserie* (Fan Units) of the DIGOS. According to this report, of Italy's 487 football supporters' clubs, comprising some 80,300 supporters, nearly half – 245 – expressed a political orientation (71 to the extreme right, 61 to the moderate right, 34 to the extreme left, and 87 to the moderate left). Some extreme ideological factions were recognised in the document as having been involved in ideological propaganda, specifically the distribution of fanzines with a political content. The report also recognised the presence of the *UltraS* at political events, as well as their participation in criminal activities with no apparent link to sports events. Political protest was enshrined in the very existence of the Italian state, and for decades some of this opposition was criminal. Football was no exception to oppositional cultures or criminal behaviour. What was exceptional was the realisation that the *UltraS* had provoked the Italian state to hire people for the specific purpose of stopping them.

These Fan Units sought to develop intelligence gathering that focused on links between extreme ideologies and football fans. The Fan Units were in weekly contact with representatives of official fan clubs and constantly monitored supporters. The police were often covert in their methods as they collected and collated information and intelligence on the more secretive *UltraS*. At times they sought assistants from inside such gatherings. The figure of the informer in police and security services was ostensibly regulated by criminal law, which aimed to balance the needs for discretion (i.e. judges could not oblige police to reveal the names of their informants) and transparency. In the latter pursuit, the legal system could not use the information in a court of law if the

---

Matches followed. Also from the European Union came the April 1996 *Guidelines for Preventing and Restraining Disorder Connected with Football Matches*, followed by *The European Parliament's Resolution on Hooliganism and the Free Movement of Football Supporters*.

informants were not available to be examined as witnesses. The ability to pay such informants was permitted by law, and police could use such monies according to their organisational practices. The police have never revealed the extent of the use of informers against the *UltraS*.

The first law dedicated to confront football violence was introduced in December 1989 and became known as Law No. 401. The legislation was, in part, a response to an event that occurred earlier that year, when fan Antonio De Falchi died from cardiac arrest following an attack by Milan hardcore football supporters during the Milan-Rome fixture. The first part of the law, however, focused on tackling illegal betting on football matches. The second part aimed to prevent and suppress violence around sporting competitions. Over the years the law has been frequently modified in an attempt to make it more applicable and rigorous. Unfortunately such changes have complicated matters; modifications have invariably been the products of urgent decrees – laws issued by the government and changed at a later date, usually with modifications by parliament. Such *ad hoc* intervention has meant that the law is complicated and therefore difficult to implement. As the hardcore football supporter phenomenon changed, so did the law.

The *UltraS* movement emerged at the beginning of the 1990s. During this period, racist and anti-Semitic attitudes became evident in the Italian *curve*. The government and parliament, with good reason, responded by passing measures attempting to repress such objectionable opinions. Law No. 401, aimed specifically at repressing the neo-fascist *UltraS,* was modified in June 1993 to contain specific criteria for punishing expressions of racial, religious and ethnic discrimination. This law also permitted the arrest of individuals attempting to bring emblems or symbols of associations into the sports arenas, as well as organisations, movements or groups having as their aim the incitement of racial hate and discrimination. This crime was punishable by arrest and between three months to one year in custody if convicted – a penalty that increases proportionally with the severity of the offence. However, the legislation and its enforcement did not deter all of those it was designed for.

Another important piece of legislation in the anti-*UltraS* armoury appeared in 1995, when Law No. 45 introduced the DASPO (Dirieto di Accedere alle manifestazioni SPOrtive). Power to apply the DASPO

– prohibition of access to places where sports events take place – was given to the *Questore* (local Police Chief); a DASPO, which lasted for one year, could be imposed on anyone convicted of crimes and, more controversially, on those not arrested or convicted in a court of law but considered instrumental in episodes of violence.[3] In reality, the DASPO could be imposed by the *Questore* irrespective of convictions or complaints against the person. The *Questore* could, therefore, demand that a person provide – in writing – the address of the place where they may be found during sports events. The *Questore* could then require the person to appear at a police station once or more during a specified period on the day of the event. The DASPO could also be applied to minors aged between 14 and 18 years who were considered a threat to public order and safety. Violation of the DASPO and non-attendance at designated 'sign on' police stations might result in a custodial sentence lasting between one and three years, or a fine ranging from E10,000 to E40,000. Arrest is also permitted in the case of breach of the terms of the DASPO. Pending trial, the courts could ban access to the places where sports events were held. The DASPO was strongly opposed both by the *UltraS* and by the entire hardcore football supporters' movement.

In 2001, Law No. 401 was modified again following the death of a Messina fan who was killed when struck by an incendiary thrown by rival fans during a match with Catania. Among the most important elements of this change was an increase in DASPO timescales and duties. Those subjected to a DASPO were now to appear at a specified police station on one or more occasions at pre-established times. The potential length of the DASPO was also increased from one to three years (or up to eight years if there were exceptional circumstances). Guilt was assumed and redress was very difficult and only available through the courts. If this happened, judges were given power to order the perpetrator to undertake socially useful activities during matches.

---

[3] According to the interpretation of the law, sporting events were defined as any competition taking place promoted by sports federations and the institutions and organisations recognised by the Italian National Olympic Committee (CONI). The measure may also be applied for misbehaviour around sporting events taking place abroad in other EU member states.

When asked about the legal nature of the DASPO and its efficacy, Dr Domenico Mazzilli, President of the National Observatory on Sport Events of the Italian Ministry of the Interior (ONMS) replied:

> The DASPO is an 'atypical' prevention measure applicable to a specific type of fans judged dangerous in terms of public security. The DASPO can also be issued for sports events taking place abroad and it can also be imposed by authorities of other Member States of the European Union for sports events taking place in Italy. The constant application of DASPO in recent years has allowed the State to ban from the stadium dangerous individuals who had committed violations of the Italian laws that safeguard public security at sports events. At this moment, 4185 DASPOs have been issued and the measure has successfully tackled violence at football matches.

Law No. 401 was modified yet again in February of 2003, with the introduction of the controversial *arresto differito* (deferred arrest). This enabled the detention of those suspected of involvement in football related violence up to 36 hours after the event (based on video-photographic evidence or other, never defined 'objective elements'). It also prohibited fans from bringing smoke bombs and petards (another type of incendiary that contains gunpowder) into the stadia. Transgression was punishable with arrest, and if found guilty, custodial sentences ranging from three to 18 months and fines of up to E500. Other amendments permitted the police to act as both judge and jury; for example, the police had the power to prevent individuals from entering the stadium if the local *Questore* considered them dangerous based on the elusive concept of 'intelligence.'

Five days after the February 2007 death of police inspector Filippo Raciti (following the violence instigated by *UltraS* against the police at the end of a Catania-Palermo match – *see* page 4), the Italian government issued a number of swingeing new legal measures against the *UltraS*. Law No. 41 demanded that football matches scheduled for stadia that had not been structurally updated (following terms laid down in 2003) would henceforth take place 'in the absence of spectators'. This decision was to be made by the *Prefetto* (the Chair of the Provincial Committee for Order and Public Security) following the recommendations of the National Observatory on Sport Events. The law also became more punitive for fans caught in the stadium or in nearby parking or transport areas with petards, batons and blunt objects. Those arrested and convicted faced imprisonment ranging from one to four years; the punishment increased if the crime delayed the scheduled start or caused the cancellation of the match. The punishment would be increased if any such act caused personal injury. Furthermore, the law limited the number of tickets any single fan could purchase to four and maintained the prohibition on football clubs selling blocks of tickets to visiting fans. On the back of every matchday ticket was now a message stressing the obligation for the buyer 'to respect the rules of the stadium' as an essential pre-condition for entry. Fans were also required to show a valid identity card (checked by stewards at the stadium entrance) as part of the admission criteria. Fines ranging from E5000 to E20,000 could be imposed upon stewards who failed to implement the law. The clubs were charged with the responsibility of issuing and selling tickets individually numbered and matched to a seat. The sale of tickets on the day of the match was prohibited. Breach of this law was punishable with fines ranging from E2500 to E10,000. The law also forbade clubs to give discounted tickets or any other benefits to fans convicted of football-related offences; the penalty was a fine issued by the *Prefetto* ranging from E50,000 to E200,000.

Raciti's death, an incident shown repeatedly on Italian national television in the days following the incident, brought about radical new thinking from the government. They had decided that his death was directly linked to the difficulty of managing sports facilities, almost all of which (but not the Olimpico in Rome) were owned by local authorities and entrusted to clubs for football matches. This situation had led to problems in the application of safety procedures, notably due to uncertainty about who was to bear the expenses of implementing structural changes and the wages of safety personnel. The government decided that control of behaviour in the stadia was to be privatised. The management of order and public security inside the stadia became the obligation of the football clubs, under the supervision of the Italian security services,

Gruppo Operativo di Sicurezza (GOS), and the *Questore*. As of February 2008, all stadia with more than 7500 seats were required to have at least one steward for every 250 spectators, as well as a coordinator for every 20 stewards. Failure to comply with these regulations brought the threat of closure. Stewards were given training and new status as 'public officers', and were required to search fans as they entered the stadium. Assaults on them were to be regarded as assaults on police officers. Dr Mazzilli explained the government's thinking on the new role of stewards:

> Via the introduction of the stewards – they have started to operate since 1 March 2008 – in the Italian football stadia, the police forces are deployed outside the stadium. It is not the responsibility of the police to be in the *curve*, the stewards have the function of hospitality, management and control of fans, obviously in collaboration with the police forces.

Other procedures were promoted to change the relationships of fans with clubs and players. The *tessera del tifoso* (fan membership card), launched by the ONMS (together with CONI, FIGC and the Italian Football League), began in March 2008. Promoted as providing a number of benefits for subscribers, the card gave priority for purchasing tickets, provided dedicated entry gates, and created a category of 'official' and 'loyal' supporters. Individuals subjected to DASPO were excluded from any official relationship with the clubs.

The effects of these new laws were immediate, explosive and, in a number of ways, unexpected. Many of them were difficult to implement, and they increased the sense of victimisation of the 'ordinary' fans and, most importantly, the neo-fascist groups. The complexity of the laws soon fitted into what is known in Italian political circles as the 'legislative jungle', a matter that became a big issue during the 2008 electoral campaign. But in essence they simply added to the already well-known inefficiency of the Italian justice system. In the entire Italian legal system in 2007, there were no fewer than 10 million legal cases pending (four million civil and six million criminal); a further 700,000 final sentences were still not completed. It also became clear that the justice system was heavily in debt, and its financial resources were inadequate to meet the needs of state prosecutors. The total debt of the Ministry of Justice amounted to E250 million. Public trust in the judicial system completely collapsed.

The situation was reflected in football circles in 2006 when four members of the *Irriducibili* were arrested. They were detained in prison for eight months, and were awaiting trial for financial impropriety involving the proposed sale of SS Lazio. In February 2007 the matter was discussed in parliament. A number of MPs were unhappy that they had been held for so long without trial. One MP, Sergio D'Elia (Secretary of the MPs' Chamber and an MP for the Radical Party with an extreme left past) explained his concerns:

> This morning [1 February 2007] I spoke with the *Irriducibili* leaders for the fourth time in 45 days. I found them nervous and anxious due to their experience. Their prison is a sort of 'advance' for a crime eventually committed: they have been not even been called in for process ... This case of the four Lazio fans is an 'ordinary' example of the Italian administration of justice, or perhaps non-administration. A citizen has the right to know the sentence they face. To wait four years for a judgment would be unfair because the sentence has to be contemporary with the facts [to be judged] or it is an injustice. This state has 40 per cent of prisoners awaiting trial... the guys are not saints, they have made mistakes and sometimes used violence, but they are not extortionists... What I want to emphasise is that they have already been found guilty in the press and in public opinion – and for this there will not be any compensation for the damages suffered; the only proper place to determine whether or not they are guilty should be the court. The only compensation possible is that, if convicted, the length of justice should be made as short as possible.

Despite these discussions, the accused were still in prison in 2009, three years later, awaiting trial. It is an extraordinary and revealing irony that their accuser, Lazio president Claudio Lotito, had been tried, found guilty, sentenced to prison for two years and fined E65,000 for the same 'supposed' crime of speculative dealing related to the club in 2005.

The Ministry of the Interior is the body responsible for security arrangements at sports stadia in Italy. Its job is to protect the freedoms and rights of citizens, the maintenance of public order and the protection and preservation of property. Further duties involve enforcing compliance with laws and regulations (be they State, regional, provincial or municipal) and the provision of emergency assistance in case of disasters and accidents. The Minister coordinates – with the assistance of the provincial public security – the activities of the Italian police forces. He is assisted in this by an advisory body of the National Committee of Order and Public Safety. Crucial to this task in each province are the titled offices of the *Prefetto* and the *Questore*. The *Prefetto* is responsible for order and public security. The *Questore* has the task of technical management, accountability and coordination of public order and public safety. To ensure security at football stadia, the Italian State commits on average 10,500 law enforcement personnel to the task. Of these 6300 are drawn from territorial forces (local police in whose area the stadium is situated). An additional 700 are drawn from special police forces (transport police, dog units), and 3500 are from specialist reinforcement units, of which some 66 per cent belong to the anti-riot units of the State Police and 34 per cent to the *carabinieri*. To enforce the raft of new anti-hooligan laws of the past 20 years, the Ministry has set up a number of representative bodies. The most important, *l'Osservatorio Nazionale Sulle Manifestazioni* (National Observatory on Sport Events or ONMS), was established in 1999 and institutionalised by law in 2005. Its considerable powers were further increased via the 2007 legislation and included the implementation and specialist training of stewards at stadia. It also introduced a threat level classification for each game based on specific indicators: the characteristics and structural requirements of the stadia, profiles of the fans (based on historical precedence, previous conflicts and recent behaviours), the type of game, the consequences of the result, and the possible link to other events. The ONMS then make suggestions to the provincial public security authorities that implement them.

The ONMS is in turn supported by the *Centro Nazionale di Informazione sulle Manifestazioni Sportive* (National Centre for Information on Sports Events or CNMS). The CNMS has been operating since 2002, collecting, analysing and processing data on football spectator violence. It is also the national contact point for the exchange of both domestic and international information around the policing of football. The establishment of CNMS was in response to the Council of Europe's concerns over security around international football. One strong recommendation was that national governments establish national football intelligence centres. The consequence of such powers and policing personnel brought an end to spectating as it had been known for decades. The ONMS established criteria and procedures to regulate banners and other material held by fans in the stadia. These include materials for creating choreography, such as drums, percussion instruments and other means of disseminating sound. The ONMS regulations permitted only flags bearing the colours of the club teams or those of countries represented on the pitch in international games. Banners that displayed a content which manifested racial discrimination, violent messages, or anything considered to be of an 'offensive nature' were banned. Also banned were megaphones, flags that might impair other fans' sight of the pitch, and all material not authorised in advance by the police.

The match-going experience changed even on entering the stadium. By 2007, all football clubs were required to provide stewards holding metal detectors at the stadium entrances. Furthermore, computerised electronic technology was required to check all admission tickets. The installation of CCTV cameras externally and inside any sport facility or stadium capable of holding more than 10,000 spectators was also a prerequisite for obtaining a ground licence.

The route taken to this state of affairs was part of the action/reaction that so typified legislation pertaining to football-related disorder. It is also important to note that in any evaluation of the Italian public order policing system, confusion is the first and most challenging barrier to overcome. The presence of five national police forces[4] on top of local/

---

[4] The central command for policing functions lies with the office of *Presidente del Consiglio* (i.e. the Prime Minister) who delegates to the Minister of the Interior in which the *Dipartimento della Pubblica Sicurezza* (Department of Public Security) is located. The *Capo della Polizia* (Chief of Police) is the head of the state police (a role created during the fascist era). The Chief of Police is also the *Direttore Generale della Pubblica Sicurezza* (Director General of Public Security) and co-ordinates the

municipal police forces makes for great difficulty in applying theoretical models to real-life situations. Nevertheless, it is safe to conclude that the model that best fits the Italian policing situation is a 'military-bureaucratic' model. All policing entities in Italy are organised using a military style hierarchical structure where little is left to discretion and strict rules of engagement apply. In this type of organisation, much is left to internal inquiries and very little to external accountability. The most important form of external accountability is provided by the Italian magistrates, who intervene when disciplinary procedures are required, but even then there is a perception that the attitude taken is: 'When faced with a decision, find a rule; when a rule cannot be found, make a rule'.

Witnessing the police forces in action against the *UltraS* clearly illustrates Italian police policy. The first is that physical force (at times excessive) is justified because it guarantees 'peace' in the wider community. The moral panic against the *UltraS* also justifies the use of physical force; being 'evil' means a police 'beating' is legitimate or at least unquestioned. In the case of the *UltraS*, the strategy used to counter them focuses on total control as well as prevention (which, while valued, is used less than repression). Such procedures provoke reactions from those on the receiving end. Marco articulated the feelings of hate and rage among the *Boys* towards the police:

… when we see them attack our friends, or when they arrest them (and you know that once in custody the police will beat you up) you remember it. If one day some police become isolated from colleagues [during our scuffles] we will hit them as punishment for police behaviour. I am angry; do you know that 90 per cent

---

five police forces: the *Polizia di Stato* (State Police, answerable to the Minister of the Interior); the *Arma dei Carabinieri* (the *carabinieri* – an army corps with police functions, answerable to the Minister of Defence); the *Guardia di Finanza* (a force specialised in public order prevention and on financial and tax crimes, answerable to the Minister of the Economy); the *Polizia Penitenziaria* (who function in the Italian prison system, answerable to the Minister of Justice) and finally the *Corpo Forestale dello Stato* (the parks police answerable to the Minister of Agriculture and Forestry, who specialise in the management and preservation of national environments and heritage parks).

of police officers use their baton reversed to cause more damage? They shoot tear gas at eye level and if you fall when they charge, they kick you. After the derby, there was a group of *Laziali* and *Romanisti* – 500 against 200 police – and there were several charges and after every charge some remained on the ground [unconscious]. In the course of these disturbances, a *Guardia di Finanza* officer went down; he received seven stab wounds and they broke a flashlight on his body. His police colleagues could not move; they could only watch. One of the big men of the *UltraS* threw the officer back to his colleagues saying, 'take him back because he is not good even to set on fire'. It was a gesture of unheard of brutality but did not tell the full story. If the police 'take you', they ask 'why did you hit our colleagues' and they kick your face. We reminded them of this on a banner that read '*pestaggi nelle carceri, pestaggi nelle caserme questa e la prova che tu sei solo un verme*' [Beating in the prisons, beating in the police cells, this is the proof that you are scum].

These feelings are not shared by the 'normal' Italian populace who, in a survey conducted in 2007, indicated that the State Police and the *carabinieri* are well respected by Italian citizens. One reason for this is that the Italian police forces, together with the judiciary, were crucial in the defeat of the domestic terrorism of the 1980s, such as the breaking up of the Red Brigades. The Italian police were able to draw on the benefits of greater resources and advanced technologies to face complex crime phenomena that require more than uninformed police intervention. The subsequent investigations led to the capture of the murderers and the suppression of the groups they acted in the name of. The police were also crucial to the successful containment of the Mafia and other criminal organisations through the capture of important fugitives such as the Mafia boss Totó Riina in 1993 and Bernardo Provenzano in 2000.

Though they are trusted, the police have recently been involved in a few football related controversies. In 2007 at the match between Roma and Manchester United, the clashes between rival fans saw police intervention. Officials at Manchester United FC accused the Italian police of brutality against their fans. The statement from the officials was quite clear in its condemnation of police tactics:

> The disturbing scenes witnessed in the Stadio Olimpico last night shocked everyone at Old Trafford. In what the club views as a serious over-reaction, local police handed out indiscriminate beatings to United supporters. In those circumstances, neither Manchester United nor AS Roma is able to call the police to account. As a result, the club warmly welcomes the government examination of the incidents and will collect witness statements from fans to submit to the Home Office.

In commenting on the Italian police action, the British newspaper the *Independent* argued: 'football is still a military operation [in Italy] where its policing is about containment of trouble inside the ground through the use, or threat, of violence'.

To date very few police officers have been successfully prosecuted in an Italian law court for misdemeanours against football fans. Nonetheless, the *nucleo mobile* or *Celere* (a specialist riot police unit), which has been repeatedly deployed at Italian football stadia, has often been accused of disproportionate use of force. A book written by Carlo Bonino, a journalist from *La Repubblica,* and published in 2009, described the lives of three members of the *Celere*. He explains the *Celere*'s world with one effective catchphrase '*odiati e hanno imparato a odiare*' [hated and they have learned to hate].

The *nucleo mobile* was successfully prosecuted in 2008 for excessive use of force, although not in relation to its policing duty at the football stadium. During the G8 meeting in Genoa in 2001, there were a number of clashes between the Italian police forces and the international anti-globalisation movement. Disorder arose in different areas of the city, supported by a range of international groups ranging from anarchists to extreme left and right-wing groups. The centre of Genoa suffered damage estimated at millions of Euros. The event will be remembered for two terrible incidents. In one, 15 protestors, armed with batons, surrounded a Land Rover with three *carabinieri* on board in Piazza Alimonda. One of the officers drew his gun and fired a shot, killing protestor Carlo Giuliani at close range. The second incident occurred a few days later, on 21 July, following another attack on a group of police officers. In retaliation the police raided the Diaz School, a building lent by the local authorities to house the protestors. The raid was brutal, in all 93 people were arrested, the majority with injuries – some serious. Many of those arrested accused the police of brutality; the police responded by claiming that they found weapons such as batons and chains on the premises. Although the case took seven years to resolve, in 2008 12 members of the police who had taken part in the Diaz operation were found guilty of brutality.

It would be ridiculous to support the *UltraS* rhetoric that 'frames' all police as violent because it is clear that there are situations in which police, especially anti-riot units, need to intervene with firmness for public safety. It would also be naive to neglect the fact that episodes of gratuitous police violence occur all over the world – such as those at the G20 protests in London in April 2009[5]. For the *UltraS*, the G8 incident in Genoa is symptomatic of the treatment they receive at the hands of the police. Marco (of the *Boys*) tells of another incident:

Almost every Sunday we have a small 'Diaz' episode. In Orvieto, 200 *UltraS* were put in a *caserma* [police barrack] and beaten up. Against Napoli, the year Roma won the *scudetto*, the police stopped our train at Torricola and all of us in the train were beaten up. The train was later stopped at Formia and when two police officers entered to question all 300 of us – perhaps they believed they were Rambo – they started to shoot their pistols at people. I was at a fountain getting water and people started to count the bullets. Someone more cunning than them knew how many bullets the guns had and then when they ran out of bullets … [laughs – he did not say but implied the police office were cornered and beaten].

---

[5] Several police officers at protests surrounding the G20 economic talks in 2009 were accused of brutality, including Sergeant Delroy Smellie, who was acquitted of striking a female protestor with his baton, and several unnamed officers who are accused of causing the death of Paul Tomlinson, who was on his way home from work when he was pushed to the floor.

The *UltraS* admit that they target the police forces, who in turn are tasked with the duty of applying the law against them. The police have chosen the strategy of tackling the *UltraS* problem by the use of tough repression. Such a strategy has its own risks. The episodes of *UltraS* direct attacks on representatives of the Italian State, such as those that occurred following Sandri's death in 2007 (*see* page 66), underscore the power and danger of an ideology like fascism rooted in a location such as the football stadium, which is attended by thousands of youths armed with a mix of myths, values and beliefs that can be collectively transformed into actions. AT received an email written in 2008, subject: 'The Real Infamy of the Italian State'. The email articulated the rage of the *UltraS* after finding out that the officer who killed Sandri was (at the time of the email) still part of the transport police of Santa Maria Novella in Tuscany. It also articulated possible threats to the police officer, 'Santa Maria Novella [the location where the officer was working] coffin of Spaccarotella [the surname of the police officer]; Gabriele with us!' The last part of the email read: 'He has killed a boy and not even seen one day of prison… And there are others who stays in prison for months or years without any proof' [referring to the prison experience of the *Irriducibili*'s leaders].

The email also displayed the increasingly subversive traits of the *UltraS* oppositional logic. In the 1970s Italian 'revolutionary' groups (of both the left and the right) were noisy, offensive and disorganised. Today's *UltraS* are much more than that. They still rage against the state that does not respect them and seeks to erase them, and the football, which they believe has no soul. But today, if the 'warrior spirit' is not understood (and why should it be by non-believers), then there may be unpredictable consequences.

Among the most controversial measures taken against the *UltraS* are banning orders – no banners permitted in the stadium, and trouble-makers (real and suspected) banned from the stadium. When asked to comment on the banners issue Dr Mazzilli answered from a strictly procedural point of view:

The national observatory adopted this directive 8 March 2007. This intervention was necessary to protect the security of the spectators, athletes and referees and all the people involved in the management of the sport event. The rule forbids the introduction in all the sports structures of banners or any other related object used for the fans choreography if not authorised beforehand by the *Questore*.

For the *UltraS* such prohibition was quite another matter; they believed that this new law/rule effectively finished the spectacle that is *il calcio*. Indeed the whole hardcore football supporter movement, 'ordinary' fans and the *UltraS* alike, have criticised the prohibitions, deeming them alarmist responses that do not respect the rights of the individual and manifest discriminatory policing. Particular criticism was also reserved for the DASPO mainly because they are imposed by the *Questore* (police) rather than a court of law and, while ostensibly subject to judicial review, have to date not been scrutinised by the Constitutional Court. Supporters also criticised the extension of the law that allows arrest up to 48 hours later if the suspect is identified through photographs or video footage as wide open to abuse. Similarly, the minimum penalty for football-related crimes is considered excessive compared with sentencing tariffs for more serious crimes committed outside the sporting context. In the eyes of the fans, this makes it impossible for the courts to impose fair and just punishment.

The Italian police have invested resources in gathering intelligence intended to prevent violent episodes at football matches. The primary strategy of the police is still perceived by the *UltraS* to be hard physical repression. Such a tactic may create a massive divide between citizens and the police and may diminish public confidence.

The police would argue that they do not seek either dialogue with or the support of the *UltraS*. Such a distance is strongly perceived by the *UltraS*; the police are considered as a danger to their values and way of life. The perception that they are treated as 'special threats' only fosters further tension, increasing the *UltraS* sense of discrimination, and goes some way to promoting their strong reactions. Giorgio explains this feeling:

UltraS does not mean gratuitous violence; we need to be careful when labelling *UltraS* 'violent'. Sometimes we are involved in violence; but then you see that in normal life a person can be stabbed for a quarrel in any city. Violence exists in society and the stadium reflects this. The stadium has been for many years a comfortable box in which to ghettoise a part of Italian youth. At the stadium there is much more repression and demonisation of the *UltraS*. Simple banners such as those in support of Giorgio Chinaglia are no longer allowed.

The 'perceived' criminalisation at the hands of police is not a sentiment shared only by the *UltraS*. Other elements of the hardcore football supporters' movement, even those who follow the interpretations of Marxism or anarchism, are similarly angered by policing strategies. The repressive policies of the Italian State have unwittingly united the *UltraS* and other hardcore supporters (regardless of their ideological connotations) around a cause. To all *UltraS*, the police are the armed wing of a repressive State. Sara (of the *Boys)* explains this thinking:

I think [the police] create tension; personally I get nervous when I see police dog units [at the stadium] and officers in riot gear. This does not help. Italian stadia are becoming fortresses; there are already emotions and rivalries among fans then if this climate of war is added, you can understand why these things [violence] happen. A girl of 20 years old like me who goes to the stadium does not want to feel criminalised; I believe many violent acts would not happen if there were less police. Too many police make me [and the *curve*] nervous; I would like to have less repression and militarisation in the stadiums. I am a female and I get angry about this militarisation. Once the police ordered me to open my purse on the train to check it – I felt like a terrorist.

When we travel to away games we always leave early because of the police searches; once we had to go to Messina and the train was scheduled to leave at 1 p.m., it left at 3 p.m. because of the police search. They treat you as a terrorist and this logically produces rancour in people.

It has always annoyed the *Irriducibili* that the media, the state and the police seem to favour the political left. To them it smacks of double standards and is part of what they consider to be a media-state alliance. The *UltraS'* methods of appealing for support around these issues have been quite successful. They are, they claim, oppressed, they are victims of 'brutal' repression, those issued with DASPOs are deprived of their freedom of choice, even if eventually declared innocent; these are all powerful weapons in their armoury of appeal. But this success has come at a price. The state dares not fail in opposing them, they are simply too powerful. The football stadium, once a bastion of freedom of thought and expression, is now in a state of emergency. Those entering and leaving are filtered, and made to reveal everything as demanded. Those not wanted are required to appear at police stations, some distance from the stadia. The unprecedented measures taken by the state have acquired the status of legitimate repression. But the *UltraS* have only themselves to blame; their political agenda has provoked a political response. Giorgio (of the *Irriducibili*) understands this but remains defiant:

> We are defined by the police as a snake that needs its head cut off. I am one of the three that compose this head and this is the reason why two of us (me and Toffolo) are *diffidati* (banned from the stadium). Nevertheless, they failed because despite this the snake is in good health and moves. We fight outside the stadium and believe me we will continue to do so.

In response, Dr Mazzilli continued to express little emotion as he reeled off technical evidence of the victory of the Italian State over the *UltraS*:

> The data we have obtained during the period since the tragic occurrence in Catania [the death of Inspector Raciti in 2007] is comforting. It is possible to say that there is a decrease in all indices relating to violence linked to football spectatorship.
> In the current championship (2008–09) there is a reduction of 72 per cent in spectator injuries at matches, 81 per cent reduction of injuries among the police forces, 83 per cent among civilians, a reduction of 39 per cent in those arrested and of 40 per cent

cautioned by the police. If we want to be more precise this is the latest data of January 2009 from *Serie A*:

The number of matches where people were injured has decreased by 28.2 per cent (from 38 to 28)

The number of matches where teargas is used has diminished by 83.3 per cent (from 6 to1)

The numbers of injured among the police forces has decreased by 41.3 per cent (from 104 to 61)

The numbers of injured among civilians has decreased by 66.1 per cent (from 62 to 21)

The numbers of people arrested has decreased by 53.1 per cent (from 129 to 60)

The numbers of people cautioned by the magistrates has decreased by 46.9 per cent (from 409 to 217)

The number of spectators at *Serie A* has increased by 10.7 per cent with a match average of 24,825 (the previous season's average was 22,430).

In March 2009, 60 *Sconvolts* (the *UltraS* of Cagliari FC) attacked the city prison by throwing missiles and threatening prison officers. Their anger was provoked by the death in prison of their leader, Giancarlo Monni, who fell ill with bronchopneumonia. On the 14 July 2009 the long-lasting judicial trial of police officer Luigi Spaccarotella (who killed Gabriele Sandri) ended with a manslaughter verdict and a six-year prison sentence, instead of a verdict of homicide and a prison sentence of between 14 and 21 years (as requested by the public prosecutor). The anger of the *UltraS* and the friends of Sandri immediately erupted. In court the *UltraS* chanted 'shame, buffoons, bastards', and the *carabinieri* had difficulty in controlling the rage directed at them. The following night, stones and bottles were thrown at the police in Ponte Milvio (an area in the north of the city near the Olimpico). The same group of *UltraS* threw small explosives at the local police station, damaging a motorcycle and a car. Two arrests were made and flags celebrating Mussolini were found in the subsequent house-raid of the arrested.

The data collected by the Ministry of the Interior is undoubtedly a credit to the work done by the Italian police, but does it imply a reduction in the radicalisation of the *curve* and suggest that the policing strategy is working? The appearance of the *UltraS Italia* and episodes such as those mentioned earlier suggest a move in the opposite direction. *La Repubblica* newspaper disputes the figures quoted by Dr Mazzilli; according to the newspaper there are now 63 *UltraS* groups, accounting for 75 per cent of all Italian hardcore football supporter groups. Whichever figures are correct there is no doubt that the *UltraS* remain a powerful force, capable of resisting if their existence is challenged.

Even with tighter controls in Italian stadia, the *UltraS* are determined not to be silenced or prevented from making their presence known

14

RISING SONS?

Certainly, we will not bow in front of their [the state and the media] psychological violence; they can arrest us or isolate us from 'our' world, but something is sure, we will always be proud and faithful to ourselves [and our ideals]. The UltraS, *in their own way, are great artists... Maybe because, different from the masses, they are able to deeply understand the ills of life ... or more simply because, in life, they are conscious of being the leading actors.*

Andrea (of the *Boys*)

Any investigation into the social movement of the *UltraS* needs to consider theoretical and empirical perspectives, from both inside and outside the football stadium. As this study has illustrated these dualities are interconnected by a belief system that drives participants to action. The neo-fascist outside the stadium gazes upon the assumed decadence of Italian society, while inside the stadium these individuals gather with ideologically inspired, like-minded souls, and any sense of passivity ends. In such a milieu individuals make the transition from theory to action without the need for consistency. Explaining this presents an academic challenge even as it disturbs the State. Further study is needed to fully understand the phenomenon.

While this book has examined the gender issues of the *Irriducibili* and the *Boys*, this is a work in progress. The phenomenon of female *UltraS* has recently been highlighted in the media. In 2008, 20 *UltraS* were charged by the public prosecutor following clashes in Rome after Gabriele Sandri's death. Among the 20 arrested for fighting the police was a 25-year-old woman. Even on the other side of the political spectrum, in 2005, 13 hardcore *Ternana Calcio* supporters – a politically left-wing group – were arrested after scuffles during a match against Perugia. Among those recorded on CCTV cameras throwing stones and incendiaries at the police were three women.

It seems most likely that the rise of women in *UltraS* groups has it roots in the fascism of the 'third millennium' as embodied by the *Casa Pound Italia*. This group supports a brand of anti-conformist, 'leftist' fascist ideology without gender preference. It is an interpretation gaining popularity in Italy. *Casa Pound Italia* supports an organisation entitled *Donne e Azione* (DEA), identified by the media as *femminismo neofascista* (neo-fascist feminism). The projects of DEA are advertised on a radio programme titled *FuturArdita,* hosted by the *Casa Pound* radio station, *Radio Bandiera Nera*.

With this theme left pending further investigation, what follows are the key themes that best explain the *UltraS*, noted in the hope that they will promote a greater understanding of their *raison d'etre* and origin among all stands of society. The existence of the *UltraS* provides an illuminating commentary on the incompetence and corruption evident in both the private and public sectors of Italian life. Using the anti-rational ideas of thinkers such as Julius Evola, the neo-fascists see their battles primarily against the 'modern' (Italian) world, which in their analysis neglects dying traditions. The growth of the *UltraS* clearly reflects the sense of marginalisation of non-leftist youth movements and, lacking the political shelter available to the left – appeals to more than the dispossessed and angry. However, their use of violence – verbal or physical – cannot easily be excused, though such activity and those who indulge in it should not be simply dismissed as being representatives of individual pathology nor as wholly marginal to contemporary Italian life.

As we have seen, *UltraS* groups such as the *Irriducibili* and the *Boys* have political convictions that are deeply anti-capitalist, anti-liberal, but also anti-conservative, seeking a revaluation of the idea of the nation as an organic community of people, which exists in opposition to a liberal, hyper-individualistic society. Yet, even as they are strongly supportive of an Italian nationalism, their politics always oppose an Italian political conformism – though crucially they have little to offer by way of visions of a new social order. Instead, their activities are based around articulating a variety of fears and a sense of political disillusionment. As a consequence the *UltraS*, and the neo-fascists with whom they share an ideology, will never take power by democratic means. At best they will constitute part of an emerging and pan-European social movement. Meanwhile they contest – with violence – their political opponents and the police sent to repress them.

Significantly they refuse to acknowledge defeat, for, as Marco (of the *Boys*) stated when questioned about his philosophy: *meglio vivere un giorno da leone that 100 da pecore* (better to live one day as a lion than 100 as a sheep). And in living the leonine lifestyle, such individuals can even face the possibility of death. Since 1962, more than 60 young men have died in events surrounding the social drama and the occasion of a Serie A/B/C football match. While such deaths are not all *UltraS*-related, the existence of the *UltraS* can be said to increase the possibility of this fate.

In their conception of society the *UltraS* appears to stress the subordination of the ego to the collective. The *curva* is certainly the one locale in the city where group values of loyalty, courage, honour and fidelity find fertile ground. The *UltraS* world might best be considered as an ideology of vengeance, which attracts people prone to emotional experiences and with unsatisfied needs. They have an enhanced sense of belonging expressed most evidently in a quasi-military organisation wherein ideas of authority, notions of charisma and personal style of command are crucial. They know they are deviant because they consider violence to be instrumental and essential for the affirmation of their rights and values. They even celebrate their deviance from what they contemptuously dismiss as *omologazione della gioventu* (youth conformism) – the commercially-duped, politically-servile followers of both contemporary Italian politics and football.[1] The *UltraS* thus act as a mass movement offering a vision for those who will be tomorrow's adults.

The *Boys* and the *Irriducibili* gather respectively in the name of AS Roma and SS Lazio, but are not slavish followers of the entities that might be considered on the surface to be their 'love objects'. Both groups are aware that club management condemns them but, in turn, believe such people are involved in the club primarily for financial self-interest which makes them liable to theft and financial betrayal. Few players of either club are revered. Many are considered to be the ultimate mercenaries whose love for the team shirt and the club lasts only as long as their contracts. In essence, then, football manifests the confusion that the *UltraS* are seeking to address.

Opposed to the processes of globalisation, yet enjoying the skills of foreign-born players and wearing football shirts adorned with the insignia of international corporate finance, the *Boys* and *Irriducibili* are at one and the same time contemptuous of the commercial logic of contemporary elite-level football. Dismissive of the game's growing materialism and its never-ending pursuit of efficiency and profit, the *UltraS* deeply appreciate those abstract qualities of faith and courage that the game provides. They are thus prisoners of the game simply because they depend on football to impart structure and meaning to

---

[1] In his 1981 study on the British far right National Front party sociologist Nigel Fielding well understood that: 'political deviance is important to this field (extreme right ideology) because it is an area in which the deviant's perception of social reality not only differs rather abruptly from that of the majority but also does so in an unusually coherent manner'.

their lives and can never walk away from the spectacle and the social drama with the layers of significance it provides.

The appeal of the *UltraS* to their members is not merely about identification with a rebellious, 'anti-system' logic, or merely a love for football. Interaction between group members is based on a mix of emotions and a sense of duty towards their *communitas*. Members are exhilarated by the group's pre-match preparations and in playing a 'cat and mouse' game with the authorities in attempts to bypass their control – both inside and outside the stadium. Being among the *Boys* or the *Irriducibili* is, for many, an imaginary act of identification with real and symbolic 'others', and with their ideals. This allows individuals such as Todde or Giorgio to play with their sense of self-image. In the variety of situations the *UltraS* both create and respond to, participants are able to pursue activities collectively that would possibly be considered repugnant – or at best, strange – if practised alone. Through such performance, participants are transported from superficiality to fantasy, as they set out to close the gap between imagined and experienced pleasures.

Shaping their self-presentation using fascist ideology's myth and values, groups like the *Boys* and *Irriducibili* seek to build an autonomous social space which confers status because it allows them to emerge from an otherwise undifferentiated crowd of discontented youth. Like their other mainstream neo-fascist counterparts, the *UltraS* find their sense of function, survival and cohesiveness in a critical and antagonistic stance towards the society from which they feel rejected. And this opposition is articulated through a lifestyle in opposition to the normal behaviour promoted and defended by a mainstream society of which they want no part.

The *UltraS* exist in a framework wherein narratives – football related and politically inspired – of idealised scenarios of masculinity are ever-present. In their behaviour they seek to combine notions of the 'warrior' with abstractions drawn from a variety of Western thinkers. They are thus a combination of theory and action and are most visible in the football stadium. Their ideological *communitas* is located in a legendary world and is founded in a shared sense of symbolism (such as the Celtic cross, specialist clothes and non-mainstream music), values (such as reverence towards Mussolini) and codes of behaviour (especially faith to their 'deviant' way of life).

There are two distinct types of *UltraS* activist: the 'elite' and the 'sympathisers'. The 'core', which includes the 'hardcore' *direttivo*, propagates and shares an ideological and cultural DNA that promotes the logic of the *communitas*. These members appear to demonstrate the convictions of the purist, and, at the same time, share a strong sense of mutual responsibility manifested most obviously in the face of rival hardcore supporters and the forces of 'repression' (the police, the State and the media). The strength and importance of the 'elite' is displayed when they are in action; such leaders – by virtue of their charisma – and if not subject to the DASPO, are always present in the vanguard in the 'battles' with other fans and police. The 'sympathisers' share the ideology of the group, but are only involved as long as membership is considered 'fashionable', or as long as a specific 'leader' renews his membership of the 'elite'.

Collectively, members of the *UltraS* exist in what is regarded as 'the post-modern condition' – one of the characteristics of which is the absence of any precisely defined purpose. They find it here; as *UltraS* they can distinguish themselves from 'others', constructing their own style to stress their own sense of authenticity, ever-articulating the 'true' *UltraS* ideal. Such feelings help the individual member of the collective to affirm his/her identity in an adversarial milieu, reinforcing the bonds among members, and at the same time inscribing the group's social definition. Hard to define and to 'capture' ideologically, the *UltraS* involve themselves in a 'guerrilla activity', using 'tenacity, trickery and guileful ruse' to provoke the societal forces of the media, the judiciary and the police by incursions that seek to cheat social constraints.[2]

However, the oppositional stance of the *Boys* and *Irriducibili* comes at a price, and assuming the role of 'social critic' entails consequences. The state – through its agents and the electoral process – is tasked to control those who are openly disillusioned with democracy and who are willing to turn to violence to resist or provoke change. Adopting and sustaining a critical posture, as the *UltraS* do, represents both a

---

[2] An analysis of their behaviour derived from French social scientist Michel de Certeau, 1984

symbolic and real challenge to the social order and this creates an inevitable reaction from the agencies of power being challenged, which is best represented by police repression, political marginalisation and social stigmatisation. Such stigmatisation notoriously threatens self-esteem at a personal and a collective level, although there are many ways of coping with such threats. One of the most common is by disengaging, which is expressed most obviously by the act of avoidance, or by fleeing from persecutors or accusers. However, for the *UltraS* a feeling of rejection from wider society actually seems to empower their collective, both as a single – named – group and as an emerging ideological movement.

Feelings of such discrimination seemed to be ever-present among all the *UltraS* interviewed for this book, but this did not constitute a reason to abandon their *communitas*. Indeed, it enhanced their levels of cohesiveness, with the 'core' of both *UltraS* groups wearing their stigma as a badge of pride, because it stated and then communicated their location in wider society, and even legitimised their place in the social drama of life.

Fascism has always demonstrated populist elements as well as certain strands of anarchism – this is what makes it a fascinating political genre. It appeals to tradition, though this, of course, can be invented. Furthermore, there are always competing 'Truths' in any system – and these too, like tradition, can be invented.

The neo-fascism the *UltraS* proclaim to follow makes no pretence of being a new ideology, instead the *UltraS* espouse old ideas topped with a heavy dose of romanticism; for neo-fascism is romantic in its vision stressing as it does a sense of community, the importance of tradition and the necessity of respect. At the same time, as a political genre neo-fascism attracts those who, even as they preach the virtues of order, are attracted by the potential their group vision holds for indulging in degrees of chaos. In this sense they are quintessentially similar to football fans the world over, who follow an entity – football's rules and principles – that has not fundamentally changed since the late 19th century. Supporters constantly portray a sense of the romantic in their club-related memories in a series of narratives that seem to be even more intense than those played out in much of contemporary society.

The oppositional behaviour of the *UltraS* has never formally contemplated the erasure of democracy. Actually, they recognise that the dictatorship model of fascism is not defensible and that the brand of fascism espoused by Mussolini needs to be re-considered in the context of contemporary Italian society. The *UltraS* and indeed the neo-fascists' existence is actually phantom politics. The 'ideologists' of the *UltraS* know the actuality of political power would be far from romantic. They celebrate the Saló Republic (so called because it was the site of the Italian Social Republic's headquarters during the Mussolini era) but distance themselves from the fascism of the regime of Mussolini because this seizing of power saw the end of idealism and the necessity of political pragmatism with all its iniquities. The *UltraS* are not pro-dictatorship but are ever-seeking new ideas for a new society and will wax lyrical about the pre-fascist contexts of modern Italy in the glorious past that they pursue. On the other hand, not all their existence is negative and oppositional. They seek consistently to set an example to peer groups and indeed provoked piety in their style and articulations – especially those that stressed non-conformity. They exemplify how to live in both a financially modest and bodily pure context. Their resistance to the exploitative logic of the capitalist system and their vehement anti-drugs message reveal these values. They seek to reach their fellow youth mainly inside (within the hardcore football supporters' world) but also outside the *curve*.

Claiming the stadium as their *agorà* they are implicitly admitting that they prefer the notion of the assembly to that of representative democracy. The *UltraS* prefer noise, slogans and, when necessary, direct action/confrontation. While the *UltraS* might see their role as bringing some sense of Athenian 'people power' to the football stadium we might consider that debates about democracy have been over-concerned with the notion of *demos* (people) at the expense of the role of *Kratos* (rule), which has frequently utilised force; strength and domination is integral to order and stability.[3] When the idea of 'assembly' was superseded by representative democracy and with it elections, political parties and charismatic leaders, the result was a democratic process that saw Europe

---

[3] This analysis of democracy is inspired by the work of Runciman, 2009.

become the global killing fields in the first half of the 20th century. Democracy suffers from founding myths; it is frequently chaotic and forever needs a sense of purpose. The *UltraS* remind us of this.

Ultimately, these 'warriors' of 21st century Italy reflect some crucial aspects of their own society – the centrality of football to Italian public life and social identities, the widespread ambivalence towards modernity, the search for fundamental values within a social system that seems to have lost its way and the alienation of youth towards a perceived corrupt and ageing society. Perhaps the irony is that if 'oppressive' forces such as the condemnatory media, the repressive police, and the 'tough' authorities, all have their way then the *UltraS* – who are in the public domain and who are known to these powerful figures, will be forced to disappear – and given the political and cultural history of Italy and its ongoing political and cultural contradictions, the *UltraS* may well be replaced. But by what, who knows?

APPENDIX:
OTHER STUDIES OF *UltraS* AND *ultrá*

The first significant Italian-based study on the hardcore football supporter (*ultrá*) phenomenon was by the Italian social psychologist Alessandro Salvini in 1988. Salvini focused on the notion of *ultrá* identity, arguing that young men joined these groups to obtain some degree of self-worth. Salvini claimed that within the *ultrá* gatherings, youths essentially learned adult social rules and that the *ultrá* group provided guidance to those whose identity was malleable and incomplete. In taking on an *ultrá* role, the individual thus assumed an identity within a framework of behaviour with 'rules'. Although not written or recorded, these rules were tacitly shared and understood by most of the participants. The most favoured trait was aggressiveness, practised because fights with rival fans could inspire self-confidence and might lead to the admiration of others and a sense of group prestige.

Salvini's study was groundbreaking for a number of reasons. Firstly, it explained that football violence might not always be practised by those of a particular socio-economic group – naturally, those who benefited least from society – because there were other reasons why a young man might want to belong to such a group. But perhaps its most interesting aspect was that it was not totally critical of the *ultrá* world. His examination of the positive aspects of such 'membership' and the idea of supporters learning how to be an adult via the football terraces was something few other observers had suggested.

Two years later the Italian sociologist Alessandro Dal Lago published a study on the *ultrá* groups in the three cities of Turin, Milan and Bergamo. His conclusions shared a similar view to an earlier report by an Oxford Brookes University research team led by Peter Marsh that considered the 'ritualistic' nature of football-related violence to be 'social-evolutionary'.

According to Dal Lago, celebrations at games and sporting events have progressively lost their cathartic function in Western society. Sporting events such as cock-fighting and dog-fighting, highly charged and symbolic spectator events that encouraged the discharge of aggression, have largely disappeared. They are considered by society in general to be morally unacceptable. In order to survive, overtly violent sports such as boxing and rugby have adopted constraining rules that seek to remove both the unjustified use of violence and the uncontrolled arousal of aggressiveness among spectators. Dal Lago argued that despite similar pressures, football continues to produce enough excitement and tension to provide a spectacle around which spectators make huge emotional, symbolic and economic investments. This tension is channelled and regulated by fan rituals, which function to express strong emotions that do not necessarily develop into violence but which always carry the potential to do so.

In his explanation of the behaviour of *ultrá*, Dal Lago developed what he calls 'three assumptions'. The first, based on the 'us-and-them' division among supporters at a match, was intrinsic to the nature of the game in that two teams were always competing for victory. This, according to Dal Lago, was most obvious in the visible differences between the fans of the two teams playing. The second was that matches were played in a place where ritual action precipitated clashes between 'friends and enemies'. Indeed, the stadium facilitated such interactions because it was an ideal place to originate symbolic conflicts by wearing different colours, singing and chanting about the other team and making collective aggressive gestures and threats. He identified two factors that influenced the intensity of such ritual conflicts. The first, and most influential, was based on the historical relationships of alliances or enmities among supporters of different teams. The second related to those events that occurred during a match that could influence the emotional equilibrium on the *curva*. Dal Lago acknowledged that this symbolic violence could sometimes descend into real violence, though he suggested that this generally occurred only when the metaphoric and ritual actions of the hardcore football supporters were misunderstood by ordinary spectators, or by the police, and were interpreted as being a threat to society.

Dal Lago's final assumption defined the football stadium as having its own rules, understood by regular supporters but which could appear incomprehensible to outsiders. In a stadium it was possible to experience different emotions from those in 'normal' life. Moreover, in a stadium, symbols and symbolic domains attained meanings that were crucially different from those found in 'normal' society. Dal Lago pragmatically divided these two realities of 'Stadium and Society', describing how, once the fans crossed the imaginary boundary between these two realities by walking into the stadium, they changed their way of acting. 'Of course, they are the same people or groups. What they have put on, however, trespassing the invisible membrane that surrounds the stadium, is another mental, cognitive and moral dress,' he says in the report. Therefore, in the 'frame' of the stadium, conflicts between supporters should be considered as rituals, with meanings best understood via the logic of football-related hostility.

Dal Lago was also very sceptical about the link between fans and political ideology, stressing the groundlessness of claims that the *ultrá* on the *curva* were ever directly linked to political groupings, or that they were even genuine expressions of political cultures. He viewed the symbols that members of the hardcore groups adopted, such as their clothes, their songs, the slogans on their T-shirts, as a random collection of items taken from different cultural sources by individual members of the group. They had no collective meaning until invested with one by observers from outside the groups. For example, the display of Celtic crosses, the singing of songs such as '*Faccetta Nera*' ('Little Black Face') and mass enaction of the Roman salute by the *UltraS Italia* in Sofia would, in Dal Lago's analysis, be regarded as displays of a ritual conflict explained by an impulse to be identified as part of the show, rather than as a political statement.

Such ideas were further enveloped in Dal Lago's borrowing of the sociological concept of *fatto sociale totale* (total social fact). This argued that an examination of any facet of society needs simultaneously to take into account several elements including the economic, the cognitive, the political, the social and the legal elements, and their impact upon individuals. In applying this concept to football – the most popular sport in the world and one in which an extraordinary number of people invest a great degree of passion and emotion – it is possible to understand how members of an *ultrá* group obtain a high degree of cultural and social visibility as well as simply rejoicing in 'the social power of the images' they create. The activities of these hardcore football supporters – both *ultrá* and *UltraS* – are a good example of this possibility, where all the elements of the carnival – the sounds, the symbols and the rituals – come together quite by chance in what French anthropologist Claude Lévi-Strauss called 'chains of meaning'.

The concept of morality was integral to other Italian explanations of this phenomenon. The sociologist Antonio Roversi's research on the fans of Bologna FC in the early 1990s sought to evaluate football violence. The main hypothesis of Roversi's work was that the hardcore football supporters should be considered as a 'moral community' which permitted its members to enjoy experiences different from their daily routines. Such gatherings, he explained, were structures that collectively followed norms and provided symbols for the participants. These represented a behavioural and cultural setting that satisfied a need for personal and social identity. This had a positive role in that it substituted for the often-decadent initiatory rituals found in education, military service and the church. However, there is a negative dimension to all of this, in that schooling in a world founded on strict values that are unacceptable to society in general may prevent them from experiencing aspects of a wider and more flexible world.

In a previous report, Roversi identified three factors to account for the enduring conflicts found in and around football. The first was the historical legacy, an ever-present aspect that arises in any assessment of the history of Italian football. As Roversi explained, 'We are still left with the fact that many new hooligan groups spontaneously take as their adversaries the supporters of those teams with whom their fathers had already done battle.'

Roversi defined the second dimension as the 'Bedouin Syndrome', 'The principle by which the friend of a friend is a friend, the enemy of an enemy is an enemy, the enemy of a friend is a friend and the friend of an enemy is an enemy.' At the same time, Roversi recognised that not all conflict can be reduced to such a dynamic, so, for his third factor, Roversi became one of the few Italian academics to acknowledge that political ideologies do indeed play a part in fuelling rivalries and violence; though he provided no proof of any extremist group involvement, beyond highlighting the use of neo-fascist symbolism.

Such ideas, although thought-provoking and indeed relevant, would certainly have benefited from the inclusion of some real evidence that focused on the *UltraS*. However, even in Roversi's 2006 evaluation of the rise of ideologically orientated football fans with an externalist approach reported no interaction between himself and the studied *UltraS* (a name by now given to overtly political football fans): 'The research that I present in this book was carried out while being comfortably seated in my office. I needed only a laptop, an internet connection and time available to navigate the internet.'

Although Roversi's works provided an important contribution to an understanding Italian football fandom, a pertinent criticism of this freedom of the researcher to mediate reality was made by 'Lorenzo', the webmaster of the AS Roma *UltraS* website, who focused on Roversi's comments on the infamous Lazio-Roma game of 2005 (*see* chapter 12). In this instance Roversi argued that two of the three Roma *UltraS* who entered the pitch to speak to the Roma player, Francesco Totti, were leaders of the *Opposta Fazione* neo-fascist group. 'Lorenzo' instead affirmed (and the *Boys Roma* confirmed) that the *Opposta Fazione* were no longer in the Roma *curva* and that the two individuals who entered the pitch – even if they were neo-fascists – were acting alone and not as representatives of any *curva* group.

But it is not just Roversi who failed to undertake in-depth, ethnographic research on the *UltraS* – indeed there has been no such undertaking. A recent study by the criminologist Vincenzo Scalia claimed to have done so but failed to detail the methodology or the theoretical framework utilised for the research. Scalia described his methodology in just one sentence, 'I consider this work as the product of ethnographic research, both as a former *ultrá* and as a current football fan'.

.

REFERENCES

The following reference list supplies sources consulted by the authors in the writing of this book. In the interests of readability we have not cited explicit references throughout the text, but any reader wishing to know more is invited to write to the authors via the publishers for clarification.

Introduction
Jones, T. (2003) *The Dark Heart of Italy: Travels through Time and Space Across Italy*. London. Faber & Faber.

Chapter 1
Armstrong, G., & Hobbs, D. (1993). Tackled from Behind. In R. Giulianotti, N. Bonney & M. Hepworth, *Football Violence and Social Identity*. London: Routledge.

Armstrong, G. (1998). *Football Hooligans: Knowing the Score*. Oxford: Berg.

Armstrong, G., & Young, M. (1997). Legislators and Interpreters: The Law and football hooliganism. In G. Armstrong & R. Giulianotti, *Entering the field: New Perspectives in World Football*. Oxford: Berg.

Blee, K. (2007). Ethnographies of the Far Right. *Journal of Contemporary Ethnography*, 36, 119–128.

Dal Lago, A. (1990). *Descrizione di una battaglia*. Bologna: Il Mulino.

Dal Lago, A., & De Biasi, R. (2002). *Introduzione all' etnografia sociale*. Bari: Editori Laterza.

Goffman, E. (1974). Frame Analysis: An Essay on the Organization of Experience. New York: Harper & Row.

Gould, D. (2002). *Football and Fascism: A Beautiful Friendship? A study of relations between the state and soccer in Mussolini's Italy*. [Unpublished thesis]. Department of History, Reading: University of Reading.

De Certau, M. (1984). *The Practice of Everyday Life*. Berkeley: University of California Press.

De Sisti, S. (1996–1997). *Politica e Tifo calcistico*.[Laurea Dissertation]. Bologna: Universita' di Bologna.

Hobbs, D., & May, T. (2002). *Interpreting the Field. Accounts of ethnography*. Oxford: Oxford University Press.

Levi-Strauss, C. (1966). *The Savage Mind*. Chicago: The University of Chicago Press.

Mauss, M. (1965). Teoria generale della magia e altri saggi. Torino: Einaudi.

Pearson, G. (1983). *Hooliganism: A History of Respectable Fears*. London: Macmillan Publishing Co., Inc.

Ricoeur, P. (1967). *The Symbolism of Evil*. Boston, MA: Beacon.

Roversi, A. (1991). Football Violence in Italy. *International Review for the Sociology of Sport*, 26(4), 311–331.

Salzman, P. (1978). Does Complementary Opposition Exist? *American Anthropologist*, 80, 53–70.

Scalia, V. (2009). Just a Few Rogues?: Football Ultras, Clubs and Politics in Contemporary Italy. *International Review for the Sociology of Sport*, 44, 41–53.

Young, M. (1991). *An Inside Job: Policing and Police Culture in Britain*. Oxford: Clarendon Press.

Chapter 2

Bianda, R., Leone, G., Rossi, G.,& Urso, A. (1983). *Atleti in camica nera. Lo sport nell' Italia di Mussolini*. Roma: Giovanni Volpe Editore.

Cresswell, P., Evans, & Goldstein, D. (2000). *The Rough Guide to European Football*, 4th Edition: A Fans' Handbook. London: Rough Guides.

Gould, D. (2002). *Football and Fascism: A Beautiful Friendship? A study of relations between the state and soccer in Mussolini's Italy*.[Unpublished thesis]. Department of History, Reading: University of Reading.

Melli, F., & Melli, M. (2005). *La storia della Lazio*. Roma: L' Airone Editrice.

Pallotta, A., & Olivieri, A. (2006). *Magica Roma. Storia dei 600 uomini giallorossi*. Roma: Un Mondo a Parte.

Pennacchia, M. (1994). *Lazio, grande Lazio*. Roma: Edizioni T-Scrivo

Pennacchia, M. (2001). *Football Force One. La biografia ufficiale di Giorgio Chinaglia*. Arezzo: Limina.

Porro, N. (1992). Sport e Sociologia in Italia. *Ludus*, 2, 1–2.

Recanatesi, F. (2006). *Uno più undici. Maestrelli: La vita di un gentiluomo del calcio, dagli anni Trenta allo scudetto el '74*. Roma: L' Airone.

Chapter 3

Bianda, R., Leone, G., Rossi, G.,& Urso, A. (1983). *Atleti in camica nera. Lo sport nell' Italia di Mussolini*. Roma: Giovanni Volpe Editore.

Cresswell, P., Evans, & Goldstein, D. (2000). *The Rough Guide to European Football*, 4th Edition: A Fans' Handbook. London: Rough Guides.

Gould, D. (2002). *Football and Fascism: A Beautiful Friendship? A study of relations between the state and soccer in Mussolini's Italy*. [Unpublished thesis]. Department of History, Reading: University of Reading.

Pallotta, A., & Olivieri, A. (2006). *Magica Roma. Storia dei 600 uomini giallorossi*. Roma: Un Mondo a Parte.

Pennacchia, M. (1994). *Lazio, grande Lazio*. Roma: Edizioni T-Scrivo

Porro, N. (1992). Sport e Sociologia in Italia. *Ludus*, 2, 1–2.

*Information relating to pages 30–36 sourced from: www.asromaultras.org

Pages 36–40: the history of Societa Sportivá Lazio football sourced from: www.ultraslazio.it

Chapter 4

Charlot, J. (1971). *The Gaullist Phenomenon*. London: Allen & Unwin

Der Brug, W., & Mughan, A. (2007). Charisma, Leader Effects and Support for

Right-Wing Populist Parties. *Party Politics*, 13, 29–51.

Garsia, V. (2004). *A guardia di una fede*. Roma: Castelvecchi Editore.

Madsen, D., & Snow, P. (1991). *The Charismatic Bond: Political Behavior in Time of Crisis*. Cambridge: Harvard University Press.

The Times. (online edition; 2009,16, August): www.timesonline.co.uk/tol/news/politics/article6798146.ece

*Source for topics discussed on pages 43–46 from: www.ascromaultras.org

Chapter 5

Beneforti, C., & De Salvo, V. (2000). *Signori Beppe, una vita da Signori. Autobiografia di Beppe-gol*. Bologna: Edizioni An.Ma & San Marco Sport Events.

Dal Lago, A., & Moscati, R. (1992). *Regalateci un sogno: miti and realtà del tifo calcistico in Italia*. Milano: Bompiani.

Giulianotti, R. (1993). Soccer Casuals as Cultural Intermediaries: The Politics of Scottish Style. In S. Redhead (Ed.), *The Passion and the Fashion*. (pp. 153–203). London:Gower.

Chapter 6

Accame, G. (1995). *Ezra Pound economist: Contro l' usura*. Roma: Settimo Sigillo.

Adinolfi, G., & Fiore, R. (2000). *Noi Terza Posizione*. Roma: Settimo Sigillo.

Baldoni, A. (1996). *Il crollo dei Miti*. Roma: Settimo Sigillo.

Blee, K. (2007). Ethnographies of the Far Right. *Journal of Contemporary Ethnography*, 36, 119–128.

Colombo, A. (2007). *Storia Nera*. Milano: Cairo Editore.

Corte, U. and Edwards, B. (2008). White Power music and the mobilization of racist Social Movements. *Music and the Arts in Action*, 1 (1), 4–20.

De Felice, R. (1975a). *Mussolini il Fascista*. Roma: Laterza.

De Felice, R. (1975b). *Intervista sul Fascismo*.Roma: Laterza.

Eley, G. (1986). *From the Unification to Nazism: Reinterpreting the German*. Boston: Allen & Unwin.

Evola, J. (1993). *Rivolta contro il mondo moderno*. Roma: Edizioni Mediterranee.

Flamini, G. (1985). *Il Partito del Golpe* . Ferrara: Bonovolenta Editore.

Ferraresi, F. (1995). *Minacce alla democrazia* . Milano: Feltrinelli.

Fong, J. (2008). *Revolution as Development: The Karen Self-Determination Struggle Against Ethnocracy (1949–2004)*. Boca Raton, FL: Universal Publishers.

Giampietro, G. (1994). *I gruppi extraparlamentari di destra 1950–1969. L 'influenza di Julius Evola*. [Laurea Dissertation]. Teramo: University of Teramo.

Gregor, A. (1979). *Young Mussolini and the intellectual origins of Fascism*. Berkeley: University of California Press.

Griffin, R. (1991). *The Nature of Fascism*. London: Routledge.

Hine, P. (1995). *Condensed Chaos: An Introduction to Chaos Magic*. Nevada: New Falcon Publications.

Ignazi, P. (1989). *Il polo Escluso*. Bologna: Il Mulino.

Jones, T. (2003). *The Dark Heart of Italy: Travels through Time and Space across Italy.* London: Faber and Faber.

Lanna, R., & Rossi, F.(2003). *Fascisti immaginari. Tutto quello che c'è da sapere sulla destra.*Firenze:Vallecchi.

La Repubblica (online edition; 2008, 01, October): www.repubblica.it/2008/10/ sezioni/sport/calcio/calciatori-fascisti/calciatori-fascisti/calciatori-fascisti.html

Mooij, M. (1998).Global Marketing and Advertising: Understanding Cultural Paradoxes. Thousand Oaks: Sage Publications.

Mosse, G. (1984). *Le origini culturali del Terzo Reich.* Milano: Il Saggiatore.

Nello, P. (1998). *Il partito della Fiamma. La Destra in Italia dal MSI ad AN.* Roma: Ist. Editoriali e Poligrafici.

Padovani, C. (2008). The Extreme Right and Its Media in Italy. *International Journal of Communication, 2,* 753–770.

Procacci, G. (1970). *History of the Italian People.* London: Penguin.

Rao, N. (2006). *La Fiamma e la Celtica.* Milano: Sperling & Kupfer.

Roversi A. (1992). *Calcio, tifo e violenza.* Bologna: Il Mulino.

Salotti, G. (2008). *Nicola Bombacci: Un comunista a Salò.* Milano: Ugo Mursia Editore.

Snow, D., Soule, S., and Kriesi, H. (2004). *The Blackwell Companion to Social Movements.* Oxford: Blackwell Publishers.

Sternhell, Z. (1989). *Nascita dell' ideologia fascista.* Milano: Baldini & Castoldi.

Streccioni, A. (2000). *A Destra della Destra.* Roma: Edizioni Settimo Sigillo.

Weber, E. (1974). Revolution? Counterrevolution? What Revolution? *Journal of Contemporary History,* 9(2), 3–47.

Weber, M. (1958). *From Max Weber. Essays in Sociology* (H. Gerth & W. Mills, Eds.). New York: Oxford University Press.

Chapter 7

Almirante, G. & Palamenghi, C. (1958). *Il Movimento Sociale Italiano.* Milano: La Nuova Accademia.

Boissevain, J. (1974). *Friends of Friends, Networks, Manipulators and Coalitions.* London: Blackwell.

Cicourel, A. (1973). *Cognitive Sociology.* Harmondsworth: Penguin Books.

Corriere della Sera. (online edition; 2009, 03, September): http://www.corriere.it/ sport/09_settembre_03/partita_livorno_adana_turchia_marco_gasperetti_ 2b578512-98a4-11de-b8d4-00144f02aabc.shtml

Corte, U., & Edwards, B. (2008). White Power music and the mobilization of racist Social Movements. *Music and Arts in Action,* 1(1), 4–20.

Crocker, J., Major, B., & Steele, C. (1998). Social Stigma. In D. Gilbert, S. Fiske & G. Lindzey (Eds.), *Handbook of Social Psychology.* (pp. 504–553). Boston: McGraw-Hill Book Company.

Dechezelles, S. (2008). The Cultural Basis of Youth Involvement in Italian Extreme Right-wing Organisations. *Journal of Contemporary European Studies,* 16(3), 363–375.

De Sisti, S. (1996–1997). *Politica e Tifo calcistico.*[Laurea Dissertation]. Bologna: Universita' di Bologna.

Ehrenrech, B. (1983). *The Hearts of Men.* London: Pluto.

Ferguson, S. (1999). *Mapping the Social Landscape: Readings in Sociology.* Mountain View, CA: Mayfield Pub Co.

Friedman, D., & McAdam, D. (1992). Collective identity and activism: networks, choices and the life of a social movement. In A.D. Morris & C. McClurg Mueller (Eds.), *Frontiers in Social Movement Theory.* (pp. 156–173). New Haven: Yale University Press

Gentile, E. (1975). *Le origini dell' ideologia fascista (1918–1925).* Bari: Laterza.

Goffman E. (1963). *Stigma: Notes on the Management of Spoiled Identity.* New York: Prentice-Hall.

Goffman, E. (1967). *Interaction Ritual: Essays on Face-Face Behaviour.* New York: Doubleday Anchor.

Heller, A. (1985). *The Power of Shame.* London: Routledge.

Hirsh, A. (2007). *The Forgotten Ways: Reactivating the Missional Church.* Ada, MI: Brazos Press.

Klandermans, B., & Mayer, N. (2006). *Extreme Right Activists in Europe.* London: Routledge.

Major, B., & O'Brien, L. T. (2005). The social psychology of stigma. *Annual Review of Psychology, 56,* 393–421.

Marcuse, H. (1964). *One-dimensional Man.* London: Routledge.

Mead, G. H. (1938). *The Philosophy of the Act.* Chicago, IL: University of Chicago Press.

Michelini, Luca. (1999). *Liberalismo, nazionalismo, fascismo. Stato e mercato, corporativismo e liberalismo nel pensiero economico del nazionalismo italiano.* Varese: M&B Publishing.

Le Bon, G. (1895/1960). *The Crowd (Translation of Psychologie de foules).* New York: The Viking Press.

Link, B. G., & Phelan, J. (2001). Conceptualizing Stigma. *Annual Review of Sociology, 27,* 363–385.

Rubenstein, J. (1992). Purim, Liminality, and Communitas. *American Journal of Sociology Review,* 17(2), 247–277.

Simmel, G. (1957). Fashion. *American Journal of Sociology.* 62, 541–558.

Simmel, G. (1957). Fashion. *American Journal of Sociology.* 62, 541–558.

Streccioni, A. (2000). *A destra della destra.* Roma: Edizioni Settimo Sigillo.

Turner, V. (1969). *The Ritual Process: Structure and Anti- Structure.* Chicago: University of Chicago Press.

Van Gennep, A. (1908). *Les Rites de Passage.* (Monika Vizedom and Gabrielle Caffee (1960)). London: Routledge.

Vannini, P. & Franzese, A.(2008). The Authenticity of Self: Conceptualization, Personal Experience, and Practice. *Sociology Compass.*2 (5), 1621–1637.

Vider, S. (2004). Rethinking Crowd Violence: Self-Categorization Theory and the Woodstock 1999 Riot. *Journal for the Theory of Social Behaviour*, 34(2), 141–166.

Turner, V. (1974). *Dramas, Fields and Metaphors: Symbolic Action in Human Society*. Ithaca, New York: Cornell University Press.

Chapter 8

Assmann, J. (1997). *Moses the Egyptian. The Memory of Egypt in Western Monotheism*. Cambridge, MA: Harvard University Press.

Braghero, M., Perfumo, & Ravano, F. (1999). *Per Sport e per Business: E' tutto parte del gioco*. Milano: Angeli

Buzzanca. A., & Di Loreto, S. (2003). *Da porta a porta*. Roma: ADN Kronos.

Dechezelles, S. (2008). The Cultural Basis of Youth Involvement in Italian Extreme Right-wing Organisations. *Journal of Contemporary European Studies*, 16(3), 363–375.

Evola, J. (1993). *Rivolta contro il mondo moderno*. Roma: Edizioni Mediterranee.

Falsanisi, G., & Giangrieco, E. (2001). *Le societá di calcio del 2000*. Cosenza: Rubbettino.

Ferrari, S. (2009). *Le nuove camicie brune. Il neofascismo oggi in Italia*. Pisa: BFS Edizioni.

George, L. (1998). Self and Identity in Later Life: Protecting and Enhancing the Self. *Journal of Ageing and Identity*, 3, 133–152.

Haenfler, R. (2004). Rethinking Subcultural Resistance: Core Values of the Straight Edge Movement. *Journal of Contemporary Ethnography*, 33, 406–436.

Hebdige, D. (1981). *Subculture: The Meaning of Style*. London: Routledge.

Hitlin, S., & Piliavin, J. (2004). Values: Reviving a dormant concept. *Annual Review of Sociology*, 30, 359–393.

Hofstede, G. (1983). Dimensions of national cultures in fifty countries and three regions. In J. B. Deregowski, S. Dziurawiec, & R. C. Annis (Eds.), *Explications in cross-cultural psychology* (pp. 335–355). Lisse, Netherlands: Swets & Zeitlanger.

Hofstede, G. (1991). *Cultures and organizations: Software of the mind*. New York: McGraw-Hill Book Company.

La Repubblica. (online edition; 2008,05, December): www.repubblica.it/2008/12/sezioni/sport/calcio/pallone-sgonfio/pallone-sgonfio/pallone-sgonfio.html

Liguori, R., & Vincenzi , M. (2002). Autogol! 2002, il campionato ha fatto crac. *Avverbi*, 60.

Macklin, G.D. (2005). Co-opting the counter culture: Troy Southgate and the National Revolutionary Faction. *Patterns of Prejudice*. 39 (3), 301–326.

Malagutti, V. (2002). *I conti truccati del Calcio. Perché il mondo del pallone é sull' orlo del fallimento*. Roma: Carocci.

Mazer, J. (2008). Locating Agency in Collective Political Behaviour: Nationalism, Social Movements and Individual Mobilisation. *Politics*, 28 (1), 41–49.

Papa, A., & Panico, G. (2002). *Storia Sociale del Calcio in Italia*. Bologna: Il Mulino.

Rafaeli, A., & Kluger, A. (1998). *The cognitive and emotional influence of service context on service quality: A model and initial findings.* Unpublished manuscript, Hebrew University of Jerusalem, Jerusalem, ISRAEL.

Rafaeli, A., & Worline, M. (2000). Symbols in Organizational Culture. In N. Ashkanasv, C. Wilderom & M. Peterson (Eds.), *Handbook of Organizational Culture and Climate.* London: Sage.

Ricchini, C., Manca, E., & Melograni, L. (1987). *Gramsci – le sue idee nel nostro tempo.* Roma: Editrice L' Unita'.

Sandelands, L. (1998). Feeling and form in groups. *Visual Sociology,* 13(1), 5–23.

Shilling, C. (1993). *The Body and Social Theory.* London: Sage.

Spradley, J. (1979). *The Ethnographic Interview.* New York: Harcourt, Brace, Jovanovich.

Weber, M. (1963). *The Sociology of Religion.* Boston: Beacon press.

Yamamoto, T., Stone, J., & Tanaka, M. (2001). *Bushido: The Way of the Samurai.* New York: Square One Publishers.

Chapter 9

Agnew, P. (2007). *Forza Italia. The Fall and Rise of Italian Football.* England: Ebury.

Bailey, F. (1969). *Stratagems and Spoils: A Social Anthropology of Politics.* Oxford: Blackwell.

Cardone, G. (2001, October 11). Scritte contro Liverani, torna la vergogna razzista *.La Repubblica [Internet].* (Available from: www.repubblica.it/online/calcio/liverani/liverani.html [accessed September 6th, 2004.]

Corriere della Sera (online edition; 2000, 01, February): www.archiviostorico. corriere.it/2000/febbraio/01/Caso_Arkan_rivolta_dello_sport_co_0_0002011589.shtml

Di Canio, P., & Marcotti, G. (2001). *Paolo di Canio: The Autobiography.* London: HarperCollins Publishers.

Friedrichs, P. (1977). *Agrarian Revolts in a Mexican Village.* Chicago: University of Chicago.

George, L. (1998). Self and Identity in Later Life: Protecting and Enhancing the Self. *Journal of Ageing and Identity,* 3, 133–152.

Hofstede, G. (1983). Dimensions of national cultures in fifty countries and three regions. In J. B. Deregowski, S. Dziurawiec, & R. C. Annis (Eds.), Explications in cross-cultural psychology. (pp. 335–355). Lisse, Netherlands: Swets & Zeitlanger.

Hofstede, G. (1991). *Cultures and Organizations: Software of the Mind.* New York: McGraw-Hill Book Company.

Klandermans, B., & Mayer, N. (2006). *Extreme Right Activists in Europe.* London: Routledge.

Pennacchia, M. (2001). *Football Force One. La biografia ufficiale di Giorgio Chinaglia.* Arezzo: Limina.

Recanatesi, F. (2006). *Uno più undici. Maestrelli: La vita di un gentiluomo del calcio, dagli anni Trenta allo scudetto del '74.* Roma: L' Airone.

Risoli, M. (2000). *Arriverderci: Swansea. The Giorgio Chinaglia Story*. Edinburgh: Mainstream.
Vannini, P. & Franzese, A.(2008). The Authenticity of Self: Conceptualization, Personal Experience, and Practice. *Sociology Compass*, 2 (5), 1621–1637.

Chapter 10
Balibar, E., & Wallerstein, I. (1991). *Race, Nation, Class; Ambiguous Identities*. London: Verso.
Cardone, G. (2001, October 11). Scritte contro Liverani, torna la vergogna razzista. *La Repubblica*. (Available from: www.repubblica.it/online/calcio/liverani/liverani.html)
Falasca-Zamponi. (2000). *Fascist Spectacle: The Aesthetics of Power in Mussolini's Italy*. Berkeley: University of California Press.
Galeotti, C. (2000). *Mussolini ha sempre ragione*. Milano: Garzanti.
Germinario, F.(2001). *Razza del sangue, razza dello spirito. Julius Evola, l'antisemitismo e il nazionalsocialismo (1930–43)*. Torino: Bollati Boringhieri.
Griffin, R. (1991). *The Nature of Fascism*. London: Routledge.
Gullestad, M. (2002). Invisible Fences: Egalitarianism, Nationalism and Racism. *The Journal of the Royal Anthropological Institute*, 8, 45–63.
Martin-Cabrera, L. (2002). Postcolonial memories and racial violence. *Journal of Spanish Cultural Studies*, 3(1), 43–55.
Il Giornale. (Online edition; 2008, 22, April): www.ilgiornale.it/a.pic1?ID=256468
Il Tempo. (Online edition; 2009, 22, February): www.iltempo.ilsole24ore.com/interni_esteri/2009/02/22/993272-omicidi_stupri_rapine_mano_sempre_stessa.shtml
Spaaij, R., & Vinas, C. (2005). A por ellos!': Racism and anti-racism in Spanish football. *International Journal of Iberian Studies*, 18(3), 141–164.
Wieviorka, M. (1995). *The Arena of Racism*. London: Sage Publications.

Chapter 11
Abravanel, R. (2008). *Meritocrazia. Per rilanciare la societá italiana*. Milano: Garzanti.
Bauman, Z. (1999). *In Search of Politics*. Palo Alto, CA: Stanford University Press.
Bonini, C. (2009). *ACAB. All Cops are Bastards*. Milano: Einaudi.
Borghini, F.(1987). *La violenza negli stadi*. Firenze: Manzuoli.
Bosetti, G. (2008, 20, November). *Perche' il potere e' nelle mani dei vecchi*. (www.repubblica.it/2008/11/sezioni/politica/paese-sbloccare/poteri-vecchi/poteri-vecchi.html)
Carboni, C.(2008). *La società cinica. Le classi dirigenti nell'epoca dell'antipolitica*. Milano: Laterza.
Camp, J. (1992). *The Athenian Agorà: Excavations in the Heart of Classical Athens (New Aspects of Antiquity)*. London: Thames & Hudson.
Corriere della Sera. (online edition; 2008, 25, October):www.corriere.it/editoriali/08_ottobre_25/dellaloggia_22106116-a252-11dd-9d1b-00144f02aabc.shtml

Corte, U., & Edwards, B. (2008). White Power music and the mobilization of racist Social Movements. *Music and Arts in Action*, 1(1), 4–20.

Davies, J. (1971). *When Men Revolt and Why: A reader in political violence and revolution*. New York: Free Press.

Galeotti, C. (2000). Mussolini ha sempre ragione. Milano: Garzanti.

De Benoist, A., & Champetier, C. (1999). La nouvelle droite de l'an 2000. *Eléments* 94 (February),11–23.

Gentry, C. (2004). The relationship between New Social Movement theory and terrorism studies: The role of leadership, membership, ideology and gender. *Terrorism and Political Violence*, 26 (2), 274–293.

Kornhauser, W. (1959). *The Politics of Mass Society*. Glencoe, IL: Free Press.

Klapp, O. (1969). *The Collective Search for Identity*. New York: Holt, Rinehart and Winston.

Klandermans, B. (1997). *The Social Psychology of Protest*. Oxford and Cambridge, MA: Blackwell.

Klandermans, B., & Mayer, N. (2006). *Extreme Right Activists in Europe*. London: Routledge.

La Repubblica. (online edition; 2009, 03, June): www.repubblica.it/2009/06/sezioni/politica/corruzione-barometro/corruzione-barometro/corruzione-barometro.html

Marchi, V. (1994). *Ultrà. Le sottoculture giovanili negli stadi d'Europa*. Roma: Koine'.

Marinelli , M., & Pili, F. (2000). *Ultrá*. Brescia: Centro Studi Ricerche Polizia [National Police research and study center].

Mariottini, D. (2004). *Ultrasviolenza*. Torino: Bradipolibri.

Morrison, D. (1971). Some Notes Toward Theory on Relative Deprivation, Social Movements and Social Change. *American Behavioural Scientist*, 14, 675–690.

Rappaport, R. (1979). *Ecology, Meaning and Religion*. Richmond: North Atlantic Books.

Regoli, R. (2006). *Ercole Consalvi. Le Scelte per la Chiesa*. Roma:Editrice Pontificia Università Gregoriana.

Roversi, A. (1992). *Calcio, tifo e violenza*. Bologna: Il Mulino.

Simi, P., Brents, B. G., & Futrell, R. (2004, 14/08). *The Politicization of Skinheads: Gangs as Social Movements*. Annual meeting of the American Sociological Association. (Http://allacademic.com/meta/p110400_index.html)

Snow, D., Soule, S., & Kriesi, H. (2004).*The Blackwell Companion to Social Movements*. Oxford: Blackwell Publishers.

Tajfel, H., & Turner, J. C. (1986). The social identity theory of inter-group behavior. In S. Worchel & L. W. Austin (Eds.), *Psychology of Intergroup Relations*. Chicago: Nelson-Hall.

Triani, G. (1994). *Bar Sport Italia*. Milano: Eleuthera.

Vincenti, L. (2000). *Diari di una domenica ultrà. 29 gennaio, Claudio Vincenzo Spagnolo*. Milano: Franco Angeli.

Walker, I., & Smith, H. (2001). *Relative Deprivation: Specification, Development and Integration*. Cambridge: Cambridge University Press.

Chapter 12

Cavender, G., Jurik, N., & Cohen, A. (1993). The baffling case of the smoking gun: The social ecology of political accounts in the Iran-Contra affair. *Social Problems,* 40 (2), 152–166.

Cavender, G. (2004). Media and crime in policy. A reconsideration of David Garland's the Culture of Control. *Punishment & Society,* 6, 335–348.

Cohen, S. (1980). *Folk Devils and Moral Panics.* New York: St. Martin's Press.

Corte, U., & Edwards, B. (2008). White Power music and the mobilization of racist Social Movements. *Music and Arts in Action,* 1(1), 4–20.

Doran, N. (2008). Decoding' encoding': Moral panics, media practices and Marxist presuppositions. *Theoretical Criminology,* 12, 191–221.

Entman, R. M. (1989). *Democracy without Citizens: Media and the Decay of American Politics.* New York: Oxford University Press.

Fairclough, N. (1989). *Language and Power.* London: Longman.

Fowler, R. (1996). *Linguistic Criticism.* Oxford: Oxford University Press.

Juris, J. (2005). Violence Performed and Imagined: Militant Action, the Black Bloc and the Mass Media in Genoa. *Critique of Anthropology,* 25(4), 413–432.

La Repubblica (online edition;2005, 13·June): www.repubblica.it/2005/f/sezioni/politica/dossifeconda6/chius/chius.html

La Repubblica. (online edition; 2008,31, August):www.repubblica.it/2008/08/sezioni/cronaca/calcio-tifosi/calcio-tifosi/calcio-tifosi.html

Marani, V. (2003). *Indagine sulla violenza negli stadi.* Roma: Ministero dell'Interno.

Panorama. (online edition; 2004, 22, March):www.panorama.it/motori/calcio/articolo/ix1-a020001023704

Porro, N. (2001). *Lineamenti di Sociologia dello Sport.* Roma:Carocci.

Chapter 13

Bauman, Z. (1992). *Intimations of Postmodernity.* London: Routledge.

Bonini, C. (2009). *ACAB. All Cops are Bastards.* Milano: Einaudi.

Campbell, C. (1989). The Romantic Ethic and the Spirit of Modern Consumerism. Oxford: Basil Blackwell, Inc.

Corriere della Sera.(online edition; 2009, 03, March): www.corriere.it/cronache/09_marzo_03/lotito_condannato_e75497e2-0807-11de-805b-00144f02aabc.shtml

Crocker, J., Major, B., & Steele, C. (1998). Social Stigma. In D. Gilbert, S. Fiske & De Certau, M. (1984). *The Practice of Everyday Life.* Berkeley: University of California Press.

De Nardo, J. (1985). *Power in Numbers: The Political Strategy of Protest and Rebellion.* Princeton: Princeton University Press.

Giddens, A. (1991) Modernity and Self-Identity: Self and Society in the Late Modern Age. Oxford: Polity.

Haenfler, R. (2004). Rethinking Subcultural Resistance: Core Values of the Straight Edge Movement. *Journal of Contemporary Ethnography, 33,* 406–436.

Hobsbawm, E.,& Ranger, T.(1983). *The Invention of tradition*. New York: Cambridge University Press.

Il Giornale. (online edition; 2008, 08, March):www.ilgiornale.it/a.pic1?ID= 334173&PRINT=S

La Repubblica. (online edition; 2009a, 15, July):www.repubblica.it/2009/03/ sezioni/cronaca/spaccarotella/ultras-vendetta/ultras-vendetta.html

La Repubblica. (online edition; 2009b, 15, July):www.repubblica.it/2009/03/ sezioni/cronaca/spaccarotella/padre-manifestazione/padre-manifestazione.html

Linden, A., & Klandermans, B. (2007). Revolutionaries, wanderers, converts, and complaints: Life histories of extreme right activists. *Journal of Contemporary Ethnography*, 36, 184–2001.

Mariottini, D. (2004). *Ultrasviolenza*. Torino: Bradipolibri.

Miller, C.T., & Kaiser, C.R. (2001). A theoretical perspective on coping with stigma. *Journal of Social Issues*. 57, 73–92.

Opp, K., & Roehl, W. (1990). Repression, Micromobilization and Political Protest. *Social Forces*, 69(2), 521–547.

Ponsaers, P. (2001). Reading about 'community (oriented) policing' and police models. *Policing: An International Journal of Police Strategies & Management*, 24(4), 470–496.

Runciman, D. 'What a Way to Run a Country', review of J. Keane's *The Life and Death of Democracy*. *The Observer* (books) 7th June, 2009.

Simmel, G. (1957). Fashion. *American Journal of Sociology*. 62, 541–558.

Strauss, A.L. (1969). *Mirrors and Masks: The Search for Identity*. San Francisco, CA:Martin Robertson.

The Independent. (online edition; 2007,08 April): www.independent.co.uk/ opinion/commentators/john-foot-italian-police-beating-up-fans-big-deal-its-what-they-do-443746.html

Chapter 14

Bauman, Z. (1992). *Intimations of Postmodernity*. London: Routledge.

Campbell, C. (1989). *The Romantic Ethic and the Spirit of Modern Consumerism*. Oxford: Basil Blackwell, Inc.

Crocker, J., Major, B., & Steele, C. (1998). Social Stigma. In D. Gilbert, S. Fiske & G. Lindzey (Eds.), Handbook *of Social Psychology*. (pp. 504–553). Boston: McGraw-Hill Book Company.

De Certau, M. (1984). *The Practice of Everyday Life*. Berkeley: University of California Press.

Giddens, A. (1991) Modernity and Self-Identity: Self and Society in the Late Modern Age. Oxford: Polity.

Haenfler, R. (2004). Rethinking Subcultural Resistance: Core Values of the Straight Edge Movement. *Journal of Contemporary Ethnography, 33*, 406–436.

Hobsbawm, E., & Ranger, T. (1983). *The Invention of tradition*. New York: Cambridge University Press.

Miller, C.T., & Kaiser, C.R. (2001). A theoretical perspective on coping with stigma. *Journal of Social Issues.* 57, 73–92.

Runciman, D. 'What a Way to Run a Country', review of J. Keane's *The Life and Death of Democracy. The Observer* (books) 7th June, 2009.

Simmel, G. (1957). Fashion. *American Journal of Sociology.* 62, 541–558.

Strauss, A.L. (1969). *Mirrors and Masks: The Search for Identity.* San Francisco, CA:Martin Robertson.

Appendix

Dal Lago, A. (1990). *Descrizione di una battaglia* [Description of a Battle]. Bologna: Il Mulino.

Dal Lago, A. and De Biasi , R. (1994). 'The Social Identity of football fans' in R.Giulianotti, N.Bonney and M. Hepworth (Eds.) *Football, Violence and Social Identity.* London. Routledge.

Levi-Strauss, C. (1966). *The Savage Mind.* Chicago: The University of Chicago Press.

Roversi, A. (1990) *Calcio e Violenza in Europa* [Football and Violence in Europe]. Bologna. Il Mulino.

Roversi, A. (1991). Football Violence in Italy. *International Review for the Sociology of Sport*, 26 (4), 311–331.

Roversi, A. (2002) *Calcio, tifo e violenza* [Football, Fanatics and Violence]. Bologna. Il Mulino.

Roversi, A. (2006) *L'odio in rete.* Siti UltraS,Nazifascismo online,Jihad Elettronica. [The Hate On-Line UltraS Website, Nazi fascism on-line, Electronic Jihad].Bologna, Il Mulino.

Salvini, A. (1988) *Il rito aggressive. Dall' aggressivita simbolica al comportamento violent: Il caso dei tifosi ultras.* [The aggressive rutual. From symbolic aggressiveness to violent behaviour: A case study of the ultras]. Florence: Giunti.

Scalia, V. (2009). Just a few Rogues? Football ultras, Clubs and Politics in Contemporary Italy. In *International Review for the Sociology of Sport*, 44 (1), 41–53.

INDEX